Adv

"Jesus, I trust in you." The message of Divine Mercy, given to us by Jesus through the writings of St. Faustina, are indeed words to live by, especially in these challenging times. Whether it's the continued fallout from the coronavirus, political unrest, or problems striking closer to home with struggles in our personal lives and families, women need to cling to this message of hope more than ever and learn more about the Divine Mercy message itself. Donna-Marie's book helps us do both and then some, and is a greatly needed and timely resource for women of all ages.

— **Teresa Tomeo**, author and syndicated Catholic
talk show host of "Catholic Connection"
and "The Catholic View For Women"

Four words effectively describe just how it is that the beauty and mystery of the feminine genius can stand up heroically to a broken and wounded world, resultant of the fall of our first parents: the Mercy of God. Donna-Marie Cooper O'Boyle's book *Divine Mercy in a Woman's Life: Milestones Along the Way* conveys this important truth.

— **Fr. Wade Menezes, CPM,** Fathers of Mercy assistant
general and EWTN series and radio host

Donna-Marie Cooper O'Boyle has taken the frequent messiness of women's lives and turned it into something astonishingly beautiful. Every woman will find herself in this book and at the same time will discover the astonishing beauty within. Well done!

— **Marge Steinhage Fenelon**, award-winning author,
retreat leader, internationally-known speaker,
and Catholic media personality

Women inspire other women. In *Divine Mercy in a Woman's Life*, Donna-Marie offers many spiritual lessons from Jesus, the Divine Mercy, and His Apostle of Divine Mercy, St. Faustina. The author also shares her own life and experiences, along with other compelling true stories, inviting the reader to pause, act, and pray for God's mercy. This book will enrich the faith of the women who read and pray with it.

— **Fr. Edward Looney**, host of the podcast
"How They Love Mary" and author of
A Lenten Journey with Mother Mary

This is a book for women of every age and in every season. The message of mercy can find a home in every season of our lives and this book guides the way.

— **Leah Darrow**, founder of Lux Catholic and
author of *The Other Side of Beauty*

Divine Mercy in a Woman's Life is a wonderful book of spiritual and theological reflections and prayers, looking at a woman's relationship with God through the lens of one of the greatest religious figures of the 20th century. Cooper O'Boyle's soul-stirring meditations, heartfelt stories, and beautiful insights on a woman's experience with Christ's Divine Mercy provides spiritual food that will nourish and strengthen the reader's prayer life in a deeply intimate and personal way. *Divine Mercy in a Woman's Life* plants the seeds of wisdom in the rich soil of human experience that, when watered by the gifts of the Holy Spirit in an open heart, will undoubtedly bring forth fruit of sacred joy in the lives of women everywhere. An absolute must-read!

— **Deacon Harold Burke-Sivers**, author,
*Father Augustus Tolton: The Slave Who Became
the First African-American Priest*

Here is a book that is original, profound, practical and potentially life-changing for readers. *Divine Mercy in a Woman's Life* is a work that will enrich, engage and expand the feminine heart. The author provides rich content full of beauty and truth that leads readers on a spiritual journey of inner healing that culminates in divine intimacy. I pray that women of all faiths will take up and read this amazing gift of grace. Highly recommended!

— **Kathleen Beckman,** author, *A Family Guide to Spiritual Warfare* and *Praying for Priests*

Donna-Marie is truly anointed by God in many ways, especially her gift of writing! This beautiful book is so powerful and such a great resource to serve to equip Catholic women to be more like the woman described in Proverbs 31:26-31. *Divine Mercy in a Woman's Life* is like a training manual for girls and a guidebook for women that uses St. Faustina's writings as a guide and leads us through the many milestones a female encounters from birth to death, giving us expert advice along the way to help us become more holy and pleasing to our Lord. Every Christian woman should own this book. And for men, it's a great book to give to your daughter, your wife, or your girlfriend.

— **Gail Buckley Barringer,** founder, Catholic Scripture Study International

Women need a lavish experience of Christ's Divine Mercy as a balm of grace. *Divine Mercy in a Woman's Life* fuses the Divine Mercy message with real life in every stage of womanhood. Because we women are so poured out, it's only necessary that we have His Mercy pour in. This beautiful book is a little spring of Divine Mercy for His ladies.

— **Alexis Walkenstein,** evangelist, producer, author

DIVINE MERCY

in a Woman's Life

MILESTONES ALONG THE WAY

Donna-Marie Cooper O'Boyle

Copyright © 2021 Donna-Marie Cooper O'Boyle.
All rights reserved.

Available from:
Marian Helpers Center
Stockbridge, MA 01263

Prayerline: 1-800-804-3823
Orderline: 1-800-462-7426
Websites: TheDivineMercy.org
marian.org

Library of Congress Catalog Number: 2021912812
ISBN: 978-1-59614-553-5

Publication date: August 31, 2021

Imprimi Potest:
Very Rev. Kazimierz Chwalek, MIC
Provincial Superior
The Blessed Virgin Mary, Mother of Mercy Province
April 20, 2021

Nihil Obstat:
Dr. Robert A. Stackpole, STD
Censor Deputatus
April 20, 2021

[Scripture quotations are from] *New Revised Standard Version Bible: Catholic Edition*, copyright © 1989, 1993 National Council of the Churches of Christ in the United States of America. Used by permission. All rights reserved worldwide.

Excerpts from the English translation of the *Catechism of the Catholic Church* for use in the United States of America Copyright © 1994, United States Catholic Conference, Inc. — Libreria Editrice Vaticana. Used with Permission. English translation of the *Catechism of the Catholic Church: Modifications from the Editio Typica* copyright © 1997, United States Conference of Catholic Bishops—Libreria Editrice Vaticana.

CONTENTS

Dedication

With great love for my children:
Justin, Chaldea, Jessica, Joseph,
and Mary-Catherine.
And my grandchildren:
Shepherd and Leo.

With a grateful heart to the remarkable women
in my life, starting with my grandmother
Alexandra Theresa K. Uzwiak;
my mother, Alexandra Mary Uzwiak Cooper;
my sisters Alice Jean and Barbara;
and my godmother Aunt Bertha, as well as my
dear Aunt Mary, Mother Teresa of Calcutta,
and dear St. Faustina Kowalska.

And with great affection to the Blessed Virgin
Mary, our Queen of Mercy, our Star of the Sea,
who leads us to Heaven.

INTRODUCTION

"I sent prophets wielding thunderbolts to My people. Today I am sending you with My mercy to the people of the whole world. I do not want to punish aching mankind, but I desire to heal it, pressing it to My Merciful Heart."

— *Diary of Saint Maria Faustina Kowalska*, 1588

*D*ivine Mercy in a Woman's Life is not a fluffy kind of book about a picture-perfect life. It gets down to the nitty-gritty, to the often-messy details of a woman's life. It offers spiritual and practical guidance, as well as huge doses of hope. This book covers many of the varied milestones of a Catholic woman's life as seen through the lens of God's love and Divine Mercy. Our sister St. Faustina will be our expert guide throughout.

The fact that this book is brutally honest as well as practical doesn't mean that it won't bring tears, make you laugh, reflect, or cheer! I suspect that you might see yourself or someone you know in some of the stories and chapters.

It was Jesus Who appointed Sr. Maria Faustina Kowalska as His Secretary and Apostle of Divine Mercy. Once a simple Polish farm girl, she became a nun in the Congregation of the Sisters of Our Lady of Mercy and appeared very insignificant to most of those who knew her. Helen lacked a formal education, having received only three semesters of primary schooling, and became afflicted with debilitating illness. Yet she was the one chosen and divinely entrusted with reminding the world about God's unfathomable mercy. Through Helen Kowalska, Jesus demonstrated the power of suffering and weakness. He always raises up the lowly and humble-hearted.

Chosen by Jesus to imitate His sacrifice and become a propagator of His Divine Mercy, St. Faustina responded to this holy call and mission with a wholehearted "yes!" God directed her on the road to Christian perfection through spiritual, mental, and physical trials and sufferings, which she accepted with pure charity in order that God's divine plan would be accomplished for the world. These trials included criticisms and mocking from fellow sisters, serious illness, and the absolute weight of the Divine Mercy message upon her shoulders when no one believed her. Saint Faustina's heroic responses to Heaven's requests give an encouraging example for us modern women to emulate!

Through His encounters with the young Polish nun, Jesus emphasizes the greatest attribute of God: His merciful love for every human person. He directs our hearts away from the sinfulness of the world and towards His Merciful Sacred Heart, from which graces abundantly flow for the redemption of the world. Jesus' visits with St. Faustina call to us to open our hearts and become devoted to the Divine Mercy.

Let us remember that St. Faustina lived in recent times — the 20th century, not in ages past. God raised her up as a saint of our time. We absolutely need the message she heroically delivered to the world. Saint John Paul II raised her to the honors of the altar by beatifying and canonizing her, making her the first saint to be canonized in the new millennium. Saint Faustina indeed helped to usher in a new advent in our Church.

On Divine Mercy Sunday, April 18, 1993, at St. Faustina's beatification, St. John Paul II highlighted the need for the Divine Mercy message and devotion. He quoted from the writings of the young mystic nun, who declared, "I clearly feel that my mission does not end with death, but begins" (see *Diary*, 281).[1]

The pontiff exclaimed, "And it truly did! Her mission continues and is yielding astonishing fruit." The Great Mercy Pope continued, "It is truly marvelous how her devotion to the merciful Jesus is spreading in our contemporary world and gaining so many human hearts!"

He asked a poignant question: "Where, if not in the Divine Mercy, can the world find refuge and the light of hope?" He said, "Believers understand that perfectly."[2]

As I write this book, I am living in a time in which we absolutely need to beseech God for more saints, a special era when we are *all* called to become saints! We need to ask for Divine Mercy for ourselves and for the world. Dear sister, let us never fail to call on our sister Faustina, a modern woman, an especially sympathetic intercessor, and a great patroness for you and for me. She is still working hard from Heaven to help us as we strive to help others. We have been put here on earth and in the Church for such a time as this!

My earnest and wholehearted prayer is that this book will bring peace to you and thoroughly nourish your mind, heart, and soul! Dig deep into your faith, my dear sister in Christ! Allow the floodgates of God's unfathomable Divine Mercy to open. Permit the ocean of mercy to flow over you and through you so that you can share it with others.

May our dear sister St. Faustina pray for you and guide you, and may God bless your journey! Jesus, I trust in You!

Yours in Jesus, Mary, and Joseph,
Donna-Marie Cooper O'Boyle
March 25, 2020
Feast of the Annunciation

HOW TO USE THIS BOOK

Just a bit about the logistics — this book's table of contents does not necessarily represent every woman's life, since not every woman will experience all of the milestones I address. Still, these chapters were included (not necessarily in chronological order) so that all women will be able to benefit from them. I have attempted to discuss as many pertinent milestones for women as possible.

Let's not forget that we women are a bit complicated. I'm sure that I can't cover every inch of every woman's complexities in this book. It would take volumes! However, I have done my best to hit many of the most common, crucial milestones for women.

I have woven anecdotes and Catholic teaching throughout the many milestones to encourage women to emulate Mother Mary's virtues and to feel affirmed in their own God-given dignity, vocation, and gifts. In addition, I hope these chapters will help to prepare women for the future and to fully live in the present, as well as to be better equipped when ministering to the girls and women in their lives. I have ended each chapter with Pause, Act, and Prayer sections for further spiritual nourishment.

I hope that, by God's amazing grace, this book will benefit readers in book groups. I pray it will be a valuable support for all Catholic women. I pray that it will be a means for my sisters in Christ to grow in holiness while learning more about St. Faustina, her *Diary*, and God's unfathomable mercy. I'll go so far as to say that I think men would benefit by reading this book, as well! They might get a valuable glimpse into how we women operate!

Today's modern Catholic women can learn much from this humble mystic, St. Faustina — once a farm girl who went off to the big city to work, went to dances, and eventually became a nun and a saint! This winsome, down-to-earth saint will guide us through this book.

Feel free to read this book straight through, or turn to specific chapters as they are relevant to you or the women and girls in your life. I hope that you do read each chapter, even if you think the topic doesn't pertain to your own life. For instance, some might choose to skip "Hitting Rock Bottom," thinking at first glance that it would not pertain to them. But they would miss the section "Distractions and Temptations to Give Up," which applies to every single woman, as well as those to whom they might minister.

Perhaps you might also choose to skip over the military chapter, figuring it doesn't apply to you. You would then miss compelling stories of heroic Catholic women whose lives are examples for all of us, whether we are connected to the military or not. I have shared loads of spiritual gems and enthralling true stories throughout this book, and I don't want you to miss any! There are stories of life-changing transformations and great miracles, too!

I would add that St. Faustina and our Lord offer such an abundance of holy wisdom to us that it's best to prayerfully savor the chapters, mull them over, and take time to absorb the material. If it's possible, you may want to go back and read them again.

All for the glory of God and the good of His people!

PART ONE
Spring

"The new evangelization that can make the twenty-first century a springtime of the Gospel is a task for the entire People of God, but will depend in a decisive way on the lay faithful being fully aware of their baptismal vocation and their responsibility for bringing the good news of Jesus Christ to their culture and society."[3]

— Saint John Paul II

When we think of springtime, images of new birth might fill our minds. After all, spring is a time of growth and new life. Depending upon where we live, after a long bleak winter, we might crave the warm spring sunshine on our faces as we eagerly await the sight of the first brave crocuses and daffodils bursting forth from the cold ground. I am always eager to see the bright yellow forsythia, and later, my favorites — lilacs!

Saint Faustina described the beauty of spring in her *Diary*: "When I went out into the garden, I saw how everything was breathing the joy of spring. The trees, adorned with flowers, gave off an intoxicating odor. Everything was throbbing with joy, and the birds were singing and chirping their adoration of God and said to me, 'Rejoice and be happy, Sister Faustina'" (1120).

Saint John Paul II, in the quote at the start of this part, speaks of a "springtime of the Gospel." In addition, he speaks of the responsibility of the People of God (that's us!) to reclaim our baptismal vows and responsibilities so that we can proclaim the Good News. We can "rejoice and be happy" because God has given many gifts to us Catholic women through which we can evangelize in various ways throughout our lives.

CHAPTER 1
Loved in the Womb

"If an ear is to grow or a flower blossom, there are times which cannot be forced; for the birth of a human being, nine months are required; to write a book or a worthy piece of music, years must often be spent in patient searching. This is also the law of the spirit. ... To encounter the mystery takes patience, inner purification, silence and waiting."[4]

— Saint John Paul II

We all started out in the womb — that dark, yet extremely comfortable first environment (even though we were upside down at times or bouncing around in tight quarters!). We were blessed to be immersed in warm amniotic fluid and rocked by our mother's every move. Our mother's body was our lifeline — her beating heart lulled us. That was life as we knew it for the first 9 months, though we have no recollection of it now. If our parents showed us love by talking, singing, or reading stories to us while we were in the womb, we have surely benefited. Certainly, these are things we can do now during our own pregnancies or our children's pregnancies. Love is powerful. It's never too early to show love to our babies!

In years past, life in the womb was mostly a mystery. We were aware that after babies were conceived, time and nutrition were required as they matured in the womb. Today, we know for certain that a lot more goes on in that hidden place, safely tucked under Mama's heart.

Scientific research confirms that unborn babies are aware of sounds from outside their mom's body. They form memories of those sounds that are then recalled after their birth. I vividly remember being in a movie theater during one of my pregnancies when sudden movie sounds roused my unborn baby, who seemed to do cartwheels in my womb! Movie theater noise is louder than we might think, and our unborn babies can certainly hear it.

According to an article in *Science* magazine, unborn babies can hear the rhythms of speech or music playing through their mother's abdomen. A journalist reported, "It may seem implausible that fetuses can listen to speech within the womb, but the sound-processing parts of their brain become active in the last trimester of pregnancy, and sound carries fairly well through the mother's abdomen."[5]

In addition, newborns much prefer their mom's voice to any other voice.[6] Many a mother (myself included) has joyfully noticed the way in which their newborn turns their little face towards her, or stops crying at the sound of her voice. The babe in arms has become familiar with his or her mother's voice from within the womb. If a sound is repeated to us often enough, we form a memory of it. That memory is activated when we hear it again. Various studies of babies' behaviors suggest that babies begin to learn language in utero. Needless to say, we should not place speakers up to a pregnant mother's abdomen to enable the unborn baby to hear what is played, hoping for some benefit for the little bambino. We certainly do not want to interfere with their rapidly growing brains or overstimulate their tiny ears. Speaking normally and often to our unborn babies is best.

Progress in the Womb

Even before a woman may know she is expecting, just weeks after conception, the roots of human behavior begin to develop. By 5 weeks, the cerebral cortex (part of the brain) will develop, which allows the sweet, growing, unique, and unrepeatable human being in her womb to eventually speak, think, learn, create, plan, and so on. At 9 weeks, the tiny one is already reacting to loud sounds. He or she begins to move, stretch, and breathe amniotic fluid, and soon will yawn, suck, swallow, feel, and even smell. By the end of the second trimester, the unborn baby can hear even better. Towards the end of the pregnancy, the baby will be able to see. There's so much more; I encourage you to do your own research.

Speaking of babies in the womb, it turns out that I was in my mother's womb for an extra month! My mother was pregnant with me for a whole 10 months and delivered a precisely 10-pound baby girl exactly 10 minutes before the clock struck midnight the night before Thanksgiving. To my chagrin, I was nicknamed the "Butterball turkey" (by my older brothers — gee, thanks a lot!) and was reminded of that "enchanting" nickname almost every year. My mother did confess to me that she had enjoyed a soft serve Dairy Queen ice cream cone as often as she could during that steamy summer when she was pregnant with me. This might help explain my hefty birth weight!

Human Life is Sacred and Amazing

I'd like to share something quite amazing about grandmothers, mothers, and grandchildren. Did you know that every single egg a woman will ever have in her reproductive system develops when she is a fetus residing inside her mother's uterus? This means that you started your life inside of your grandmother! When your mother was in your grandmother's womb, the egg that would later be *you* resided inside there, too! In addition to this, if you conceive a daughter, your future grandchildren will be eggs inside of your daughter while she is inside of you! I think that's incredible to ponder!

Whether or not you will be blessed with babies in your womb or children placed in your arms through adoption, every single one of us women was once cradled in our mother's womb. Our unique, unrepeatable life began at our conception. Indeed, God has a great plan for us. Though our path on the pilgrimage of life might be crooked, dark, or obscure at times, God's amazing grace and infinite mercy will lead us through it all, hopefully to eternal happiness with Him in Heaven.

PAUSE

Take some time to ponder the wonders and holy mysteries of human life in the womb.

ACT

Praise God for all human life — born and unborn!

A PRAYER OF MERCY

"Let every beat of my heart be a new hymn of thanksgiving to You, O God. Let every drop of my blood circulate for You, Lord. My soul is one hymn in adoration of Your mercy. I love You, God, for Yourself alone" (*Diary*, 1794).

Dear Jesus, please help me to always do
what is in my power to protect human life.
Please have mercy upon my soul.
I trust in You!
Mother Mary, help me, protect me, and guide me.
Saint Faustina, please pray for me.
Amen.

CHAPTER 2

As a Baby

"But after a while, I was left alone with the Infant Jesus who stretched out His little hands to me, and I understood that I was to take Him in my arms. Jesus pressed His head against my heart and gave me to know, by His profound gaze, how good He found it to be next to my heart."

— Saint Faustina (*Diary*, 1442)

As baby girls, we are totally dependent upon our caregivers. Sadly, not every baby will grow up in a happy or stable home. Yet, we hope and pray that every baby will be showered with the love that he or she deserves. In our last chapter, we discussed the incredible growth that occurred in secret during our first nine months of life. Our lives began in an environment very unlike our lives outside the womb. For most of us, life as an unborn baby was pretty predictable (not that an unborn baby can predict!).

Now let's consider our birth, when we came out from darkness into light — usually, it was very bright hospital light — having left the warm comfort of our mother's body (almost 100 degrees Fahrenheit) to enter the colder air of the wider world. A stark and drastic change, for sure. We must also consider the means that were used to get us out of the womb, whatever they might have been. In addition, there was the poking and prodding that went on (thermometers, blood draws, and the like), as well as the sudden, strange sensation of clothing. Needless to say, our little bodies were shocked, and we were forced to somehow adjust. Hopefully, it was with lots of love, our mother's comforting voice, and the warmth of her body against our own.

Speaking of love and babies, St. Alphonsus Liguori said of our love for Jesus, "If the Redeemer had come to be feared and respected by men, he would have come as a full-grown man and with royal dignity; but because he came to gain our love, he chose to come and to show himself as an infant, and the poorest of infants, born in a cold stable between two animals, laid in a manger on straw, without clothing or fire to warm his shivering little limbs: 'Thus would he be born, who willed to be loved and not feared.'"[7]

We might take some time to prayerfully ponder Jesus as a baby, and His birth.

Home Is in a Mother's Eyes

I love the expression, "Home is in our mother's eyes." I'll share a true story to illustrate. Mother Teresa's nuns once took in a little girl whom they found wandering the streets of Calcutta, India. She was dirty and starving. They cleaned her up, clothed her, and fed her well. After a few days, the little girl went missing. The sisters finally found her under the shelter of a tree, along with her mother and siblings. The little girl had left the security of the convent to go back to the love of her mother. Her family might have been bereft of a physical home. Their real home, however, was in their mother's eyes. A mother's love is powerful.

Speaking of eyes, did you know that making eye contact with a baby changes the brain activity in both the baby and the person looking at them? Their brain waves actually sync up! According to an article in *Time* magazine, the gaze between the two creates what researchers call "'a joint networked state' that facilitates communication between the two of them."[8] They surmise that "the babies' 'neural synchronization' is kicked up a notch by an adult's gaze" and that "neural synchronization may provide a mechanism by which infants construct their own earliest social networks."[9]

You may be surprised to learn that a newborn's brain is in an unfinished state at birth. Their 100 billion neurons need to be connected in networks. This happens as the growing baby experiences the world around him and forms foundational attachments with his or her parents, family, and caregivers. Loving gazes between caregivers and babies form and reinforce important neural connections.

A newborn can see best at close range — a distance of about 8 to 14 inches. Isn't it interesting that the distance from a mother's eyes to her infant's eyes while she is feeding and holding him is the exact measurement necessary for this synchronization and neural connecting to occur? God doesn't miss a single detail. He has it all figured out. A beautiful and life-long bonding forms through our loving gaze.

Ushered Into the Church Through Baptism

My mother was born weighing in at only a pound and a half. Can you imagine that? The doctor had to look closely to determine whether she was a girl or a boy — she was that tiny! Because of the danger of her dying, she was baptized right away. Her parents knew the importance of ushering their little baby into the Church. Though God is a loving God, and in His great mercy must certainly bring all little babies who pass away straight to Heaven (born and unborn), my grandparents acted quickly to ensure my mother's access to salvation.

My mother was kept warm against my grandmother's body, as well as with a hot water bottle in a shoebox lined with cotton, at a time when incubators and sophisticated equipment were nonexistent. I thank the good Lord that my mother did survive. My mother grew up, married, and had eight children of her own.

Speaking of baptisms, St. Faustina was baptized on August 27, 1905, at St. Casimir Church in Świnice Warckie just two days after her birth. The Baptism took place during a cholera plague, and people had been warned not to visit that area. Saint Faustina's parents, Marianna and Stanislaus, might have been eager to have their baby girl baptized to ensure her entrance into Heaven in case she was stricken by the deadly plague.

"Holy Baptism is the basis of the whole Christian life, the gateway to life in the Spirit *(vitae spiritualis ianua)*,[10] and the door which gives access to the other sacraments" (*Catechism of the Catholic Church*, 1213). We are not Catholic merely because we go to Holy Mass, or because we know or live our faith. First and foremost, we are Catholic because we were baptized. When the holy waters of Baptism were poured over our heads and we were prayed over, we became members of the Catholic Church — the Body of Christ, a sharer in the life of the Trinity. Baptism is a powerful Sacrament that ushers us straight into the Church.

The Church instructs us that "through Baptism we are freed from sin and reborn as sons of God; we become members of Christ, are incorporated into the Church and made sharers in her mission: 'Baptism is the sacrament of regeneration through water in the word'"[11] (*Catechism*, 1213).

Jesus Himself submitted to a form of Baptism at the hands of St. John the Baptist. Even though the Baptism was intended for sinners, Jesus desired to set an example. He also instituted the Sacrament by commanding His disciples to proclaim the Gospel to all nations and to baptize them (see Mt 28:19).

Pope Benedict XVI pointed out the beauty and power of Baptism. He said, "Heaven opens above us in the Sacrament." With regard to its ongoing effects, he stated, "The more we live in contact with Jesus in the reality of our Baptism, the more Heaven will open above us."[12]

In another address, he said, "Baptism is this new birth that precedes our own action. With our faith we can go to meet Christ, but he alone can make us Christian and give to our will and to this desire of ours the response, dignity, and power to become children of God."[13] The pontiff closed with a prayer to the Blessed Mother, reminding us that we should demonstrate who we are in our words and deeds — mostly in our deeds.

In these pages, we will discuss how to live out our Catholic life in words and deeds as daughters of God. Saint Faustina and some of the other saints will be right here to help us!

We begin our earthly pilgrimage as a little baby totally dependent upon others. Our lives begin to be shaped by experiences and environments. Our merciful and loving Father in Heaven has a great plan for each of us. In time, we mature, and with the Sacrament of Baptism under our belts (and over our heads!), we move forward towards our unique mission.

PAUSE

Take a moment to ponder the amazing gift of life and how God in His great love has a plan for each and every human person.

ACT

Thank God for the great gift of life and the Sacrament of Baptism. Onward, Christian soldier!

A PRAYER OF MERCY

Thank You, dear Jesus, for the marvelous gift of human life, the Sacrament of Baptism, our experiences, and our caregivers. Help me to be attentive and loving in responding to the needs of babies.
Dear Jesus, please have mercy upon my soul.
I trust in You!
Mother Mary, help me, protect me, and guide me.
Saint Faustina, please pray for me.
Amen.

CHAPTER 3

As a Girl

"I saw the Infant Jesus near my kneeler. He appeared to be about one year old, and He asked me to take Him in my arms. ... He cuddled up close to my bosom and said, It is good for Me to be close to your heart. ... Because I want to teach you spiritual childhood. I want you to be very little, because when you are little, I carry you close to My Heart, just as you are holding Me close to your heart right now."

— Saint Faustina (*Diary*, 1481)

Blessed as she is with childlike innocence and a heart full of wonder, life is a fascinating adventure for a little girl. We pray that children are protected from anything that will tarnish or harm their precious innocence. What is our part? How do we help preserve children's innocent hearts, and how do we remain pure, preserving a childlike heart in ourselves?

We can certainly take time to ponder, "What was it like when I grew up? What has influenced my foundation and formation?"

Our lives are filled with experiences and encounters, many of which help to shape who we turn out to be. Very early on, sensory experiences help to mold us, affecting us throughout our lives. That is one reason why it is essential for us Christians to surround ourselves with like-minded and faith-filled people. They can surely help us to stay on the straight and narrow path that leads to Heaven.

Parents and grandparents can strive to be more cognizant of the friends who associate with their children and grandchildren.

In addition to these stimuli and experiences, genetics come into play in children's development, affecting how the brain is hardwired. At the same time, life is a continual learning experience. The people around the child and those who associate with her will essentially become the child's teachers, in one way or another. In addition to learning from formal teaching, children discover and assimilate a great deal simply by observing those around them, especially their caregivers.

It's important to keep in mind that we are always teaching our children, because children don't miss a beat! They are very astute and can read our body language and pick up various cues from our speech or behavior. Needless to say, not every child will grow up in a nurturing, safe environment. Love and care, or lack thereof, is a critical influence on children in their earliest years. Most children who receive enriching childhood experiences from attentive, loving caregivers will grow up to feel secure and thrive. On the other hand, most children who receive less attention and loving care from distracted, ill-equipped, or stressed caregivers will suffer. They may experience anxiety and be less able to cope in certain difficulties. We may have the opportunity to help others in these situations as well as to take our own circumstances to prayer, do our best, and trust God to make up for our deficiencies.

"Let the little children come to me, and do not stop them"[14]

Children are quite naive about the ramifications of their first friends' influences on their lives. They are simply looking for someone to play with. But, because children usually spend a lot of time with their peers, these friends will have a major impact on their psychology and development. Their influence will have both positive and negative effects. Parents, grandparents, and caregivers need to continually keep a close eye on the interactions between children, and be present to nip bullying in the bud as well as to encourage positive friendships.

"God opposes the proud, but gives grace to the humble" (Jas 4:6). When the apostles argued about who was the greatest among them (see Lk 9:46-48; Mt 18:1-4), Jesus swiftly settled their differences of opinion by bringing a little child into the equation. Jesus told His followers that to get into Heaven, they had to be like a child.

How do we receive the kingdom of God as a child? How do we humble our hearts, acquire a childlike dependence upon God, and not rely on our own devices? After all, the world urges us to grow up strong and mighty — to be successful. Saint Augustine gave a succinct answer. He said, "Man, grown old through sin, is rejuvenated through grace."[15] It is with God's grace that we are freed from sin and can acquire the necessary virtue of humility.

Jesus told St. Faustina that He wanted her to learn spiritual childhood from Him. Because of this, He often appeared to the young nun as the Infant Jesus. Can we even imagine this grace and privilege? Because our Lord Himself taught His "Secretary of Divine Mercy" about the need to have a childlike heart, St. Faustina became a docile student in the school of spiritual childhood. Saint Thérèse of Lisieux (1873-1897), a modern-day saint associated with spiritual childhood, was also a favorite saint of St. Faustina's. Both St. Faustina and St. Thérèse died at a young age — St. Faustina at 33 years of age and St. Thérèse at only 24 years of age.

Saint Thérèse explained what her "little way" meant. She said, "It is to recognize our nothingness, to expect everything from God as a little child expects everything from its father ... to be disquieted about nothing, and not to be set on gaining our living."[16] In other words, she sought to live the eternal life of Heaven in this life. Similarly, St. Faustina wrote in her *Diary*, "And I rejoice immensely in His greatness and am delighted that I am so little because, since I am little, He carries me in His arms and holds me close to His Heart" (*Diary*, 779).

Take time to pray and ponder what it means to depend upon God like a little child — to trust Him — to be "little."

PAUSE

Take a moment to ponder your own fascinating adventures as a little girl. Stretch your mind back as far as you can go. Think about your friends' influences on you, and yours on them. Is there anything you would change if you could now?

ACT

Carve out some time for extra prayer with our Lord and His Holy Mother. Ponder your present friendships. Are they holy? Think about your influence on the children in your life. Is there anything you can change to make the relationships better? How can you be more childlike in your faith? Endeavor to take some steps to do so.

A PRAYER OF MERCY

Dear Jesus, please carry me in Your arms and hold me close to Your Sacred Heart. Please teach me spiritual childhood. Please have mercy upon my soul. I trust in You!
Mother Mary, help me, protect me, and guide me.
Saint Faustina, please pray for me.
Amen.

CHAPTER 4
Rite of Passage

"Do not conform yourselves to this age
but be transformed by the renewal of
your mind, that you may discern what is
the will of God, what is good and
pleasing and perfect."

— Rom 12:2

The world can seem like a confusing place to a teen girl. Everyday life is both exciting and utterly challenging for her. If she gets involved with the wrong crowd, she most likely will be steered off course. On the other hand, choosing wholesome friendships can lead her in the right direction.

Let's take a quick look at what happens in the minds, hearts, and bodies of teen girls.

A teen girl's body develops and changes throughout puberty, which begins sometime between the ages of 7 and 13, varying with each girl. Hormones are released and the pituitary gland is working hard, while the ovaries are stimulated and estrogen is produced to mature and prepare the girl's body for pregnancy. These new hormones and chemicals moving through the body are essentially turning a teen into an adult.

A girl's body will begin to develop curves. Hair will grow in places it hadn't grown before (underarms and pubic area). Her breasts will develop, and body fat will increase in her hips.

As puberty progresses, she will get her first menstrual period. This could come as a frightening surprise if the young woman is not informed in advance about this life-changing experience. During this time, much to her chagrin, acne might be triggered by puberty hormones. Since gaining weight during this phase of life is normal and necessary, it is detrimental and unhealthy for girls to diet to try to avoid it.

With so much societal pressure on girls and women to be super thin (even the impossible size zero), many young girls secretly believe that they absolutely need to look just like a super-skinny (airbrushed) fashion model. Therefore, it's essential for parents, grandparents, and guardians to keep a constant eye on things such as mood swings, weight loss, and fears, and to remain readily available for open communication.

Along with these major physical changes come emotional ones, too. This is a critical time in a young woman's life. She may be overly sensitive and experience strong emotions. She might feel embarrassed, vulnerable, alone, anxious, or afraid. Your calm, loving words and presence can be a young woman's safe harbor through difficult hormonal episodes and emotions, and during any other challenge. A warm hug, for instance, can speak volumes when words are not helpful.

First Friends: For Better and For Worse

Though we might not realize it at the time, our early friends help to shape our lives — for better or for worse. For me, growing up as the seventh of eight children and being the youngest daughter was both fascinating and frightening. My older brothers and sisters had already paved the way for me, so I didn't need to prove anything to anyone. Still, I had to find my way and ultimately, myself. Life in a large, blue-collar Catholic family was challenging. I did not live a peaches-and-cream kind of life, though I am deeply thankful for all the experiences I had, for I know that without a doubt, they helped shape me into who I am today. I continue to pray for the graces and experiences that I need to be further molded into the woman who God wants me to be.

For most of my childhood, I lived in an affluent town, though we were as far as you can get from being affluent! My father wanted to get us out of the big city, which had grown worse in terms of crime. So he moved our crazy big family to a simple home set on a couple of acres of land out in the country. Miraculously, my parents were able to swing securing the mortgage, though they lived paycheck to meager paycheck.

I vividly remember looking over my shoulder many a time as a young teen in my new town, interiorly terrified that one of my classmates (who were always dressed to the nines) might see me go into the local thrift shop with my mother. With no money to spare, the eight of us Cooper kids wore hand-me-downs. At that point in my life, I felt extremely embarrassed. I worried, "What if someone at school would see me wear something bought from the thrift shop? What if it had been theirs?" That would have been the absolute end of my world.

Nowadays, it's quite normal and even trendy to shop at consignment shops and the like. It's a bit funny to look back and recall the dramatic fears and helpless feelings that I had once endured. As an adult, it's a bit sad, too, to recognize the internal suffering that many young girls go through because of the judgment (real or imagined) of their peers. Yet, knowing about their struggles can help us to be more aware and available to them.

Girls Can Be Heartless

It's a miracle that we emotionally survive our teenage years! Certainly, there are many kindhearted girls. Still, girls can be heartless, and sometimes they choose to bully other girls. This is for any number of reasons, including jealousy, envy, immaturity, and insecurity. In addition, female social cliques are formed, and the girls who are not members can suffer deeply. Someone even decided to make a movie about this ever-present trend with teen girls. It's a 2004 teen comedy called "Mean Girls."

I had my own "Mean Girls" experience growing up. One day as I was hurrying through the school corridors to get to my next class, a folded-up note came hurling through the air and landed atop the books piled high in my arms. I had no idea where the strange-looking triangular note had sailed from, so I continued on my way to avoid being late. Later, my world fell out from under me as I read the note, while my eyes brimmed with burning tears. Three so-called friends had teamed up to write a demeaning note to me. Thoroughly devastated, I wondered how I could go on after that. Yet, I had to pick myself up and move forward. I won't lie. It was tough. Growing up as a teen is difficult. Teens crave affirmation. They want to fit in. They often feel awkward and insignificant, too. They might not realize to Whom they really belong, and so get caught up in the stinging feelings and offenses they endure in the moment.

How different things could be if only we realized during times like these that "this too shall pass," and that our trials and tribulations can help to form us. That said, hopefully, these young women will not be too embarrassed or ashamed to share their social miseries with a loving relative or a trusted sympathetic teacher. Those whose daughter, granddaughter, relative, or friend is being bullied are called to help alleviate the trials and tribulations of those around us, and to seek to bring an end to suffering wherever we can do so in accordance with our faith and Christian morality. We should bear in mind it can be a tremendous help for a girl to know that when she realizes who she really is — a beloved child of God, and therefore it is to Him she really belongs — she can get through the strife more easily. With God's grace and loving assistance from those around her, she will heal from her wounds and grow into a strong woman who will fiercely protect others from evils such as bullying and right wrongs when she is able.

Transformed by God's Grace

The Sisters of Our Lady of Mercy, St. Faustina's order, took care of wayward girls. Most all came from rough backgrounds before arriving at the convent. They might have never been taught about God or how to tell right from wrong. Saint Faustina's heart went out to them, and she aimed to save their souls with God's grace. Her prayerful perseverance and the sufferings she offered for them helped to convert them. Once when she was enduring crippling doubts, she begged Jesus to make one of the wards go to Confession that very day. She told Jesus this would reassure her that it was indeed He Who was speaking to her about Divine Mercy. She noted in her *Diary*, "At that very moment, the girl asked to go to confession." The priest was called by the surprised Mother who had charge of the class, and the girl made her confession with "great compunction" (*Diary*, 74).

Young girls these days have a lot of stress and worries to contend with. We all need to be attentive to youth who might be going through something difficult at home or at school and are afraid or too shy to ask for the help they need. We can also lovingly and prayerfully guide them towards wholesome, healthy, and even holy friendships, as well as an active life in the Church.

PAUSE

Ponder whether you were affected by cliques and bullies as a teen girl. Have you suffered from them or contributed to them? Take that to our Lord in prayer.

ACT

Do not be conformed to this world. Pray and be transformed by God's grace! Do all you can to impart God's love and mercy to young girls and teens. A smile, a hug, a kind word, and prayer can go a long way!

A PRAYER OF MERCY

Dear Jesus, please forgive my shortcomings and
sins. Help me to uplift the hearts of young girls
and teens. Dear Jesus, please have mercy
upon my soul. I trust in You!
Mother Mary, help me, protect me, and guide me.
Saint Faustina, please pray for me.
Amen.

CHAPTER 5

Raised in a Single-Parent Household

"The slightest storm would drown me, engulfing my boat in the swirling depths, if You Yourself did not watch over me, O God, at each instant and moment of my life."

— Saint Faustina (*Diary*, 1322)

Single-parent households might be more common these days, rather than the exception to the rule, so we might not give much thought to the lives and struggles of these families unless we are part of one ourselves or close to someone who is. Yet, we should pay attention to them. Many children suffer invisibly and silently because they lack the love, support, or attention of one of their parents. This can be due to divorce, death, or military deployment, to name a few reasons. Many single-parent families who are committed, trying hard, staying alert, and adhering to their faith will indeed do well. We will look at various scenarios in this chapter.

Separated Through Military Deployment

Military life can be frightening. There are many unknowns. Family members are often intimidated by factors beyond their control, especially the fact that their loved one might be in harm's way. Military families sometimes operate as single-parent families when one of the spouses is deployed. It's unavoidable. Children in military families can feel isolated, and deeply miss the love and attention from the missing parent. One U.S. Army wife shared with me that while trying to be the sole parent present, she had often felt alone, as well as resentful towards two-parent families. Those of us who know a military family can reach out to the family members during deployments to lend a hand. Our gentle, loving works of mercy can help bring comfort and stability to a difficult situation.

Army wife Diane Bridon told me that she often worried about her husband's safety. She said she was afraid of "losing my husband in war, or that he might even be killed by an angry soldier at work, since he is a commander of eight hundred-plus soldiers and has to, at times, administer military justice." Diane told me that every deployment is difficult. She felt that she had to change something. So, during one particular Lenten season, Diane made a life-transforming decision. She set out for church as often as possible to adore our Lord. With every visit to our Lord, Diane's faith life took quantum leaps. She became less fearful and lonely. Naturally, Diane's transforming attitude helped her children as well. She said, "I saw myself growing closer to Christ, and the lonesomeness I felt earlier because of the absence of my spouse began to dissipate."

The Bridon family devised ways to remain connected even during deployments. Diane shared, "In our house, we did not allow any deployments to become negative, even though it was a really sad situation." She and her children rallied to shore up her husband. They were sad to see him leave, but Diane explained, "Once he was gone, we concentrated on supporting him, keeping everything going at home so he could focus on the mission at hand." They hung in for him so he wouldn't worry about them. They sent him care packages themed by holidays and special occasions. They even kept their family Sunday dinners alive while he was deployed by connecting through video conferencing "even if it was early in the afternoon for us." Their efforts paid off, keeping them from feeling too disconnected.

Military wife Nancy Belmont shared with me, "I did not cope very well during my husband's first deployment. I was very isolated." She and her newborn daughter lived in a small German village quite a distance from the post where her husband was stationed. "Twice a week," she said, she "would travel to post for Mass and our Catholic Women of the Chapel meetings." She said she endured the deployments but that she "wished away most of that year." She didn't want that to happen again.

Nancy continued, "When my husband deployed the second time, we were back in the States and I had two children." She was "determined to handle the situation differently." She decided to "band together with two other Army wives who had children the same age as mine."

These young families gathered together every Sunday for a special, shared family dinner. "We didn't care if our houses were tidy," she explained. "The joy of each other's company and the relief that we didn't have to cook dinner every night sustained us." These dinners were a great release from being on their own and gave every one of them "something to look forward to each week." The friends became close and relied upon one another to help with each other's children when circumstances called for it. Nancy recalled, "When I was horribly sick with the flu, one of these ladies insisted she bring me groceries. After one look at me, she took my children back to her house so they could play and I could get some rest."

Fifteen years after their first meeting, Nancy said, "They are still two of my closest friends and champions." They often recall the times years ago when their families grew together. She told me, "I'd never encountered friends like them before and I've never forged such strong bonds since. We knew we needed each other in a special way," she explained. "We worked to honor that connection every day of the deployment, and our relationship has endured, blossoming into a life-long friendship."

Apathetic Spouse

Some women struggle with the fact that their husband does not share their Catholic faith, or if he does, isn't practicing or interested. He sits back and leaves the faith education up to his wife. Thus, she might feel alone in her teaching — sometimes even like a single parent. Some amount of discouragement is normal. However, I sincerely hope that she will not become too discouraged. Through persevering efforts, she can indeed accomplish her goal in ensuring the children are raised solidly in their Catholic faith. Hopefully, with prayer, one day her husband may step up to the plate.

Broken Families

It's never easy growing up in a broken family. Though, as I mentioned previously, single-parent families (separated in divorce) are more common now than in times past, their stigmas and struggles don't simply disappear. Kids may feel let down, different, wounded, insecure, alone, scared, misunderstood — the list goes on. They might not vocalize all of their feelings, but instead try to get by in survival mode. Parents, grandparents, and caregivers can be instrumental in aiding the children to express what is on their hearts and help them get any necessary counseling. Their loving presence can be just the medicine that the children need.

Another kind of broken family is one in which one of the parents dies. The surviving parent and their children feel great loss and need time to grieve. With God's grace, life will go on. Memories are recalled, and new memories can be created. These families need loving help and guidance, too. If we know someone in this situation, we can prayerfully discern ways we can help them, and then carry out those works of mercy. Certainly our prayers for these families will be beneficial for them, and for our own souls as well. Our Lord desires that we help one another.

This reminds me of a time when one of my young daughters was feeling at a loss over an upcoming father/daughter dance. She hadn't wanted to tell her friends that her father had abandoned the family, which actually happened during the end of my pregnancy with her.

Well, a wonderful friend from our parish stepped in. He became Jessica's date and dance partner. Jessica no longer felt odd or afraid of what her friends would say. It turned out to be a lovely evening.

Nothing Can Separate Us

As devastating as they might be, separations, divorces, and deaths do not separate us from the love of God. He loves us very much and is present to us in all the dark corners of our lives, though we might not fully realize it at the time. We are reminded by the Apostle Paul:

> Who will separate us from the love of Christ? Will hardship, or distress, or persecution, or famine, or nakedness, or peril, or sword? As it is written, "For your sake we are being killed all day long; we are accounted as sheep to be slaughtered." No, in all these things we are more than conquerors through him who loved us. For I am convinced that neither death, nor life, nor angels, nor rulers, nor things present, nor things to come, nor powers, nor height, nor depth, nor anything else in all creation, will be able to separate us from the love of God in Christ Jesus our Lord (Rom 8:35-39).

Saint Faustina went through many struggles and two dark nights in the spiritual life (which I discuss in my book *52 Weeks with Saint Faustina: A Year of Grace and Mercy*). While she didn't experience a single-parent household, this woman religious' deep spiritual insights and experiences can still be helpful for those who have. Though very prayerful, the young nun often felt plagued by doubt. Can we blame her? No one, not even her superiors, believed her claims for quite some time. They thought she was faking her illnesses and making up Jesus' visits to her asking for the Divine Mercy message and devotion to be propagated. The young mystic's doubts were exacerbated by the evil one, who caused much havoc. How did she respond? Saint Faustina made many acts of trust to Jesus. Before she even fully understood the signature line in the Divine Mercy Image ("Jesus, I trust in You"), she believed that she glorified God by her acts of trust (see *Diary*, 190). We can do the same.

PAUSE

Take a moment to ponder any broken or single-parent families that you know or have known. Is there something you can do to help through prayer, word, or deed?

ACT

Pray an extra Rosary or Divine Mercy Chaplet for single-parent families.

A PRAYER OF MERCY
(Saint Faustina's Simple Act of Trust)

"Do what You will with me, O Jesus; I will adore You in everything. May Your will be done in me, O my Lord and my God, and I will praise Your infinite mercy" (*Diary*, 78).

Dear Jesus, I feel as St. Faustina has felt — that the slightest storm will engulf me. Please protect me from every storm each day and grant the graces I need to keep from "drowning."
Please have mercy upon my soul.
I trust in You!
Mother Mary, help me, protect me, and guide me.
Saint Faustina, please pray for me.
Amen.

CHAPTER 6
Discovering My Identity

"A woman's dignity is closely connected with the love which she receives by the very reason of her femininity; it is likewise connected *with the love which she gives in return.*"[17]

— Saint John Paul II

D o we ever truly understand our worth in God's eyes? Perhaps we will in Heaven; however, our Catholic identity begins when the holy waters of Baptism flow over our heads. Our souls are marked with a spiritually indelible character, and we become members of the Catholic Church. We discussed this important Sacrament earlier. Our parents are usually the ones who choose this life-transforming Sacrament for us when we are babies. But for those of us who weren't baptized as infants, it's a Sacrament we choose out of a desire to become members of the Body of Christ.

The Sacraments of the Catholic Church, which are gifts from God instituted by Jesus, are essential to our development as Catholic Christians and certainly help us to discover our identity as Catholic women. Of the seven Sacraments, there are three Sacraments of Initiation; they are Baptism, Confirmation, and Eucharist. After Baptism, we receive our First Penance and then our First Holy Communion at around 7 years old, which the Church calls the "age of reason," since a 7-year-old is capable of understanding whether what they are doing is right or wrong. Therefore, it is a good time for them to receive the Body and Blood of Christ for the first time. They can choose to welcome Jesus!

Canon law requires that children have a sufficient knowledge of the Eucharist after careful instruction and preparation so that they will be able to receive with faith and devotion.[18] Naturally, as the children grow and as their faith is nourished, their understanding, devotion, and faith will mature.

Eucharist as Source and Summit of Christian Life

The *Catechism* instructs us:

The Eucharist is "the source and summit of the Christian life."[19] "The other sacraments, and indeed all ecclesiastical ministries and works of the apostolate, are bound up with the Eucharist and are oriented toward it. For in the blessed Eucharist is contained the whole spiritual good of the Church, namely Christ himself, our Pasch"[20] (1324).

Because Jesus humbled Himself in the Incarnation of the Word to share in our humanity, we are enabled to have a share in His divinity. As we tread along our life-long pilgrimage, we are nourished by the Bread of Life each time we receive our Lord in Holy Communion. As we work hard at striving for sanctity, our longing for the Eucharist is ever deepened. We absolutely need the Eucharist for our spiritual survival.

I'm reminded of dear Mother Teresa, whom I knew personally. She often spoke about the Eucharist and how she and the Missionaries of Charity (MC) sisters depended upon the power of the Most Holy Sacrament of the Altar to carry out their work. She said they needed to receive Jesus in the broken bread of the Eucharist at Mass every morning in order to receive the strength and graces they needed to go out and take care of the broken bodies of the poor. We need our Lord as well. Being blessed with a special gift for receptivity, women are naturally predisposed to unite with Christ's self-gift in the Eucharist.

Saint Faustina was very devoted to Jesus in the Eucharist. In fact, her full religious name was "Sr. Maria Faustina Kowalska of the Most Blessed Sacrament." The young mystic's life was centered on the Holy Eucharist, even as a child. Later, as a young nanny, Helen would sing Polish hymns about Jesus in the Eucharist as she cared for the children. All throughout her *Diary*, we see that Faustina writes about the importance, strength, and beauty of the Eucharist. She adored and praised Jesus all through her days and even into her nights. She attributed everything that she was and every bit of strength that she had to the sustenance she received from the Holy Eucharist. Faustina wrote, "If the angels were capable of envy, they would envy us for two things: one is the receiving of Holy Communion, and the other is suffering" (*Diary*, 1804).

Saint Faustina asserted in her *Diary* that she was a living tabernacle for our Lord. She tells us that the Eucharistic Jesus stays with us! Specifically, she wrote, "Today, I have come to understand many of God's mysteries. I have come to know that Holy Communion remains in me until the next Holy Communion. ... My heart is a living tabernacle in which the living Host is reserved" (*Diary*, 1302). These are powerful words to ponder in our hearts.

Dozens of times in her *Diary*, the young mystic described seeing the rays of mercy coming from the Host as they do in the Divine Mercy Image; at times, they were covering the world (see *Diary*, 420, 441, 1046).

On one occasion, Sr. Faustina was having trouble praying because she was very exhausted. Nevertheless, longing for Jesus in Holy Communion, she hurried to the chapel for Holy Mass. Afterwards, Jesus told her, **"Know, My daughter, that the ardor of your heart is pleasing to Me. And just as you desire ardently to become united with Me in Holy Communion, so too do I desire to give Myself wholly to you; and as a reward for your zeal, rest on My Heart"** (*Diary*, 826). Can we even imagine this?

Saint Faustina then became immersed in the Lord "like a drop in a bottomless ocean." She wrote, "I drowned myself in Him as my sole treasure" (*Diary*, 826). Another time, Jesus told His little bride, **"In the Host is your power; It will defend you"** (*Diary*, 616).

Confirmation

As a young woman matures, she can choose to embark upon the Sacrament of Confirmation, which imparts a strengthening of the gift of the Holy Spirit within us. In this way she continues her journey in choosing the Catholic faith. Indeed, we need the Holy Spirit on our pilgrimage through life. The *Catechism* tells us, "Confirmation perfects Baptismal grace; it is the sacrament which gives the Holy Spirit in order to root us more deeply in the divine filiation, incorporate us more firmly into Christ, strengthen our bond with the Church, associate us more closely with her mission, and help us bear witness to the Christian faith in words accompanied by deeds" (1316).

Like Baptism, Confirmation marks our soul spiritually with an indelible character, and therefore is received only once.

Confession Is the Fountain of God's Mercy

The Sacrament of Reconciliation is essential to our spiritual lives. It is truly a pathway to peace of heart and will bring us into the state of grace once again. It also strengthens us for the journey ahead because through it we receive graces to fight off temptations. We need to humble ourselves and confess our sins to receive God's graces and forgiveness. Once, Jesus told St. Faustina how to make a good Confession and what actually happens there — how He meets us. The level of our trust determines the level of our receptivity to His grace and generosity.

Specifically, He told her:

> **Daughter, when you go to confession, to this fountain of My mercy, the Blood and Water which came forth from My Heart always flows down upon your soul and ennobles it. Every time you go to confession, immerse yourself entirely**

in My mercy, with great trust, so that I may pour
the bounty of My grace upon your soul. When
you approach the confessional, know this, that
I Myself am waiting there for you. I am only
hidden by the priest, but I Myself act in your
soul. Here the misery of the soul meets the God
of mercy. Tell souls that from this fount of mercy
souls draw graces solely with the vessel of trust.
If their trust is great, there is no limit to My generosity. The torrents of grace inundate humble
souls. The proud remain always in poverty and
misery, because My grace turns away from them
to humble souls (*Diary,* 1602).

In addition to confessing our sins and receiving forgiveness from God, we need to forgive those who have harmed
us. Though this is difficult at times, we must remember that
our Lord can forgive us our sins only to the extent that we are
willing to forgive others. We pray in the Our Father, "Forgive
us our debts, as we also have forgiven our debtors" (Mt 6:12).

We have discussed the essential Sacraments we need to
form our identity. Now, let's look at another need.

We Need Our Mother

Everyone needs a loving mother. Not every woman grows
up with a loving mother for a myriad of reasons. Their mothers
might have been ill equipped to handle the responsibility, for
instance, or unable to show the proper love that their daughters deserved. We can pray for these mothers and daughters.

The Blessed Mother can surely help a young girl or a
woman to discover her identity in Christ. We should never
fear reaching out in prayer to Mary, who wants to mother us.
We might hesitate, assuming she is too far away or that she
couldn't possibly understand what we are going through. We
must remember that Mary was human like us, and like us, she
needed to be steadfast in her faith and prayer life. Mary suffered intense pain, which included holding her precious Son's

lifeless body in her arms after He was taken down from the Cross. She knows our every pain and sorrow. She is well aware of the challenges we face — our joys and our sorrows.

Jesus told John, "Here is your mother" (Jn 19:27). Jesus gave us the exquisite gift of His own Mother when He was breathing His last breaths on the Cross. Mary had always been a co-redemptrix with her Son. She desired only God's will and humbly accepted that she was the chosen one when the Angel Gabriel came to her at the Annunciation. Saint Louis de Montfort wrote, "What Lucifer has lost by pride, Mary has gained through humility. What Eve has damned and lost by disobedience, Mary has saved by obedience."[21]

Mary entrusted herself completely to God and remained ever-present with Jesus from the very beginning (when she conceived the Son of God by the power of the Holy Spirit), united to Him through the Cross — and she is still working hard from Heaven to save our souls.

We will discuss Mother Mary at greater length in later chapters. For now, let us ponder the eminent gift of Mary and be encouraged to reach out to her regularly. She will help us to discover our authentic feminine identity.

I'll quickly note that St. Faustina loved the Blessed Mother intensely and kept prayerful company with her. Through her holy mentor, Faustina learned a great deal about the spiritual life as Mary led her daughter to a special union with her Son. Faustina wrote of one such occasion in her *Diary*: "I am spending this time with the Mother of God and preparing myself for the solemn moment of the coming of the Lord Jesus. The Mother of God is instructing me in the interior life of the soul with Jesus, especially in Holy Communion. It is only in eternity that we shall know the great mystery effected in us by Holy Communion. O most precious moments of my life!" (*Diary*, 840).

We'll discuss how a woman can discover her God-given gifts later on (Chapter 19). For now, let us ponder our identity as Catholic women and turn to Mother Mary often to ask her to guard the purity of our souls, hearts, and bodies.

PAUSE

Take some time to meditate on your identity as a Catholic woman. How have the Sacraments of Initiation helped to shape your life? How do they perhaps help you now in discovering your feminine identity?

ACT

Ask Mama Mary to be with you in your Sacraments and as you continue to discover your womanly identity. Keep walking forward in faith, frequenting the life-giving Sacraments. By your Confirmation, you are a soldier for Christ! Onward, Christian soldier!

A PRAYER OF MERCY

Dear Lord, King of Mercy, please forgive me for my many sins. Please transform my heart. "Mary, Immaculate Virgin, take me under Your special protection and guard the purity of my soul, heart and body. You are the model and star of my life" (*Diary*, 874).

Dear Jesus, please have mercy upon my soul.
I trust in You!
Mother Mary, help me, protect me, and guide me.
Saint Faustina, please pray for me.
Amen.

CHAPTER 7
Someday, My Prince Will Come!

"Love is patient; love is kind; love is not
envious or boastful or arrogant or rude.
It does not insist on its own way;
it is not irritable or resentful."

— 1 Cor 13:4-5

To be young and in love. That first crush — that first kiss!
Is that what it is all about? Well, when we are young girls,
we most likely think so. We yearn to be loved and cared for. We
long for loving arms around us, pulling us close to comfort us
and let us know that all will be well. We want to know that we
are protected — that we are loved. A strong father or father
image provides this stability. However, not every girl is blessed
in this way.

We should desire true love. But where and how do we
find it? How do we know if the handsome "prince" galloping
towards us on the white horse is the real deal or the devil in
disguise? I was certainly tricked by the illusion of a charming
prince at one point in my life. We will get into that later (see
Chapter 25). For now, let's take a look at St. Faustina's prince.

Saint Faustina might have been waiting for her prince to
come. After all, she partook in public dances with her friends.
Her Prince indeed arrived. Our Lord was her Prince and had
called to St. Faustina's heart and soul when she was just 7 years
old. Little Helen was praying at a Vespers service before the
Blessed Sacrament at St. Casimir Church in her hometown

when she heard a call to a religious vocation. She wrote in her *Diary*, "I experienced the definite call of God, the grace of a vocation to the religious life ... for the first time, I heard God's voice in my soul; that is, an invitation to a more perfect life" (7). Though Helen's parents were faithful Catholics, there was no one around that helped her by fostering her vocation, and her parents, being poor, did not want her to enter the convent for lack of a dowry. They also valued her as the most conscientious and responsible of their children, and were hoping to have her help and support around home and the farm as they became more frail with age.

Later, when St. Faustina was 18 and her parents refused her permission to enter religious life, she tried to "stifle" the "incessant call of grace" that she said caused her anguish, because though God was calling to her, her parents gave a flat out "no!" As St. Faustina explained it, "I turned myself over to the vain things of life" (*Diary*, 8). She shunned God interiorly and felt miserable; however, she felt she had no other options.

Try as she might to turn from God's call, eventually, she wrote, "God's grace won out in my soul" (*Diary*, 8). Her Prince did indeed arrive! Basically, Helen would end up eloping with God.

Let's back up to see what happened. In July 1924, Helen was with one of her sisters, trying to have a good time, but instead she experienced "deep torments." She would later record in her *Diary*, "As I began to dance, I suddenly saw Jesus at my side, Jesus racked with pain, stripped of His clothing, all covered with wounds, who spoke these words to me: **How long shall I put up with you and how long will you keep putting me off?**" (*Diary*, 9).

Can we even imagine this? Wow.

Suddenly, as she recalled in her *Diary*, "the charming music stopped [and] the company I was with vanished from my sight; there remained Jesus and I" (9). Helen had to figure out what to do — and quickly! Jesus vanished, and Helen was left to grapple with the intensity of it all while everything else stood frozen in time. She pretended to have a headache to hide what had just taken place in her soul. And then she slipped away from the dance unnoticed. That's when she made her way to the Cathedral of St. Stanislaus Kostka, where Jesus would reveal to her what she should do next. That very evening was the beginning of her holy journey to become a nun and God's Secretary of Divine Mercy.

Our Father in Heaven loves us all with an everlasting love, and His loving arms are around us. But, if we were not raised as a believer, we might not realize that He is with us and always has our best interests in mind. God's love is unconditional, and He will never ultimately disappoint us. God tells us, "For surely I know the plans I have for you, says the LORD, plans for your welfare and not for harm, to give you a future with hope" (Jer 29:11). God promises us eternal life.

Saint John professed, "For God so loved the world that he gave his only Son, so that everyone who believes in him may not perish but may have eternal life" (Jn 3:16). There is no love stronger than this!

"Boys Only Want One Thing!"

If adolescent girls do not receive solid Christian guidance as they mature through growth spurts and puberty changes, and as they long for loving relationships, they very well might head in the wrong direction, chasing after what they think is true love. They are not yet mature enough to understand their mixed emotions and the fact that adolescent boys and girls develop and mature differently. For instance, girls go through puberty ahead of boys. It is a turbulent time when a girl's struggles for independence, along with her need for peer acceptance and the pull of peer pressure, can feel utterly overwhelming.

You might have heard words of caution, sometimes even shouted out by a caring guardian: "Boys only want one thing!" Though these guardians likely mean well, they seldom elaborate or take the time to lovingly sit down with their girl to correctly explain the birds and the bees. They might be embarrassed themselves when it comes to teaching sex education, or they might not be equipped to teach it correctly.

Chances are good that most young girls hear a lot of misinformation from their peers, as well as too much encouragement from an unbalanced society to throw caution to the wind and get mixed up in unhealthy relationships and sex. The culture certainly pushes a false identity on girls and women, bombarding them with crazy mixed messages that are often far too difficult for young, vulnerable, hormonal teen-aged girls to discern.

As discussed in Chapter 3, it's essential for parents, grandparents, and guardians to keep a close eye on a young girl's activities and friendships, and to be a solid and loving part of their lives. In addition, it's most important to put safe parameters in place for children. Adolescents can use these rules when they need a safe way out of a bad or dangerous circumstance. Let them know that they can save face and excuse their bowing out of a situation by calling on the rules that are out of their control.

To help our girls, we can find additional, meaningful ways to spend time together, encourage them to talk to a trusted adult in times of need (even if it won't be us), discuss ways to manage any stress, and emphasize the importance of not losing sight of their Christian identity when within a peer setting. Encourage your daughter or granddaughter to feel secure in her own shoes — to be her own person — a daughter of God possessing a magnificent dignity and purpose.

Are We Raising the Bar?

Truth be told, a holy young woman can awaken a man's heart to be good. Her pure love and encouragement deepens his vision and refines his works. I cannot help but think of Venerable Fulton J. Sheen, who challenged women to raise the bar. He did not mince words. You have probably heard it before, but it certainly bears repeating. He said, "When a man loves a woman, he has to become worthy of her. The higher her virtue, the more noble her character, the more devoted she is to truth, justice, goodness, the more a man has to aspire to be worthy of her." And then he made an unheard-of claim.

"The history of civilization could actually be written in terms of the level of its women," he exclaimed. [22]

Wow. Can we pause to really take his poignant words to heart?

Let's ask ourselves a couple of important questions. Are we women exhibiting virtue, noble character, and a love for justice, truth, and goodness? All of the time? I don't think so.

Sadly, with all the confusing mixed messages aimed at them, countless women and girls have lost sight of their true dignity, beauty, and greatness in cooperating with God's magnificent plan. And if we are confused about our own dignity, how are we to help the men? We must first be right with God and understand what loving God is all about before everything else in our lives will fall into its proper place.

Our sister Faustina comes to the rescue. She wrote, "And God has given me to understand that there is but one thing that is of infinite value in His eyes, and that is love of God; love, love, and once again, love; and nothing can compare with a single act of pure love of God" (*Diary*, 778). If only we women could learn this foundational truth early on in life. We are so fortunate that our friend Faustina put her holy sentiments and experiences into the words she penned in her *Diary*.

"Oh, with what inconceivable favors God gifts a soul that loves Him sincerely!" she continued. "Oh, how happy is the soul who already here on earth enjoys His special favors!" Certainly sweet Faustina was herself one of these treasured souls. The young mystic added, "And of such are the little and humble souls" (*Diary*, 778).

※ ※ ※

PAUSE

Take a few moments to ponder the fact that we women should be raising the bar. Ask yourself if you are exhibiting virtue, noble character, and a love for justice, truth, and goodness. Why or why not?

ACT

Love is patient. Love is kind. Raise the bar!

A PRAYER OF MERCY

Dear Lord, King of Mercy, please forgive me of
my many sins. I am sorry for the times that I have
shunned You through my bad choices and in
refusing to listen to Your calling.
Help me to seek the true love that will deeply
transform my heart — Your love.
Jesus, I trust in You!
Mother Mary, help me, protect me, and guide me.
Saint Faustina, please pray for me.
Amen.

CHAPTER 8
Graduation

"Amid the roaring waves I sail peacefully,
trustingly, and gaze like a child into the
distance without fear, because You,
O Jesus, are my Light."

— Saint Faustina (*Diary*, 1322)

Most likely, everyone reading this book has had the benefit of an education. Perhaps not everyone has graduated from school or had the opportunity for a college education. Saint Faustina never officially graduated from school. In fact, she received barely a year and a half of primary education, because the older children left the small school she attended in order to make room for the younger children who were coming in. Interestingly, despite her lack of education, Jesus would appoint St. Faustina as His Secretary of Mercy. Amazing, isn't it? Our Lord often uses those whom others might consider to be insignificant in some way. God always uses humble souls to reach and transform hearts.

Graduation from high school, college, or university usually ushers one into a new life of some sort. We shove off onto the high seas! Everyone has their own unique path — sometimes it takes a long while to discover ours. In addition, our path might vary many times throughout our lives.

Here I am reminded of words that St. Faustina wrote about trust:

The barque of my life sails along
Amid darkness and shadows of night,
And I see no shore;
I am sailing the high seas.

The slightest storm would drown me,
Engulfing my boat in the swirling depths,
If You yourself did not watch over me, O God,
At each instant and moment of my life.

Amid the roaring waves
I sail peacefully, trustingly,
And gaze like a child into the distance without fear,
Because You, O Jesus, are my Light.

Dread and terror is all about me,
But within my soul is peace more profound than the
     depths of the sea,
For he who is with You, O Lord, will not perish;
Of this Your love assures me, O God.

Though a host of dangers surround me,
None of them do I fear, for I fix my gaze on
     the starry sky,
And I sail along bravely and merrily,
As becomes a pure heart.

And if the ship of my life sails so peacefully,
This is due to but one thing above all:
You are my helmsman, O God.
This I confess with utmost humility (*Diary*, 1322).

Saint Faustina was completely aware that without God's
help she would be drowned in the storms of life — she would
sink. Yet she does not fear the host of dangers around her. She
fixes her eyes on the hopeful, starry sky. She sails away bravely,
peacefully trusting God, allowing Him to be her helmsman —
giving Him complete control of her life.

As a young woman graduating from school or university,
we are thrust into an uncertain world that seems to be getting

more troubled and convoluted by the day. It truly is an exciting, albeit scary time when we embark upon a new chapter in life — to get on that boat and sail off towards our future. It is impossible to learn everything about life from books or professors. We have to experience life in order to truly learn.

After graduating, we look ahead at the dark ocean of life and are afraid that once we are out on the rough sea, we will no longer see the shore behind us. What if we come across fierce storms? What if we can't see through the dense fog? We might resist the call of God to our soul to set out into the deep — to trust Him at the helm. Yet, when we can prayerfully let go of our fears and trust God wholeheartedly, we will have true peace of heart as God guides us into the future.

Trusting God starts today. We can pray to emulate St. Faustina's great trust and "gaze like a child into the distance without fear" because Jesus is our Light. A childlike faith coupled with a good dose of prudence will take us a long way. As a parent, grandparent, aunt, sister, or friend, we can be a great encourager to a young woman who is graduating. We can let her know that she can trust us and come to us at any time. Our prayers, congratulatory good wishes, and encouragement will indeed help and will boost her self-esteem.

Getting That Degree

We move out of our comfort zones when we move ahead into the future. Getting that degree and forging ahead takes hard work but also courage. It is tempting to retreat to a pre-graduation or pre-degree safe harbor. After all, we feel secure there where things were predictable. But, with prayer and determination, we can venture out. We should try not to listen to the naysayers (who could be ourselves!). The first deaf-blind person to earn a bachelor of arts degree, Helen Keller, urges us on with her bold statement, "Life is either a daring adventure or nothing."[23] Keller described her life not able to see or hear as being "at sea in a dense fog."[24]

In addition, it's important to ponder the fact that, by the time we graduate and have our degree in hand, the workforce may have changed. Circumstances might make it difficult to pursue our field of choice. Some of us might be dealing with something unexpected — a loss of a loved one, a serious illness, or an unplanned pregnancy. Our lives might be changed for the time being or forever, and we embark upon a different path. There are a myriad of reasons why our plans and dreams might change or become rerouted. There might be a time in the future to revisit those earlier plans.

We can try our best to pause, reflect, and truly offer our situations to the Lord, asking His help. We can learn from St. Faustina, who discovered the importance of surrendering her heart wholly to God. When faced with fears and difficulties, she did not rely on her feelings, but rather upon faith. She stated, "In the midst of the worst difficulties and adversities, I do not lose inner peace or exterior balance, and this discourages my adversaries. Patience in adversity gives power to the soul" (*Diary*, 607).

Our sister Faustina teaches us to trust God, be vigilant, and not lose heart.

As I mentioned in the last chapter, St. Faustina knew she was called to religious life, but did not receive the support she absolutely needed from her parents due to lacking the necessary money for her dowry. So her dreams seemed crushed for a time. She asked her father again a year later, and his answer was the same: "No!"

Saint Faustina felt she had no other choice but to go the way of the world — at least partly. She would work as a domestic servant in the big city of Łódź and live in an apartment with her cousins. We know the rest of the story. (Well, not totally, because I believe that St. Faustina is still working hard in Heaven!) She was finally able to pursue her dream and enter the convent. God far surpassed her humble expectations, I might add! He formed her into a great saint — His Secretary and Apostle of Divine Mercy!

What Do Women Do?

Let's take a look at some of our abilities and concerns as we finish out our chapter on graduation, a time when a woman might aspire to make her mark on the world.

I'll tell you just seven things we women do! These traits are not exclusive to women, of course, but they are some of our strengths:

1. **We love!** God gave us soft hearts, after all!

2. **We search. For what?** For a better life, for peace, for happiness, for truth, for something better. But hopefully, we always search for God. However, sometimes in our search, we could get sidetracked. Many times, our search, our thirst is not quenched, and we don't feel satisfied. We might be searching in all the wrong places. We'll talk about this in Chapter 10.

3. **We fix!** Or we try to fix. Perhaps men are better known for this, but we have it in us, too! We want justice — it's in our makeup to make things better.

4. **We nurture!** It's what women do!

5. **We discover!** Ultimately, prayerfully, we discover God and our God-given gifts!

6. **We lead!** Hopefully we lead others in the right direction — towards God, and family first. Mother Teresa always said, "Love begins at home." When our family is cared for, we might broaden our reach to neighbors, community members, and people in the workplace or our parish.

7. **We protect!** Ever seen a mama bear? I have! I live in the woods of rural Connecticut. You don't mess with a mama bear protecting her cubs. We women have this in us, too — a protective spirit!

What Are Women's Concerns?

Countless issues come to mind, but I'll name just seven right now:

1. **Their family.** For mothers, it's their kids, especially, that they stay on the right road, and that they are happy and healthy.

2. **The world outside our doors.** It can look pretty scary.

3. **The future.** What does it hold for us?

4. **The past.** We might have regrets, but we must remember St. Faustina's counsel on living in the present moment, which we will discuss more as we go along.

5. **Our health, healthcare, bills, and money.**

6. **Sexual harassment in one form or another.** (I must note that though sexual harassment is a common experience among women, this doesn't mean it is inevitable in our lives. Our faith teaches chastity to men and women. Sexual harassment is a sin on the part of the harasser.)

7. **Body image.** This is a huge one! We are never satisfied. We mature women (myself included) want to look like we did 15 or 20 years ago! I'm telling you right now — it ain't gonna happen! Let go of that dream! We chase after a very unobtainable standard due to a myriad of demands for perfection. Women are bombarded with these demands by the culture. Sometimes they're very tough to ignore. However, we need to learn to be happy in our own skin.

Saint John Paul II reminded us that women have great strength and dignity and that they have been entrusted with a great task. In his apostolic letter *Mulieris Dignitatem* (*On the Dignity and Vocation of Women*; *MD*), he said, "The moral and spiritual strength of a woman is joined to her awareness that *God entrusts the human being to her in a special way.* Of course, God entrusts every human being to each and every other human being. But this entrusting concerns women in a special way — precisely by reason of her femininity — and this in a particular way determines their vocation" (*MD*, 30, emphasis in original).

We women are gifted with strength and dignity! Let that sink in! Let's keep his words in mind and move on to another question.

What Can Women Do?

A lot! Some of us women might feel stymied over our lack of control in life, but we can certainly pray. We certainly need to! Prayer is powerful. We can lift our eyes towards Heaven and its rewards and follow God, not the world. We can strive to be a radiant example of authentic feminine beauty.

⁂

PAUSE

Take a few moments to ponder what St. Faustina did when faced with fears and difficulties. She did not rely on her feelings, but rather upon faith (see *Diary*, 607).

⁂

ACT

Women are gifted with strength and dignity! Pray to discover yours! Try to be a model of true feminine beauty through the virtues of faith, hope, and love that reside in your heart. Move forward performing works of mercy with God's grace! Trust God! Let Him steer the ship.

A Prayer of Mercy

Dear Lord, King of Mercy, have mercy on me, a
sinner. Please help and protect me. Grant to me
the "peace more profound than the depths of the
sea" that St. Faustina spoke of, if that be Your holy
will. Please, dear Holy Spirit, enkindle my heart.
I want to move forward with God's amazing
grace, equipped with His teachings. I pray that
I will help all in my path, today and always
— imparting God's mercy to them.
Jesus, I trust in You!
Mother Mary, help me.
Saint Faustina, pray for me.
Amen.

CHAPTER 9
Launching Out

"And he said to them,
'Follow me, and I will make
you fish for people.'"

— Mt 4:19

How do we launch out on our own — whenever that might be in life? This could be an experience we go through more than once — when we are young and make our first steps into the adult world, and later on when we launch out again, perhaps moving on from an old chapter of our lives. It's possible it could be a conversion of sorts. At times, we turn the pages of our lives amid trepidation. Whom should we trust? Ourselves? God?

Saint John Paul II explained that each of us has a special calling in God's plan, and that we need to listen carefully to Him. He said, "The Lord tells the Prophet Jeremiah that his vocation was *part of God's eternal plan* even before he was born." He elaborated, "These words remind us that *each person has a place in God's plan* and that *each of us should carefully listen to God's voice in prayer in order to discover the special calling we have received in Christ.*"[25]

We need to listen carefully.

In the four Gospels, Jesus says, "Follow me" at least 20 times. The Bible contains more than 30 verses about "following" God. Jesus said, "I am the light of the world. Whoever

follows me will never walk in darkness but will have the light
of life" (Jn 8:12). He calls to us and makes clear that He will
indeed lead us to the light and only the light.

We need to trust His words.

Indeed, Jesus calls to us — each and every one of us.
He says, "Come, follow me." Saint John Paul II explained it
this way:

> In the hidden recesses of the human heart the grace
> of a vocation takes the form of a dialogue. It is a
> dialogue between Christ and an individual, in which
> a personal invitation is given. Christ calls the person
> by name and says: "Come, follow me." This call,
> this mysterious inner voice of Christ, is heard most
> clearly in silence and prayer. Its acceptance is an act
> of faith.[26]

How do I hear this call from Christ? Am I meant to
marry? Is God calling me to religious life, or single life? What
career should I pursue? Saint Teresa of Avila said she pretty
much forced herself to become a nun simply because she knew
it would be good for her. As years go by, Christ's call to us may
vary in terms of what He asks us to do. Later in life, His call
might simply be to stay faithful to the duties of our daily lives
(not necessarily an easy task).

Life Is a Mystery

Life is a mystery. We may have many great plans and
dreams but never see them come to fruition. God might have
another idea! Our lives might unfold in ways we had never
imagined. Mine sure did. But that is another story![27]

We must trust God with our lives. He surely knows what
is best. Saint John Paul II reminds us, "Every vocation is a
deep personal experience of the truth of these words: '*I am
with you*' (*Ex* 3:12)."[28]

Because we are on the subject of plans and dreams, I am
reminded of how we are to trust God even with the little details
of our daily life. Often a brand new "to-do" list suddenly forms

in my mind — all the things I realize I would like to do as I am lying in bed and opening my eyes to greet a new day. This, mind you, is in addition to the already-written list from the night before. The new list sounds completely reasonable as I recline there, ready to throw my legs over the side of the bed and head to the shower. However, truth be told, almost every day, my "to-do" list takes on a life of its own. I try to stick to my lists, but there are times when I go to bed that night lamenting over what I did not accomplish.

I have to ask myself a couple of questions: *Am I piling too much on my plate? Or, perhaps, are those interruptions to my day (or night) encounters from God — His gifts to me, allowing me to serve others?*

I need to recognize that God might have another plan, one that is more important for me that day. For instance, the frightened elderly neighbor who showed up at my front door with a nosebleed when I was in the middle of doing a webinar; the neighbor calling at 2 a.m. with an urgent need when I thought I was going to catch up on some sleep; the continual phone calls; the never-ending communication coming in from various parts of the world from folks needing some sort of help — all these are wonderful opportunities to pause from whatever it is I'm doing to lovingly serve others in need.

We can dream and plan, but we must be open to God's will.

Let's Not Be Tricked!

It's so easy to get lost along our search for the Truth — our hunt for meaning in our lives. Too many alluring things beckon us to follow, and the devil is so cunning that he makes sure to disguise his darkness in pretty little packages. If we are not extra careful, we can fall into the evil one's traps many times over.

Consider the frog that is boiled to death without ever being aware of it. Venerable Fulton J. Sheen mentioned this deceptive method of killing whereby the temperature of the water is turned up imperceptibly. He said, "At no point during the increase of temperature will the frog offer resistance. It

will never realize that the water is too hot — until it's dead."
Sheen goes on to explain, "That's the way we are spiritually.
We just become used to the temperature of the world."[29]

That is tragic, because as beloved Sheen tells us, "We
don't realize that it is gradually possessing us, until we are in its
grip." He gives sage advice: "So we are doing battle therefore
with triteness, shallowness, and dullness, and we have to resist
and begin to go in the other direction."[30]

We need to be on guard, resist those sparkly, disguised
packages from the evil one, and be careful not to get accustomed to the "temperature of the world." If we keep our eyes
on the Lord, ensuring that we make time for Him, speaking
to Him often in prayer and frequenting the Sacraments, we
will stay on the straight and narrow path that leads to eternal life. Surrounding ourselves with like-minded friends and
associates will help a lot. It's way too easy to get used to the
"temperature" of our environment, so we want to make sure
our environment is holy.

Landing a Career

Saint Faustina didn't launch out into a secular career
because she was a professed religious sister, yet we can learn
from her work. When she was a young teen, Helen worked as a
domestic, caring for children. She was beloved by the children
and their parents alike. She loved our Lord and lifted her heart
to Him through Eucharistic hymns and prayers even as she was
engrossed with the task at hand.

As a nun, St. Faustina worked in a bakery, in the bakery
shop, in the kitchen, answering the convent gate, and serving the people who came begging. She also worked in the
gardens when she was strong enough. She was a fastidious
worker and her hard work bore great fruit — literally! In the
greenhouse and the garden, she nurtured the plants, helping
them to grow in great abundance. I wonder if she used holy
water in the garden!

The young mystic recorded in her *Diary,* "Help me, O
Lord, that my hands may be merciful and filled with good

deeds, so that I may do only good to my neighbors and take upon myself the more difficult and toilsome tasks" (163). The saint-in-the-making was always concerned with pleasing our Lord and helping those around her. She had a big heart and persevered in toiling and praying for others.

Once, when suffering from tuberculosis, St. Faustina was sent to the congregation's residence in Derdy. When she was not praying the Rosary, doing some spiritual exercises, breathing deeply the fresh, crisp air, or taking the required two-hour rest each afternoon, she would work in the kitchen. She cooked for seven sisters and more than 30 girls living there. She was assigned a certain unruly girl as a kitchen assistant. It was there among the pots, pans, and potatoes that her holiness made a grand impression on the troubled girl.

Mother Serafina Kukulska, the superior in Walendow at that time, would testify later on that no one wanted to work with this girl. However, through Sr. Faustina's godly influence, the girl was dramatically changed. Faustina might not have realized at the time what an impression she was making. No doubt Faustina left it up to God as she prayed earnestly, gave direction, and doled out lots of love to a girl who might never have been loved properly.

It's the same with us. By God's amazing grace, we can help to transform lives by our loving example.

God Always Has a Plan!

One of my favorite anecdotes about Sr. Faustina's work relates the time she was having much trouble lifting the heavy pots of potatoes from the stove to drain off the boiling water into the kitchen sink. She felt she wasn't strong enough, based on the numerous times she had struggled with the weight of the pots and accidentally spilled scorching hot water (and sometimes potatoes) all over the linoleum kitchen floor! She decided to speak with the Mother Directress because she did not want to waste any more food or burn anyone. There were other sisters more suited for the task. Despite Faustina's earnest request, what did the Mother Directress say? Well, it was certainly not helpful to the distressed nun, who was simply told that she would acquire the skills.

Sister Faustina went to her Lord and Master and asked Him what to do. She immediately heard, **"From today on you will do this easily; I shall strengthen you"** (*Diary*, 65). What a consolation it must have been! That evening, she had an amazing experience, which I recalled in my book *52 Weeks with Saint Faustina*:

> When she lifted the pot cover to release the steam and peered inside, Sr. Faustina nearly fell over. This time, it wasn't because of the weight of the pot.
>
> Instead of cooked potatoes, an abundance of the most beautiful red roses this sister had ever seen perfectly filled the pot! The mystic was completely taken by surprise. For one brief instant, Sr. Faustina could not comprehend the miracle's meaning. Suddenly, a distinct voice within her revealed the answer. **"I change such hard work of yours into bouquets of most beautiful flowers, and their perfume rises up to My throne"** (*Diary*, 65).[31]

God always has a plan! He uses our weaknesses and makes us strong. He swoops in with nothing short of a miracle! While we most likely will not see an abundance of lovely red roses in our pots of food, we should feel confident knowing that we can always learn from Jesus, realizing that He is pleased with our work when it is done lovingly and offered to Him.

Trust and Grace

Every morning, we arise afresh in Jesus, our Light. Let us not allow our days to get off to the wrong start by being concerned about yesterday's worries. Ask Jesus to relieve you of the burden of old worries with fresh morning hope. Prayerfully start anew each day.

Jesus wants us to trust Him with our lives. When we are young and launching out for the first time, we might lack the maturity to fully trust our Lord. Certainly, with God's grace, we can trust Him at any age or stage of our life.

We must remember that Jesus will grant to us every grace that we need — that is, when we trust Him. He told His Secretary of Mercy, **"The graces of My mercy are drawn by means of one vessel only, and that is — trust. The more a soul trusts, the more it will receive. Souls that trust boundlessly are a great comfort to Me, because I pour all the treasures of My graces into them. I rejoice that they ask for much, because it is My desire to give much, very much. On the other hand, I am sad when souls ask for little, when they narrow their hearts"** (*Diary*, 1578).

PAUSE

Ponder the way in which you do your work, what-ever that may be. Do you put your whole heart into it? Recalling how our friend Faustina worked in the gardens, in the kitchens, and at the gates, what can you learn from her? Keep in mind that she went to the Lord with her troubles and strove to do her best.

ACT

Don't conform to the "temperature" of the world. Keep praying. Have faith in God. Trust Him. Go the distance. Don't stop!

A Prayer of Mercy

Jesus, You told St. Faustina that the graces of Your
mercy are drawn by means of the vessel of trust.
Please help me to wholeheartedly trust
You with my entire life.
Please have mercy upon my soul.
I trust in You!
Mother Mary, help me, protect me, and guide me.
Saint Faustina, please pray for me.
Amen.

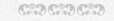

Act of Faith

*Saint John Paul II said we accept God's call
"in an act of faith."*

"O my God, I firmly believe
that you are one God in three divine Persons,
Father, Son, and Holy Spirit.
I believe that your divine Son became man
and died for our sins and that he will come
to judge the living and the dead.
I believe these and all the truths
which the Holy Catholic Church teaches
because you have revealed them
who are eternal truth and wisdom,
who can neither deceive nor be deceived.
In this faith I intend to live and die.
Amen."[32]

PART TWO
Summer

"I want to hide myself in Your Most Merciful Heart as a dewdrop does in a flower blossom. Enclose me in this blossom against the frost of the world. No one can conceive the happiness which my heart enjoys in this solitude, alone with God."

— Saint Faustina (*Diary*, 1395)

The season of summer might evoke happy memories of lazy summer days from childhood, as well as bright expectations for our future summers. This part of our book is anything but lazy as we delve into a variety of powerful milestones in a woman's life. Saint Faustina speaks of her desire to be hidden in Jesus' Merciful Heart as a dewdrop in a flower blossom to be protected from the "frost of the world." Like our sister Faustina, let us endeavor in the summer of our life to draw near to our Lord's Merciful Heart.

CHAPTER 10
Searching

"In God's eternal plan, woman is the one in whom the order of love in the created world of persons takes first root."

— Saint John Paul II (*MD*, 29)

"I Am Woman." Remember the 1971 hit song by Helen Reddy, making women out to be strong and invincible? The song and its lyrics celebrated female empowerment and became a sort of anthem for the women's liberation movement. It is true that women are strong. We are very strong. Let us not forget that. And, yes, that inner lioness comes out of us at times. Ask any mother! Of course, we need to be mindful to always act appropriately when letting that roar out!

A little further along in the 1980s, we heard about women bringing home the bacon and frying it up in the pan in the "Cause I'm A Woman" perfume commercial. It implies that women "can have it all." However, as a Catholic woman speaking to you through the pages of this book, I need to add that we must not lose sight of our beautiful, God-given feminine gifts. We cannot allow anyone's worldly definition of a real, strong, authentic, or whatever kind of woman dictate to us how we should be. It is God alone who defines our womanhood. In addition, we need to be mindful about what we are pursuing in our lives.

We will discuss our beautiful feminine gifts in Chapter 19, but for now, we want to look at what we are searching for in life — at some of the distractions and demands for perfection we face as women; at how we can resist temptations to veer off the path and give up; and at love and our true dignity and mission — and get some help from St. Faustina, and the Blessed Mother, too!

There's a lot to take in, so take your time — pray and savor.

What Can Distract Women From God?

We innately thirst for the Truth, for God, for a better life, for solutions to our problems, and for peace and justice to prevail, but in our search for all this, we can get off track — most likely more than once. The world, of course, is a big distraction, right? The culture — the bombardment from the advertising industry that targets women since we are the number-one consumers — is another big distraction. The internet and social media are also problems if not used correctly, because for one thing, they can present a false sense of reality, promising "perfect everything!"

We might begin to lament that our lives are not Pinterest or Instagram perfect, like the images projected on our screens. We can get caught up in other "realities" rather than focus on the people whom God has given us to nurture, guide, and be guided by: our family, our neighbors, friends, community members, and actually, everyone we rub elbows with.

It sounds funny, but we can also get in our own way. If our noses are mostly inserted in our devices and smartphones, or if we are overly involved in too many committees and commitments that we think we *have* to be involved with, then we will have scarcely any time left to talk with our Creator, the One who helps us to find our way to Him!

If we are so preoccupied, how can we be aware and attentive to life as it unfolds around us? We can lose our way to God because we get in the way — yes, we can be a problem!

Also, we women can feel very weary and even battered by the constant expectations and demands of others, and by the noisy culture in which we live. Our Lord calls us to Himself.

He has said, "Come to me, all you that are weary and are carrying heavy burdens, and I will give you rest" (Mt 11:28). His words should comfort our souls. His presence will give us a deep and abiding peace. And we women who know Jesus' love and peace need to bring it to others!

Let us ask ourselves if we possibly might be looking for "perfection" and beauty in all the wrong places. In our pursuit for so-called perfection, we can waste so much time and lose opportunities to do what God wants us to do. Why do we want to be perfect according to the world's standards? God calls us to be perfect in HIS eyes!

Demands for Perfection

The simple fact that we are women subjects us to countless demands that can get in the way of acknowledging who we really are in God's eyes. These demands can also hinder our search for God and deter us from launching out into life.

By the way, dear sister in Christ, I need to tell you — there is no such thing as a "size-zero" woman! I mentioned this in Chapter 4 when talking about younger girls. So I want to ask, if there is no such thing as a size zero (in my humble opinion), why kill yourself? It's all made up — a very clever marketing tool! This goes for all the other lies targeting women, too. We simply cannot waste our time and energy chasing after some unobtainable level of perfection.

Most of the advertising is airbrushed anyway. It's completely fake. I know that *you* don't fall for this, but sadly, some women do. We can't blame them for not being able to see clearly through the murky waters, but we need to help them! Our dignity and value can never truly be determined by the number on a scale, our clothes size, a youthful appearance, or anything else!

Many women have been scarred by painful early experiences. Remember the "Mean Girls" experience I discussed in Chapter 4? Well, we women have a tendency to carry around a bunch of baggage, and it's killing our spirit! Yes, those traumas and awful experiences have indeed hurt us deeply, but we need to ask God for healing so that we can stop weighing ourselves down. Holding on to the pain is like trying to walk softly while carrying the world on our backs.

Take the time to read what St. John Paul II had to say so beautifully about women's gifts in his 1995 *Letter to Women* (#2) and in *Mulieris Dignitatem*. He lamented the fact that throughout the centuries, women had been pushed to the margins of society, viewed as sex objects, and not acknowledged for their amazing gifts, among other issues (*Letter to Women*, 3, 4, 5).

It's no wonder that women struggle! Let us do our very best to use our God-given gifts and help others to discover theirs.

That Thing Called Love!

Let's get back to that thing we do as women that I mentioned in the "Graduation" chapter: We love. We have big hearts. It's quite obvious. Just take a look around and you'll see countless women caring for others in multiple ways. God made us that way — to receive love and to give love.

In *Mulieris Dignitatem*, St. John Paul II said, "Woman can only find herself by giving love to others" (*MD*, 30).

This is powerful! Let us women ponder these words. We can only find ourselves by giving love to others!

We will discuss this further in our "Spiritual Motherhood" chapter, but to state it briefly, every woman is a mother to others, whether biologically, adoptively, or spiritually. It is innate. Women are given motherly hearts by God specifically to care for others, to nurture relationships, encourage, uplift, ease pain, bring peace, and to soothe the savage beast — to mother them!

This is real beauty!

Saint John Paul II shares with us, "The moral and spiritual strength of a woman is joined to her awareness that *God entrusts the human being to her in a special way*" (*MD*, 30, emphasis in original).

What is the key word here? A few come to mind: "human being," "entrusts," and "awareness." I want to talk about *awareness.*

Awareness is key! Awareness regarding God's amazing gift of the human being to us women is required of us so that we can fully comprehend our vocation as feminine women. If I am caught up in the values (or lack thereof) of the culture, the mass media, excessive shopping, possibly idiotic reality television, and spending endless time on the internet, I might be totally unaware of God entrusting others to me. The problem isn't just my lack of time to hear God and converse with Him. It's also that other things that are not holy will pollute my heart and make it much more difficult for me to find my way out of the muck, especially if I am becoming numb to their ill effects (or even enjoying them).

And if God is counting on us women to make a beautiful difference in our world by drawing others to Him through our lives of Christian love — well, we will have failed Him. We will have fallen for the "apple," as did Eve.

So again, we need to be mindful about what we get involved in and pray to find a proper balance between our self-care, our families, community service, and apostolic work. As I said earlier, women have tender hearts, and we can easily love many people and things, but we must not neglect the very people our Lord has given us to care for. We must be careful not to get caught up in senseless worldly attachments.

It's a good time to mention the necessity of holy self-love. To love our neighbor as ourselves, we have to possess love and care for ourselves. To be selfless, we have to be engaging in healthy, holy self-care, or else we will have nothing to give. That said, let's be sure not to burn the candle at both ends by getting so overly involved in activities that we exhaust ourselves.

Mother Teresa forever preached that "love begins at home." Let's be sure we have our priorities straight. Our Lord will guide our priorities if we ask Him in prayer.

Blessed Fr. Michael Sopoćko's Advice

Saint Faustina eventually had a wonderful spiritual director who helped her a great deal in spreading the Divine Mercy message. (I say "eventually" because it took some time before anyone actually believed her.) She repeatedly asked Jesus to give her a spiritual director. Jesus allowed His bride to meet her director during an interior vision (see *Diary*, 34), so when she finally met him, she already knew him!

The esteemed theologian Fr. Michael Sopoćko (1888-1975) was a professor of theology, a military chaplain, and a confessor to many converts. He was the first priest who fully believed St. Faustina. At first, he was leery about getting involved as Faustina's director, but her superior practically pleaded with him. God's will won out! Blessed Sopoćko jumped in with both feet and became instrumental in the propagation of the message of Divine Mercy. Because he was obedient to God's call and all of what it entailed, he has been beatified! Hopefully, he will someday also be canonized!

One of the many articles that Blessed Sopoćko wrote was titled "Trust in God." In it, he discussed the right balance in our trust in God, the many ways we trust God, how to help the dying with trust (which we'll discuss in Chapter 34, "Preparing for Death and Eternal Life"), and much more. I'll share his wise words with you here, but first I want you to know that St. Faustina noted in her *Diary* that Fr. Sopoćko's writings were very pleasing to Jesus.

Regarding our approach to trusting in God, he wrote:

> When we trust in God, we do not rely on human means alone, for in this world nothing — not even the greatest strength and riches — will avail unless God Himself supports, strengthens, comforts, teaches and protects us. We must, indeed, take any measures that we regard as necessary, but we cannot rely only on these; we must put our whole trust in God. This trust should be the golden mean between

what is known as Quietism, and over-activity. The advocates of this excessive activity are in a continual state of turmoil, for, in all they do, they rely solely on themselves. Trust in God causes us to do our work conscientiously, down to the smallest detail, but it saves us from the unrest of those who never allow themselves a breathing-space. It would, on the other hand, be sheer laziness to leave everything to God, without trying to do our duty as well as we could.[33]

Resisting Temptation

During our search through life, we are faced with many choices as well as scores of temptations. Which way will we go? Will we get sucked into a life other than the one God has planned for us? This can certainly happen when we are faced with struggles and roadblocks or become disillusioned by lies from the culture. Should we persevere, change our minds and get lackadaisical, or turn the other way completely? The choices we make in this life directly affect our eternal life. This does not mean that things can't be turned around later on. However, if we continue to strive to lead a holy life, we need to prayerfully make effective and appropriate choices.

As I mentioned in Chapter 7, even St. Faustina turned away from God's graces. Saint John Bosco advised, "When tempted, invoke your Angel. He is more eager to help you than you are to be helped! Ignore the devil and do not be afraid of him: He trembles and flees at your Guardian Angel's sight."[34]

Thomas á Kempis advises us that it's wise to nip temptation in the bud! He said, "Above all, we must be especially alert against the beginnings of temptation, for the enemy is more easily conquered if he is refused admittance to the mind and is met beyond the threshold when he knocks."[35]

Here I Am, Lord

Jesus told His disciples to cast their nets in the deep waters. Summing up our chapter on searching, dear sister, we should ask ourselves: "*Are we going to seek and follow God halfheartedly?* Or will we be on fire with His love, striving to do His holy will?"

Jesus told St. Faustina that He suffered so much in the Garden of Gethsemane because of lukewarm souls! He said the souls of the lukewarm **"wound My Heart most painfully."** He revealed to Faustina, **"My soul suffered the most dreadful loathing in the Garden of Olives because of lukewarm souls. They were the reason I cried out: 'Father, take this cup away from Me, if it be Your will'"** (*Diary*, 1228).

And Jesus gives the solution: **"For them, the last hope of salvation is to flee to My mercy"** (*Diary*, 1228).

CRO CRO CRO

PAUSE

Take a moment to ponder how you have navigated your life thus far. What has distracted you from getting closer to God? How might you trust Jesus more wholeheartedly? Ponder the fact that humanity as a whole has been entrusted to every Catholic woman, and that specific human beings have been entrusted to your loving heart. Are you *aware* of this amazing gift?

CRO CRO CRO

ACT

Be humble and prayerful. Give yourself "breathing space." Keep going! Trust God! Follow Him wholeheartedly!

A Prayer of Mercy

Dear Jesus, please help me to resist temptations and walk forward in faith to serve You and my neighbor. Jesus, please have mercy upon my soul. I trust in You!
Mother Mary, help me, protect me, and guide me.
Saint Faustina, please pray for me.
Amen.

CHAPTER 11
Losing One's Faith

"Fight like a knight,
so that I can reward you."

— Jesus to St. Faustina (*Diary*, 1760)

O nce upon a time, I used to work out at a health club in an attempt to stay physically fit. I must admit that I became a bit obsessed with the spinning classes! I really enjoyed exercising because I wanted to keep my body healthy. After some time, I became employed at that same health club, running a preschool that I founded. Ironically, as soon as I began that job, I no longer had time to work out — so I didn't!

The same thing can happen to our prayer life if we are not careful. If we busy ourselves with too many other things, or if we simply neglect our prayers, our faith "muscles" will atrophy, and we will lose our way. Without prayer, our souls will die. It might sound ironic, but we can even get so caught up in holy work that we neglect to pray.

We absolutely need to carve out time to pray every day. Scripture tells us, "Pray without ceasing" (1 Thess 5:17). We are warned, "Stay awake and pray that you may not come into the time of trial; the spirit indeed is willing, but the flesh is weak" (Mt 26:41). Unquestionably, we are called by our Lord to lead vibrant prayer lives in order to worship Him, but also for strength to survive the many temptations we face to give up, turn away, or fall asleep.

Now let's take a look at women's desires, discover how we could possibly lose our faith, and discern how we can preserve it.

What Do Women Desire?

What do women want? Is it "peace on earth and good will towards men," my normal response to my family when they ask me what I would like for Christmas? (I drive them crazy! They would rather I ask them for a tangible gift.)

Yes, it's true: We women want peace, happiness, order, justice, love in the family, and to be understood, too. We want change for the better.

Yet we live with much uncertainty because in reality, we do not have control of many things. We might think our life should be one nice, straight line, ascending to better things. But life often does not work that way. We might need to take the scenic route, maybe even more than once!

When St. Faustina was just 7 years old and felt a strong calling from God, she wouldn't have known that the road to sanctity would be so hard and that she would suffer through two dark nights in the spiritual life. Yet all throughout her difficulties, God's graces became her comfort (as they will for us, too).

On our journey through life, there will be bumps in the road. There will be twists and turns. There will even be darkness at times. In my memoir, *The Kiss of Jesus*, I talked about the crazy twists and turns in my life, and the dark corners, pain, suffering, and abuse I endured.

I disclosed things I had never talked about publicly in the past. They were dark things that I felt were best left secreted in the dark — that is, until I realized by God's grace that I needed to share my hard times with others so I could offer a great big dose of hope to those who are struggling or have lost their way.

However, as I was writing that book, I physically shuddered at times. In a sense, I needed to relive the experiences in order to tell about them. God was with me then, too.

I wrote about being left at the side of the road with my 3-year-old daughter, just a couple of weeks before giving birth to my third child by Caesarean section. Of all people, it was my then-husband who deserted us there, after stating, "I'm leaving!" Then he got out of the car and hitchhiked away.

I wrote about the physical abuse I endured behind closed doors from my second husband, a man I married after being granted an annulment, a supposed "upstanding citizen" — even a daily Mass attendee. And I shared about being held captive by a crazed man with automatic weapons in an apartment earlier in life!

But God had a plan. He always does. And amazingly, He also put a couple of saints in my life: Servant of God Fr. John Hardon, SJ, and St. Teresa of Calcutta (Mother Teresa)! I weave their wisdom into just about everything I write. I never imagined at the time how these saints would deeply impact my life and ultimately help me to help others.

So, back to our journey towards God: While we want a nice, clean, straightforward route to God, it most likely won't happen that way. But we can certainly hold on to great hope in our hearts knowing that God will always be with us, and will provide us the graces we need to walk in faith, even in darkness. He will take our hand. We need to trust Him.

When I did finally sit down to write my memoir, I could clearly see the threads of grace that were woven all throughout my life.

We can learn much from our sister Faustina, who chose to pause and pray when faced with fears:

O My God. When I look into the future,
I am frightened,
But why plunge into the future?
Only the present moment is precious to me,
As the future may never enter my soul at all.

It is no longer in my power
To change, correct or add to the past;
For neither sages nor prophets could do that.

And so what the past has embraced I must
entrust to God.

O present moment, you belong to me,
whole and entire.
I desire to use you as best I can.
And although I am weak and small,
You grant me the grace of Your omnipotence.

And so, trusting in Your mercy,
I walk through life like a little child,
Offering You each day this heart
Burning with love for Your greater Glory (*Diary*, 2).

These are powerful words. There is no doubt that it can
be very difficult to pause and be still when life pulls us in so
many directions. Yet we need to dig our heels in and dwell in
the present moments of our lives. Staying in the present also
helps us to stay true to our prayer lives, especially if we have
made a conscious decision to pray.

Don't Give in to Discouragement

It doesn't take long to give in to discouragement. I talk to
countless women who get in touch with me because they have
become deeply discouraged for a variety of reasons and need
prayer and advice. Sometimes their discouragement is due to
stresses and strains, lack of sleep from caring for their lively
family, or handling other pressing responsibilities that wear
them out. As I discuss in other parts of this book (see Chapters
8 and 10), women face a continual torrent of demands for
perfection and eventually might become discouraged that they
haven't measured up to the crazy expectations of others.

Saint Faustina often felt alone in her mission and even
experienced doubt, especially because no one believed her.
Under the weight of it all, she had to make wholehearted acts
of trust. She related in her *Diary* how once she actually fell to
the floor and cried out to Jesus:

I came to my cell. The sisters were already in bed — the lights were out. I entered the cell full of anguish and discontent; I did not know what to do with myself. I threw myself headlong on the ground and began to pray fervently that I might come to know the will of God. There is silence everywhere as in the tabernacle. All the sisters are resting like white hosts enclosed in Jesus' chalice. It is only from my cell that God can hear the moaning of a soul (19).

Elsewhere, St. Faustina recalled, "Once when I was being crushed by these dreadful sufferings, I went into the chapel and said from the bottom of my soul, 'Do what You will with me, O Jesus; I will adore You in everything. May Your will be done in me, O my Lord and my God, and I will praise Your infinite mercy'" (*Diary*, 78).

The young mystic explained, "Through this act of submission, these terrible torments left me." On top of that, Jesus gifted her with an incredible consolation. Faustina recalled, "Suddenly I saw Jesus, who said to me, **'I am always in your heart.'** An inconceivable joy entered my soul, and a great love of God set my heart aflame." She explained, "I see that God never tries us beyond what we are able to suffer."

We need to take these words to heart. God will always supply everything that we need to overcome difficulties, great or small.

Saint Faustina continued, "Oh, I fear nothing; if God sends such great suffering to a soul. He upholds it with an even greater grace, although we are not aware of it." This next part is key in our lives as well. Faustina wrote, "One act of trust at such moments gives greater glory to God than whole hours passed in prayer filled with consolations. Now I see that if God wants to keep a soul in darkness, no book, no confessor can bring it light" (*Diary*, 78).

Saint Faustina teaches us that trust in God is essential in our spiritual lives. From the very beginning of her religious life, the Secretary of Divine Mercy trusted God, even if she didn't realize it. The signature on the Divine Mercy Image would end up being, "Jesus, I trust in You." It is a profound statement — one that we can lovingly utter over and over throughout our lives.

Overcoming Guilt

A parasite sits upon our shoulders, sucking the life out of us. It's called "guilt." Women often feel guilty, and the weight of that guilt can cause severe problems. Quite often, women are raised with some sort of guilt. I know a young mother who, when buying her little son a new pair of shoes, was made to feel guilty by her own mother who had lived through the Great Depression. It's tough enough to raise a family, but when a young mother is made to feel guilty by her own mother for providing for them — well, that is hard as well as perplexing. Many things can contribute to crippling pangs of guilt.

Certainly, guilt can be a good thing — especially when it is tugging at your conscience because of a need to make amends. However, I believe that women tend to feel guilty even when they are not at fault. That's a problem, because we women are meant to lead vibrant and joyful lives in service of our Lord and others. Add excessive guilt to the picture, and that most likely won't happen. Guilt can wrap us in chains.

Saint Faustina struggled with guilt. One time, she poured her heart out to Jesus, telling Him she was sorry that she didn't pay enough attention to Him one particular day. She had been inundated with many people seeking her undivided attention during her visit home to her family. She later wrote in her *Diary*:

> When I entered the chapel to say goodnight to the Lord before retiring, and apologized for having talked so little to Him when I was at home, I heard a voice within my soul, **I am very pleased that you had not been talking with Me, but were making My goodness known to souls and rousing them to love Me** (404).

We, too, can learn from this that we should not feel guilty when spending necessary time with or tending to our loved ones and those in our care. We should know that our dear Lord knows *everything* about us, including every demand, every need, and every pull on our attention. He wants us to serve those whom He gives us to serve — those in our midst and those who call upon us for help (if we are able). I often tell young mothers that it would be wrong to abruptly stop caring for their children in order to kneel down and start praying to fulfill a particular prayer practice. Lovingly taking care of people in our lives *is* a prayer. It's an *active* prayer.

However, we need to try our best to "reschedule" our praying times when they get rearranged by life, and not to neglect prayer. Jesus also wants us to carve out time for conversations with Him whenever we are able. We need to remain in the state of grace and pray at every opportunity. We lift our hearts to Him. Our lives can become a living prayer to our Lord.

Learning to overcome guilt and finding true balance in our love of God and neighbor will free us to live the life we are meant for.

Forgiveness

The world tells us to hold onto grudges. But St. Faustina knew the power of forgiveness. She wrote in her *Diary*, "He who knows how to forgive prepares for himself many graces from God. As often as I look upon the cross, so often will I forgive with all my heart" (390).

Forgiveness can be a tough pill to swallow, but lack of forgiveness can really mess us up. It robs us of peace. We might have trouble accepting someone's apology because of the lingering pain caused by their negative actions, but to be free of this bondage and allow our wounds to be healed by God, we must die to self and, with God's grace, learn to forgive and accept forgiveness. It's the only way to true peace of heart.

One time, Jesus asked St. Faustina to reflect on how she treated others. He said, **"My daughter, in this meditation, consider the love of neighbor. Is your love for your neigh-**

bor guided by My love? Do you pray for your enemies? Do you wish well to those who have, in one way or another, caused you sorrow or offended you? Know that whatever good you do to any soul, I accept it as if you had done it to Me" (*Diary*, 1768).

Another time, Jesus appeared to her at Holy Mass and taught His Secretary a powerful lesson in forgiveness. Saint Faustina recounted, "During Holy Mass, I saw Jesus stretched out on the Cross, and He said to me, **My pupil, have great love for those who cause you suffering. Do good to those who hate you.**" She was troubled and answered, "O my Master, You see very well that I feel no love for them, and that troubles me" (*Diary*, 1628).

Jesus explained, **"It is not always within your power to control your feelings. You will recognize that you have love if, after having experienced annoyance and contradiction, you do not lose your peace, but pray for those who have made you suffer and wish them well"** (*Diary*, 1628). These are words that we should all take to heart!

Jesus also told Faustina, **"If someone causes you trouble, think what good you can do for the person who caused you to suffer"** (*Diary*, 1760). Clearly, we not only need to forgive, but according to our Lord Jesus, we should do good to the person who has offended us. It might take heroic effort, but God will grant us the graces we need. Doing good to that person doesn't mean that we need to invite them over for dinner; rather, it means sincerely praying for them.

⬥ ⬥ ⬥

PAUSE

Take a few moments to ponder any discouragement or guilt in your life. Think also about the need to forgive or to accept someone's forgiveness. Is something holding you back? Are you able to lovingly help someone to discover the need for forgiveness in their life? Are you able to help alleviate a false feeling of guilt in someone's life? Can you help someone who might be losing hope or has hit rock bottom? There is much to ponder. Your loving prayers and acts of mercy can be transforming.

Act

Trust God. With God's grace, let go of any "baggage" you are carrying in your heart. Pray about works of mercy you can carry out to help someone who is in need. Endeavor to pray extra Chaplets of Divine Mercy if you can, to help those in most need.

A Prayer of Mercy

Dear Lord Jesus, please make me strong.
Please help me to forgive, to overcome guilt,
to not give in to discouragement, and to submit my
life to Your holy will. With Faustina, I will say,
"[T]rusting in Your mercy, I walk through life like a
little child, offering You each day this heart burning
with love for Your greater glory" (*Diary*, 2).
Jesus, please have mercy upon my soul.
I trust in You!
Mother Mary, help me, protect me, and guide me.
Saint Faustina, please pray for me.
Amen.

CHAPTER 12
Joining the Military Family

"Through prayer, I live in you, Lord.
I live in you as a baby in its mother's womb
with its breath united to hers and its heart
beating in rhythm with hers."[36]

— Cardinal Nguyễn Văn Thuận (1928–2002),
prisoner of war

My heart goes out to military families. As a young teen, I observed my own mother's tears when two of my brothers were fighting in the jungles of Vietnam. She was so worried that they might not survive the war. I knelt by the side of my bed each night pleading with God to bring them home. Thank God they both came home alive.

My brother Gary has since gone to his eternal reward, eventually succumbing to cancer after having been exposed to chemical weapons. My brother Tim is fighting cancer as I type this. He too, was exposed to chemical warfare. War is terrible and affects our soldiers, airmen, seamen, marines, and their families much more than we can ever imagine.

Many Kinds of Battles

In my book *By Dawn's Early Light: Prayers and Meditations for Catholic Military Wives*, I wrote:

War affects those who fight it, those back home who support their soldiers, and their loved ones who are constantly worrying about them. So many uncertainties are associated with military life ... Soldiers are affected by stress and strain — physically, emotionally, and mentally. They fight a war not only on the battlefield but also in their hearts and minds. We need to pray for their spiritual, emotional, and physical protection. Their families need many prayers as well.[37]

The Vietnam War also affected me through my fiancé, in addition to my brothers. I was engaged to a Vietnam veteran, an ex-marine. Unfortunately, posttraumatic stress disorder (PTSD) caused him to suddenly snap. He had a nervous breakdown and ended up holding me captive, threatening to murder my family and me! It was a very long and horrific ordeal, to say the least. Thank God I eventually got out safely.

Much later, I met a woman who had picked up my memoir, *The Kiss of Jesus*, at a Catholic conference. The words on the dust jacket had her intrigued, because she saw that I had once been held captive by a Vietnam veteran. She shared something with me that she had not disclosed to anyone else. This woman stood at my book table at a book signing event, leaned in, and poured out her woeful tale. As tears glistened in her eyes, she told me that her husband, a Vietnam veteran, had snapped from the effects of PTSD and had beat her up seven times while she was pregnant. Thank God, she was able to escape his clutches after the baby was born. My heart was pierced, hearing her share her harrowing experiences. We must pray that he and other tormented veterans and their families will get the help that they need.

As difficult as war and its consequences are, most military families are wonderful. Years ago, I was invited to speak to a woman's group at West Point in New York. The women knew me as a Catholic author and wanted me to give them a retreat day. I thoroughly enjoyed my visit with them. As the day was coming to a close, I told the women that I would like to write a prayer book just for them — for military women. And I did!

It's the book I quoted from above, *By Dawn's Early Light,* though I wrote it for more than the wives — it is for every woman associated in some way with the military, including women serving in the armed forces.

Learning and Loving Through Military Life

While speaking at West Point, I met an Army wife named Elizabeth Tomlin. We've stayed in touch over the years, becoming close friends, and so it seemed natural to interview her for this book. Elizabeth's father was a United States Marine, and she grew up on naval and marine installations around the world. So military life feels natural to her.

Elizabeth's husband, Greg, joined the Army in a pre-September 11 world. She shared, "When he was commissioned, the U.S. military was involved in peacekeeping operations in Kosovo." However, she added, "The world changed forever on September 11, 2001." From that day forward, "Greg's career has always been with the knowledge that the U.S. is at war."

Elizabeth recalled somberly, "It was certainly unforeseeable for a 21-year-old standing on the lawn of the College of William and Mary that, 19 years later, we would still be at war, but we are." She said, "That knowledge I think brings an urgency to Greg's training and a definite striving for excellence so that when he and his soldiers deploy, they are as prepared as possible."

That said, Elizabeth also told me that "military life is joyful." This Army wife sees being a military spouse as part of her vocation. "I have to keep my family going while Greg stays away for extended periods of time." She said, "I have to do my part on the home front, even when, as they say, 'the years are short but the days are long.'"

Elizabeth has worked with the Military Council of Catholic Women (MCCW), which is the women's ministry for the Archdiocese for the Military Services, USA. She was the MCCW president from 2014 to 2016 and still serves on its board of directors. The MCCW's mission is to "connect, unite, and inspire military women to grow in their Catholic faith."[38]

Elizabeth sees the MCCW as "unique among women's ministries" because, she said, "we share our Catholic faith as well as our identity either as military spouses, service members, or retirees." She believes that "the Catholic camaraderie, paired with our military *esprit de corps*, affords us the opportunity to form strong friendships with people who share our faith and lifestyle."

My friend learned through the years that sisters in Christ in the military are truly *there* for one another. As Mary did for her cousin (see Lk 1:39), military women often run in haste to serve their fellow sisters in Christ. Elizabeth remarked to me that "the friends I have met in MCCW are my best and lifelong friends. We take care of each other." The military women of faith help to strengthen and serve one another.

Elizabeth recalled a time when an unexpected dish of love was delivered to her front door during a sorrowful time in her life. "One of the kindest things someone ever did for me was that a woman I barely knew sent a pan of lasagna over to my house when I had to have surgery following a miscarriage." She is thoroughly convinced that "that's what Catholic military women do for each other — we show up when it matters."

"When I was new at being a military spouse," Elizabeth recounted, "I had a fiercely independent attitude. I rarely sought help, and I was reticent to accept help." It might have taken a while, but, she said, "something I have learned over the years is to accept help from your sisters in Christ, even if you could manage to accomplish something on your own." She added, "My military sisters in Christ in the MCCW are always the first to volunteer to pitch in and lend a hand."

"Paul reminds the Galatians to 'bear one another's burdens,'" Elizabeth said (Gal 6:2). She explained, "When we allow our community to help us, we let others express their love of Christ to us," adding, "It's a good and generous thing to accept help, and if you let someone lessen your burden, you'll be able to help others without becoming burned out or exhausted." That's an important lesson for us all!

Now let's look at another Catholic woman's life-altering military experiences.

A Difficult Life Redeemed

A U.S. Air Force wife I know shared a memorable story with me. I'll call her "Ann" to protect her identity. Ann's daughter Jill was almost 5 years old when Ann's husband, Ryan, was deployed to Turkey. He served there for eight months. Three weeks before he was to come home, Ann's telephone rang in the middle of the night. She picked up the phone.

"Ann, it's me, Ryan."

Ann was very surprised because he had never called in the middle of the night before.

She asked him, "Are you okay?"

"No," he answered, and began to cry. He said, "I just want to come home."

Ann replied, "I know. You will, in just a few weeks!"

Ryan continued to sob. Ann tried her best to reassure him from so many miles away: "I told him that Jill and I loved him very much, and we were excited for his return!"

Ann and Jill's world would soon turn upside down. One week before Ryan was to return home, he called to discuss his arrival. Ann recalled, "This time his tone was very different — a manner that I had never heard from him in the nine years we had been together."

She was baffled. "He seemed unsure in his statements towards me, but said he had doubts about our marriage." Ann could not wrap her mind around this sudden change. She said, "I had no idea what he meant. He would not elaborate." Ann did not like his coarse tone. Fear pulsated throughout her body. "He made it seem that he wasn't sure if he wanted to come home to us and it sounded like if I didn't pick him up from the airport, he would arrange other means."

They argued over the phone. "We hung up, finally agreeing that my folks, his folks, Jill, and I would be there." Ann added, "But that did not come without great resistance from him."

Ann recalled, "This was not our first deployment. We had done this many times before." Again, she tried to decipher what had transpired. She shared with me, "His choice of words and tone gave me a lot to be concerned about!"

When the conversation was over, Ann sat on the edge of the bed in the dark, weeping. She said, "My gut was telling me that he might be seriously considering divorcing me!" She couldn't shake the fear of abandonment. "I had been with him for over nine years."

She was completely bewildered.

Her Airman Comes Home

The day arrived to get Ryan at the airport. Family members were waiting and excited! Ann said, "I was nervous in every sense of the word. I was hoping beyond hope that his issues had passed."

Ryan came off the airplane and greeted Ann with a half of a hug. Ann noticed immediately that Ryan was not wearing his wedding ring. Ann shared, "I was pretty shocked."

Ann could feel her heart breaking. She tried to hold herself together while she was around everyone as they welcomed him home.

The next few days and nights were extremely painful for Ann. She shared, "I began trying to figure out what Ryan wanted to do and if we could save our marriage." She said, "He was distant, but reassured me that there was no other woman." Ann said, "His responses were vague, and he felt our marriage was probably over."

"I couldn't understand what had changed. Why did he feel this way? There were no explanations." Despite the confusion and heartache, they had to prepare for their upcoming military move to North Carolina. During that assignment, Ann said, "He would be gone for hours at odd times and come back really late." Over time, he became unreachable by phone.

"I would encourage him to go with me to visit Jesus in the Blessed Sacrament." Ryan told Ann that while there, God told him to leave her. Because of the stress, Ann had barely been sleeping and eating. Not only was she in survival mode, she said, but she began to feel herself sinking.

She Had Placed Her Faith in Her Man

She pondered, "I loved him with all my heart and soul. I put my whole self-worth in this man. I felt completely and utterly worthless, unloved, and undesirable." Her stomach was in knots. She could barely cope. "The fear of raising a child alone and losing the man I loved was gut wrenching," she recalled. "Imagining life without him became very bleak … I was slowly dying inside."

"The pain that swelled within me began to make me feel numb." Ann began slipping into a deep black hole. She said, "My days began to run into each other, and sleep was scarce." Ann hid from her daughter when she was home so that Jill would not witness her mother in a state of severe depression. "I would lock myself in the bedroom or bathroom crying silently alone." Ann felt her life as she knew it spiraling out of control. "I could not see a light at the end of this tunnel — it was very dark inside."

Ann began to inflict physical harm on herself, "banging my head against the walls continuously when my daughter was not home." She shared, "As my world was crumbling all around me, I succumbed to sliding into the deepest pit of despair." She said she tried to harm herself several times.

Ann, Ryan, and Jill made their move to North Carolina, but Ryan stayed at the barracks while Ann and Jill lived nearby in an apartment. Mother and daughter did their best to pray for reconciliation and to wait.

The Crucified Jesus and Mary's Intercession

"Crying myself to sleep every night, I began to have a reoccurring dream of a crucifix appearing in front of me in a church," Ann said. "I started to pray the Rosary daily, asking for Mary's intercession." It turned out that Ann had to pass a Catholic Church on her way to the Air Force base. She said,

"I often felt the need to stop and go in, but didn't act on it."

"Finally, one day, I gave in to that tug, that urge to stop and go in."

When she walked into the main chapel, she looked up. "Right before my very eyes, I saw before me the exact same crucifix that had appeared in my dreams!"

Ann's heart began to beat fast. She recalled, "My knees felt like they were going to buckle!" Still, she walked up closer to the crucifix and knelt down before it.

"As I bowed my head down to pray, I began to hear Jesus speak within the depths of my very being. 'My child, you are not alone. I know your pain. I stretch out my arms to you because you are worth it!'"

Tears began to stream down Ann's cheeks. She heard Jesus speak to her heart.

"I ask you to let go of this and give it to Me. Trust in Me."

Ann took it all in as she wept and prayed. "This was a very humbling moment in my life. My body had been shaking and trembling with weakness, but now I began to feel caressed by His love and presence."

Ann looked up to the Lord Jesus hanging on the Cross, and she entrusted everything into His hands.

She shared with me, "I had put all my self-worth into a man, and when he left me for another woman, my self-worth could have left with him, but now I finally understood that my worth is solely dependent on being a daughter of God, made in His image and likeness."

In the days ahead, through countless prayers, Ann began to realize that no matter how undesirable she felt, "I was desired by our Lord!"

"Jesus' love and mercy gave me hope that continued to reassure me that He is the light at the end of this tunnel and that I just needed to stay focused on Him," she said.

Months later, Ann felt forced into a divorce. Though it was very painful, she told me, "Much good has happened since that divorce. I eventually petitioned the marriage tribunal and was granted an annulment." She added, "Today, I am married in the Catholic Church to a wonderful man and have two more children."

As sorrowful and difficult as Ann's journey was, God redeemed her and showed her the way to Him. Jesus' great love and Divine Mercy has saved her life.

PAUSE

Take a few moments to ponder the military people in your life. Have you ever expressed to them your gratefulness for their sacrifices? Could you pray for all military personnel and their families?

ACT

Soldier on, fulfilling the duties of your state in life! Give help to others. But also be open to asking for help. God is with you! He always was and always will be!

A PRAYER OF MERCY

Dear Jesus, please help me to be more attentive to the people You have placed in my life — to be generous with my loving prayers and kind words. Please, Jesus, have mercy upon my soul.
I trust in You!
Mother Mary, help me, protect me, and guide me.
Saint Faustina, please pray for me.
Amen.

CHAPTER 13
Falling in Love

"This is my commandment, that you love one another as I have loved you."

— Jn 15:12

We have all heard countless love stories. Some involve knights in shining armor and damsels in distress. Others are modern versions of those romantic tales. I'm sure you have heard or seen a million of them yourself. The fictional love stories that we see portrayed on the big screens might draw a tear, warm our hearts, or make us smile.

But what about real love? How does that come about? How does it endure? When speaking about love, I often mention Mother Teresa and how she taught the world that real love often hurts. It requires sacrifice to truly love someone, whether they're a stranger or not.

We most likely enter our own love story with a hopeful heart, a few butterflies in our stomach, warm fuzzy feelings, and perhaps a few goosebumps! Not every love story has a happy ending, though, I'm sorry to say. Sometimes love is blind, as the saying goes, so we need to be careful. We may not choose with whom we fall in love, but we need to choose how we love them, discerning whether our love should be romantic or neighborly.

Some sweet true-love stories took on new, sacrificial meaning in the middle of the worldwide COVID-19 pandemic, a crazy time. The pandemic hasn't changed the fact that a Catholic wedding is not simply an event. It is a very special and foundational Sacrament. We will get into that more in Chapter 22. For now, let's just say that when COVID hit, many betrothed couples opted to go ahead and get married without the fanfare. They wanted their sacramental bond to begin rather than wait a year or more until it would be safe to assemble a hundred-plus guests. They tied the knot by pronouncing their vows before a priest and a few loved ones. They will have their big shindig at a future date. May God bless them for not holding off their marital covenant and their future just because they couldn't have a party.

My own marriage had an interesting beginning: My husband and I first laid eyes on each other through a sort of blind date! We had been getting to know one another through phone calls and countless emails, having "met" through mutual friends. When the time to meet finally arrived, my husband-to-be was getting sweaty palms while waiting in his truck for me! Love can make you nervous! Falling in love adds lots of emotion to our lives — as you can see from the story I'm going to tell next.

The Girl on the Yellow Bicycle

At the start of the Christmas season, 16-year-old Lisa moved into a new home with her family. She sorely missed her old neighborhood but pushed through the winter months hoping to adjust. One summer day, she took her yellow English racer out for a spin through the neighborhood. Along the way, she passed a maroon Pontiac Grand Prix. She noticed two boys about her age in the car, but she continued peddling. "Little did I know," she recalled, "that the boys had decided that the guy in the passenger seat of the car, who did not know me at all, would call me to go bowling." The driver told his friend, "The girl on the English racer goes to school with my sister." He would get Lisa's name and phone number.

Back at home after Lisa's bike ride, the phone rang. She said, "My dad was speaking to the boy, who got nervous and forgot the name given to him by his friend." Quick on his feet, the boy said, "Can I please speak to the girl who rides the yellow English racer?"

That was the beginning of their beautiful love story. Lisa said, "The new neighborhood had failed to measure up until that point." Needless to say, Lisa said yes to that first date. Lisa and Andy have been married now for 42 years. "Having had four children and now 11 grandchildren," Lisa said, "we thank God for all these many years and all of their fruitfulness." They are faithful Catholics and believe in the power of prayer. Lisa shared, "Prayers to St. Joseph and many Rosaries of the Blessed Virgin Mary have brought us through thick and thin." I'll add to this that Andy came into the Church over the course of their marriage.

Lisa remembered, "On this day as I reflect, I say yes, yes, and yes again to love and to life with this boy, now a man. We started out holding hands and now, after all these years together, we are still holding hands. Once again, I say, 'Yes, I love you.'"

Of course, no two love stories are exactly alike. I can't tell you how you will or should fall in love. You'll surely figure that out on your own.

Let me share with you another love story.

Selfless Love Pierces the Heart

In 1941, my mother's sister Mary was married to Bill. Soon after, Bill went off to fight in World War II. Mary was expecting and gave birth to her first child. With no permanent home, Mary moved in with my mother, and lived with her growing family for at least three years.

No doubt Mary was deeply grateful for my mother's selfless opening of her home. She must surely have endured worries and struggles with her husband fighting a war on the other side of the ocean, necessitating the sacrifice of raising her little daughter alone for those years.

Finally, Mary's soldier made it home safely from the war. A few years later, Bill was diagnosed with cancer. He suffered for a long while, undergoing numerous treatments. My aunt

Bertha (sister to my mother and Mary) was a young teen at the time. She shared with me, "All the while, Bill never told Mary that he was dying." However, Mary also knew of Bill's terminal diagnosis from the doctors, but never told Bill that she knew.

Aunt Bertha was so impressed and touched by what her older sister confided in her. Bertha told me, "That is when I realized what 'love' is: Till death do us part." She added, "He was very stoic and brave not wanting her to know his pain. She took great care of him until his dying day." Authentic love is stronger than pain and death.

Now let's shift gears a bit and talk about Christ's incredible love for us and ours for Him.

The Living Water

We absolutely need the Living Water that Jesus desires to give us. To get to the heart of the matter, we should discuss two powerful words: "*I thirst.*" No doubt you've heard the account in John's Gospel of the Samaritan woman meeting Jesus at Jacob's well (see Jn 4:1-29). Through this story, we become aware that the mystery of prayer is illuminated by the "well" where we go to seek God.

The Samaritan woman showed up at noon — the hottest part of the day — forced by Jewish custom to avoid others. She was being ostracized for living with a man to whom she wasn't married. Jesus knew just when to find her.

Jesus was speaking to a woman out in public, something that, at that time, was unheard of for a reputable man. On top of that, the woman was a Samaritan, a member of a people despised by the Jews. Yet Jesus persisted with His loving confrontation, asking the woman about her husband.

At first, the woman beat around the bush, trying to disguise her sinful life. By God's grace, she came to recognize to Whom she was speaking. Suddenly, her heart was transformed as she began to understand the deep love of her Savior and His insatiable thirst to receive mankind's love in return. She became a missionary, running back to her village to bring the incredible, life-changing message of our Lord's love and Living Water to her people.

Saint Augustine discussed this remarkable, historic meeting between the Samaritan woman and Jesus, telling us that in a certain sense, Jesus comes to meet every human being and finds us "beside the well where we come seeking water." He explained that Jesus is always the first to seek us. His request for a drink expresses His thirst for our love. He tells us that the desire that Jesus has for our love "arises from the depths of God's desire for us." We can find this explanation in the *Catechism* (2560).

Even though we may not realize it, "Prayer is the encounter of God's thirst with ours. God thirsts that we may thirst for Him"[39] (*Catechism*, 2560). Saint Augustine's profound insight gives us a new way to view prayer: Amazingly, God thirsts for us and wants us to thirst for Him! He calls us to be in union with Him.

Let us also consider that the Samaritan woman possessed an apostolic spirit. As soon as she received such a beautiful gift from Jesus, she didn't keep it to herself. She ran back to the village to tell the people about Jesus' Living Water. She wanted her people to have it, too.

Love Requires Sacrifice

This reminds me in a way of a woman to whom Mother Teresa brought a serving of rice.

Once, a man showed up at Mother Teresa's convent door to tell her about a starving Hindu family with eight children. Mother quickly gathered up the rice she had planned to cook for supper that evening. She and the gentleman set out quickly in search of the family. Upon finding them, the saint of the gutters recalled, "I could see the specter of hunger drawn on the faces of the little children when we found the family. They looked like human skeletons."

With great joy and a warm smile, Mother Teresa handed over the parcel of rice. However, before the mother of the house cooked it up, she immediately divided the portion in half and excused herself, quickly exiting their tiny abode. It didn't take long for her to return. Mother Teresa asked where she had hurried to. The Hindu mother had gone next door to deliver half of the gift of rice to her hungry Muslim neighbors.

That woman's love for her neighbors touched Mother Teresa to the core. She shared, "What struck me was that she knew, and because she knew she gave until it hurt. That is something beautiful. That is love in action! That woman shared with great sacrifice."[40]

Mother Teresa often spoke about how Jesus thirsts for our love. The humble saint of the gutters experienced Jesus' thirst in a mystical way.

"I Thirst"

Mother Teresa heard Jesus calling her to give her life in service of the poor and the rejected, those whom she called "the poorest of the poor." In doing so, she would satiate Jesus' thirst.

This humble saint lived her life striving to do that by taking care of the least of us all over this planet. I was blessed to see this remarkable, holy woman in action. I have also observed the deep reverence and understanding of our Savior's thirst in all the MC sisters whom I have met.

The words "I Thirst" mark every MC chapel throughout the world. In the many MC convents I have visited in various parts of the world, these two simple yet profound words are painted on the wall beside the tabernacle to remind all who enter the chapel that Jesus thirsts for our love, and that we should thirst for His love, too.

In her *Diary*, St. Faustina recalled Jesus' passionate words to her, spoken from His Cross during an apparition. "During Holy Mass I saw the Lord Jesus nailed upon the cross amidst great torments. A soft moan issued from His Heart. After some time, He said, **I thirst. I thirst for the salvation of souls. Help Me, my daughter, to save souls. Join your sufferings to My Passion and offer them to the heavenly Father for sinners**" (1032).

Jesus calls to each one of us to help save souls by prayerfully joining our sufferings to His Passion and offering them to God the Father.

Sometimes, I think we tend to forget that God also seeks our love! Perhaps we never knew this. This notion of thirst for love between us and our Creator is something we need to ponder more deeply and act on. Try to take time to meditate on this, and if possible, while in the presence of Jesus in the Blessed Sacrament.

In John's Gospel, we read about instances of Jesus' thirst, such as, "After this, when Jesus knew that all was now finished, he said (in order to fulfill the scripture), 'I am thirsty'" (Jn 19:28). There are other occurrences in John's Gospel that help us understand Jesus' words about thirst (for instance, as we discussed in the "Living Water" section, when Jesus is thirsty and asks the Samaritan woman for a drink). In addition, Jesus' declaration "whoever believes in me will never be thirsty" (Jn 6:35) and His words spoken in the Temple during the Feast of Booths, "Let anyone who is thirsty come to me, and let the one who believes in me drink" (Jn 7:37-38), expand our understanding of "I thirst."

Saint Faustina knew just where to find our Lord to receive His Living Water. She visited Him in the Blessed Sacrament and communed with Him when receiving Holy Communion. She wrote in her *Diary*:

> My heart is drawn there where my God is hidden,
> Where He dwells with us day and night,
> Clothed in the White Host;
> He governs the whole world,
> He communes with souls.

> My heart is drawn there where my God is hiding,
> Where His love is immolated.
> But my heart senses that the living water is here;
> It is my living God, though a veil hides Him (1591).

Other saints, including St. Teresa of Avila, discussed Christ's Living Water and the Samaritan woman. In her *Way of Perfection*, the Spanish saint wrote of how all are invited to taste of this water: "But, as He [Christ] said we were all to come ... I feel sure that none will fail to receive this living water unless they cannot keep to the path [of prayer]."[41]

We Catholic women long for our Lord's Living Water. He comes to meet us as we draw our water — as we go about whatever it is that we do. He is there waiting. He desires to gift us this life-giving refreshment.

He gives us the gift of thirst! Let's allow that to sink in.

Perhaps you can ponder those two simple yet powerful words, "I thirst," and a few questions as well:

- How do Jesus' words speak to my heart?
- How can I attempt to satiate His thirst for love?
- Do I try to avoid Jesus by showing up at the well at noon — that is, by avoiding chances to encounter Him?
- Am I ashamed of my life or the choices I have made? Rather than try to hide or avoid the issue, can I confess my sins and accept Jesus' Living Water — His forgiveness and great love?
- Can I go to Jesus with an empty vessel?

Let's endeavor to go to the "well of prayer" at the foot of the Cross and soak in Jesus' amazing love for us. Pray and ponder there in front of Jesus at the tabernacle, whenever you are able to go. You might not be able to stay for an hour, but any visit as time allows is good. Many times, our prayers will be just a moment here and there at Jesus' feet, lifting up our hearts to Him while we trudge through our busy days, trying to attend to all of the things we need to do for our families, as well as praying for those in our care.

While we are with Jesus after we have received the Bread of Life in Holy Communion, at the foot of the Cross in meditation, or while visiting Him in the Blessed Sacrament, let's be sure to thank Him for the gift He has given to us women of caring for others, and for all the gifts He bestows upon us to help us do so.

You'll notice that Jesus' words from the Cross ("I thirst") were uttered in the present tense, making them current. We should recognize that Jesus still proclaims "I thirst" today.

Remarkably, Jesus truly thirsts for our love! Let that sink in. Let us fall madly in love with Him!

Other Loves in Life

We need to put our Lord first in all things, and then He will assist us in our love life. Be sure that "falling in love" is not simply an infatuation. Put the love to the test. Will that special man put you first before anything else (except for God)? Is he lusting after you? I hope not. Lust is not love.

Pray about your relationships. Ask God to help you. Certainly, our Blessed Mother will look after you. Seek her in earnest prayer and ask her to find the right man for you, if it is God's will that you should fall in love and court your future husband. I said "if it is God's will" because not every woman is called to the Sacrament of Marriage, which, of course, is where romantically falling in love is supposed to culminate. Some women are called to religious life and others to the single life, which we will discuss in further chapters.

What is your love story? No matter what, love will continue to unfold in our lives.

PAUSE

Take some time to ponder the loves in your life. Meditate upon Jesus' amazing love for you. Think about your conversations with Him. Do you give Him enough time? Do you listen quietly in prayer? When you meet our Lord at the well of prayer, will it be at noon, like the Samaritan woman's encounter? Or will it be at every opportunity, raising your heart to Him?

ACT

Go to Jesus — trust Him and fall madly in love with Him. He is waiting for you by the well of prayer.

A PRAYER OF MERCY

Dear Lord, open my heart to receive Your Living Water. Please guide me in all my relationships.
Jesus, please have mercy upon my soul.
I trust in You!
I want to trust You with all my heart.
Mother Mary, help me, protect me, and guide me.
Saint Faustina, please pray for me.
Amen.

CHAPTER 14
Paths to Sanctity for Singles

"O my God, my only hope,
I have placed all my trust in You,
and I know I shall not be disappointed."

— Saint Faustina (*Diary*, 317)

Marriage or the convent? When it comes to a woman's vocation, this could be a question that onlookers ponder. Down through the ages, cultural expectations had been that the natural progression for a young woman was probably either pursuing a future spouse or that she was destined for the convent. Even today, if a young woman is not engaged or married, people begin to wonder, "Why does she not want to marry? Doesn't she want a husband, and a family?" This notion is difficult for the single woman who is trying to figure out her path in life.

No matter whether we're married or single on earth, the whole Church and everyone in it is called to have a spousal relationship with Jesus Christ (see Eph 5 and *CCC*, 1658). As we grow in holiness, no matter whether we are married, consecrated religious, or single, we are all invited into a mystical betrothal, and ultimately mystical marriage with the Divine Word (as St. Bernard, St. Theresa of Avila, and St. John of the Cross all teach). Some single women are in that state for their entire lives by divine providence, and divine providence always leads each one of us (if we are cooperating with that providence) into the vocation or state in life that is most conducive to our holiness as unique individuals.

The single life might come as a total surprise, or it can be a state of life that one has consciously chosen. A woman might choose to be a consecrated virgin (remaining single and making a religious commitment, but not entering formal religious life). A woman might remain single because marriage just never came about. Her Prince Charming didn't show up, or perhaps he was not meant for her. Thus, Divine Providence has arranged the circumstances (mental or physical health, or other situation) by which it's made clear to the woman that marriage or religious life is not meant to be.

This was the case for my friend Mary Talarico. Mary considered religious life, but, she said, "After many sessions with our priest at the time, I became discouraged and thought I didn't have the stamina to live the life of a nun."

In addition, Mary has admittedly had her heart broken more than once. In her mid-20s, she was in a relationship with a young man whose lifestyle clashed with hers. She became very unhappy.

Mary told me, "One day I read in the newspaper that the U.S. government was looking for secretaries to work overseas." This greatly appealed to her, and she decided to take the required exam. Shortly thereafter, she received a letter from Washington informing her that she had passed. Enclosed was a ticket to Washington!

"My brother thought I was a bit too drastic in my decision to make such a move," Mary noted. Naturally, he was sad to see her leave. Mary shared, "We laughed over this as he said that most people move to another neighborhood or city, 'but not my sister! She moved abroad to get away from the man who was messing up her life!'"

Mary had many experiences working abroad. One of them was immensely harrowing. She recalled, "On one occasion when I was on my way to my next assignment, I changed my travel plans at the last minute. I was supposed to be on the same flight and accompany one of the visitors who was to be a guest speaker at the [U.S.] Embassy in Israel." She explained, "To my horror and dismay, if I had taken that flight, I would have been murdered, because the gentleman I was to accompany and the person next to him were both killed by the Red Brigade. I often think that God has a reason to keep me here. That was the closest near-death experience that I have encountered."

How Did We Get Here?

Some women are single because they don't feel a calling to either marriage or religious life. Being single might also be temporary — a woman might be prayerfully waiting for further direction. In any case, for the most part, the single woman carries out her vocation in the midst of the world, whether living alone, or with family or roommates.

There are assorted challenges associated with the single life. One single woman I know (I'll call her "Cindy") told me, "I fight loneliness, and sometimes I get nervous at night living alone by myself." Watching her young-adult friends get married and start a family at times puts a distance between her and them. Cindy explained, "The things we had in common faded as their lives changed."

Being single can indeed be lonely. A single person can get tired of hearing the same question when they choose to dine out: "Just you?" They might feel self-conscious that people are staring at them. They might feel singled out. (Honestly, no pun intended!)

Mary, whom I mentioned previously, said she is very thankful that "God has blessed" her "with a long and beautiful life," and pointed out that "when I was growing up, you were considered an old maid if you were not married by 21."

She shared, "I spent the majority of my adult life overseas, and being a single woman [there] was different from the American mentality." She said, "In America, people asked me why I chose not to marry."

It's true that we live in a "couples" world, which could cause us to forget about the single people. We can also inadvertently discriminate against single women by supporting mostly "couples only" events. Our parishes might only invite families to bring up the gifts at Mass or other sorts of participation. We should lend a hand to start Catholic groups for singles.

Truth be told, "Love is the fundamental and innate vocation of every human being" (*Catechism*, 2392).[42] Certainly, love is the vocation for the single woman. We are all called to give love and receive love.

The *Catechism* instructs:

> We must also remember the great number of *single persons* who, because of the particular circumstances in which they have to live — often not of their choosing — are especially close to Jesus' heart and therefore deserve the special affection and active solicitude of the Church, especially of pastors. Many remain *without a human family* often due to conditions of poverty. Some live their situation in the spirit of the Beatitudes, serving God and neighbor in exemplary fashion. The doors of homes, the "domestic churches," and of the great family which is the Church must be open to all of them. "No one is without a family in this world: the Church is a home and family for everyone, especially those who 'labor and are heavy laden'"[43] (1658, emphasis in original).

We aren't called to pity the single state of life or to make single people feel odd in some way, but rather open our homes and welcome our single neighbors, break bread with them, and, above all, pay attention to them, especially if they are lonely or isolated. Our faith and our lives need to be shared. God calls us to this love, and, in fact, we need the love of our single friends, too!

There are many positive aspects to the single life. For instance, one single woman I know told me, "Being single allows me time to discover what it is that I enjoy because you can try anything!" She added, "I really enjoy being open to wherever the Spirit would move me next. I know the possibilities for a single woman are endless!"

The Hands and Feet of Christ

Single women have a special calling to the apostolate, as well as time to discern a vocation. When not called to religious life, single women usually have more flexibility with their schedules because they're usually not bound to family responsibilities, and so are able to serve through various parish and community activities. In addition, single women might be well suited to certain professions that require more time and dedication, such as medicine and education.

Lindsey, a 30-year-old single woman, told me, "I believe that we can live our faith every day by being the hands and feet of Christ here on earth." She certainly practices what she preaches! She is very involved with parish life, volunteering in her local soup kitchen, praying outside a local abortion mill, and helping out in a prison ministry.

My friend Mary is grateful that, due to the way her life has unfolded, she is more readily available to help out at her parish and wherever there is a need — for instance, taking care of her mother when she was stricken with Alzheimer's disease. Mary also told me, "Because I have so much time on my hands and have no hobbies, I feel I should give the extra time to help in our parish office, as that is where I can be the most helpful." She also became an extraordinary minister of Holy Communion "to bring Communion to the parishioners of my parish who are in nursing homes." Mary also started a book club at her parish.

My friend Joan Lewis, whom you might know from her EWTN television series, "Joan's Rome," has also been quite busy as a single Catholic woman. Like many other single Catholic women, Joan didn't plan her vocation. It unfolded for her.

One evening, while I sat at her dining room table, I would become privy to the details about how it all happened. In the intimate setting of Joan's home, situated very near St. Peter's Basilica, my friend disclosed, "I did not choose to give up family for a career." She explained, "I wanted a happy marriage and family like my parents had, like my myriads of aunts and uncles and, later, my many cousins had."

That didn't happen for Joan.

"The Lord had other plans, even though it took me awhile to realize they were His!" Though Joan didn't marry and have a family, she said, "God, in His wisdom, gave me a very large and very beautiful and very extended family." She considers all of her beloved friends all around the world her "second families."

Her family expands even wider than her circle of relatives and friends. She told me, "I am very close to the North American College, the U.S. seminary in Rome, close to the rectors, to the priests and nuns on its faculty, and I follow the path to the priesthood of so many terrific young men — another 'family' for me."

Joan loves to cook and entertain dinner guests. Several ambassadors to the Holy See have broken bread at Joan's table. She said, "I am honored to have as friends a number of cardinals and bishops of the Roman Curia and scores of priests, as well as those who are residential prelates." She has traveled around the world to cover news events for the Church. With a Holy See diplomatic passport tucked in her bag, working as a member of the Holy See delegations to the United Nations conferences, Joan has covered the International Conference on Population and Development in Cairo, the World Summit for Social Development in Copenhagen, the World Conference on Women in Beijing, the Habitat Conference on Human Settlements in Istanbul, and two conferences in Doha, Qatar. She visited with St. John Paul II on numerous occasions. Being a member of the Vatican Information Service afforded Joan the opportunity to read everything the pontiff wrote. She said, "I learned a great deal, and my faith grew as a result."

Sitting at her dining room table that evening, Joan humbly shared that if she hadn't been a single woman, she wouldn't have been able to carry out all her interviews or her charity work, or offer hospitality to so many who visit her home.

Consecrated Virginity

There is another opportunity for Catholic women within the single life: becoming a consecrated virgin. This ancient vocation was the first form of consecrated life in the Church, but it fell into disuse when religious communities flourished. This rite was restored in 1970 and has been flourishing since that time.

My friend Louise Paré is a consecrated virgin and has shared a bit of her journey with me. I first met Louise through the publishing industry, where she worked for 42 years. Louise shared, "What a blessing to be able to spread God's word in that way!" Since her retirement in 2016, Louise has been serving as a spiritual director and retreat speaker at her diocesan retreat center in Michigan.

For Louise, her calling started with a dramatic encounter with Jesus that stirred her heart at a tender age.

Louise recalled that during the Cuban Missile Crisis, "the sisters at school asked us to go home and pray for protection from war. I said something profound like, 'Don't let the Russians bomb us.'"

"God responded to this simple schoolgirl prayer," she said, "by flooding my whole being with a deep personal knowledge of His love for me." This profound encounter would become engraved upon Louise's little heart.

"I didn't know anything at that point about consecrated life, but that knowledge of God's personal call never left me." Later in life, Louise recalled, "When it came time to discern God's call for my life, I realized that I could not choose anything else because this loving union with God was so deeply ingrained in me."

When Louise was in her 20s, she recognized "something strange was happening in my life." She had begun to set her alarm clock to wake herself up early in the morning, she said, "so that I would have time to pray." This practice helped her to realize how much her relationship with Jesus meant to her.

She recalled, "I was not the type of person to get up early

if I didn't have to. But I saw that spending that time with Him was very important to me, and it was worth some sacrifice." This practice has stayed with her to this day. She said, "I put prayer first in my day so that it does not get squeezed out by other things." Louise knows how days can take on a life of their own, and that it is essential to carve out time for God.

"Life is busy," Louise said, "and many things are beyond my control. But if I cannot pray first thing, I plan when I will be able to pray." She has her priorities straight; yet as in everyone's prayer life, sometimes there is a struggle: "Prayer can be challenging, and for all of us, it is hard to overcome our sinfulness and be conformed to the image of Christ." Louise offers wonderful advice: "It requires faith, perseverance, and sometimes a lot of courage. But it is worth the struggle!"

A Consecrated Virgin Is More About "Being" Than "Doing"

Louise has been a consecrated virgin for 28 years. She shared what it actually entails and what it means to her. "Consecrated virgins are free to practice any of the spiritual traditions," she said. Consecrated virgins do not take vows. "There are no specific promises as you might find in a religious order," she noted. "Instead, the heart of the commitment is to an exclusive and all-encompassing love."

"The rite of consecration," Louise said, "focuses on the relationship with Jesus." She added, "The virgin is encouraged to give herself fully to Him, completely surrendered, to live as His bride, to love and serve His Church." Sound simple? As Louise put it, "In one sense, it is very simple. In another sense, it is deeper than you can imagine."

Louise explained, "A consecrated virgin is so much more about 'being' than 'doing.' It is completely tied up in the gift of myself in love to the Lord, and He in turn gives Himself to me. It forms the very core of my being."

Graces continue to flow throughout a consecrated virgin's prayer life and commitment. "I find the desire growing in me that everything I do in my life be an expression of my consecrated life," she said. "That union of God needs to pour into every aspect of my life."

Louise felt blessed to visit Rome in 1995 for an international pilgrimage of consecrated virgins and had the wonderful opportunity to meet St. John Paul II. She said, "He was a great supporter of this vocation, and I still believe he prays for and supports consecrated virgins in a special way."

In his encouraging address, the pontiff taught:

> Love Him as He desires to be love in your concrete life: "If you love Me, you will keep My commandments" (Jn 14:15; cf. 14:21). Love Him as is fitting to your spousal condition: assuming His same sentiments (cf. Phil 2:5); sharing His way of life consisting in humility and meekness, love and mercy, service and joyful availability, untiring zeal for the glory of the Father and the salvation of the human race. The state of consecrated virginity makes the praise of Christ more spontaneous, listening to His word quicker, service to Him more joyful, and the occasion of offering Him the homage of your love more frequent. *Yet consecrated virginity is not a privilege, but rather a gift of God*, which implies a strong commitment in following Him and being His disciple.
>
> The following of the Lamb in Heaven (cf. Rev 14:6) begins on earth, walking down the narrow path (cf. Mt 7:14). Your *sequela Christi* will be more radical, the greater your love is for Christ and the more lucid your awareness of the meaning of virginal consecration. In the Apostolic Letter *Mulieris dignitatem*, dealing with the "Gospel ideal of virginity," I recalled that, "in (consecrated) virginity is expressed ... the radical nature of the Gospel, which consists in leaving everything and following Christ" (n. 20).
>
> Your being *disciples of Christ* will be more intense, the more you are convinced that Jesus is the

one Teacher (cf. Mt 23:8), whose words are "spirit and life." Dear Sisters, remember that your place is, like that of Mary of Bethany (cf. Lk 10:39), at the feet of Jesus, listening to the words of grace that come forth from His mouth (cf. Lk 4:22).[44]

Unlike women in religious orders, consecrated virgins do not live in community. Louise explained, "They live on their own and are responsible to the diocesan bishop for living out their vocation faithfully. Their primary community is their parish life, and they belong to their diocese in a particular way." She also shared, "Consecrated virgins must supply for their own financial support, and this can take many different shapes."

Consecrated women work in a variety of professions. "Many work in service to the Church," Louise explained. The various forms of work "give [consecrated virgins] an opportunity to serve others as an expression of their life as disciples."

The Gift of Jesus

With permission from her diocesan bishop, Louise told me, "I am blessed to have the Blessed Sacrament reserved in my home." She said, "This is not a given for any consecrated virgin, but a number of bishops have granted this permission to consecrated virgins within their diocese." What a gift!

Louise said, "This is a profound privilege, and one I never take lightly. I recognize that I am profoundly blessed." She explained, "This vocation embodies such a deep gift of self to our Lord and a true spiritual marriage, and this presence of Jesus in the Blessed Sacrament in my home really underscores the depth of that relationship." Louise shared, "It humbles me and it awes me to have Him present in such a tangible way."

Having the Blessed Sacrament reserved in her own home perfectly complements Louise's vocation, which, she said, is "a deeply contemplative life." She continued, "This consecration is the path God has called me to in order to be joined in union with Him. Praying before the Blessed Sacrament is a natural extension of that call. Being with God in silence is important in my time of prayer."

"The Psalms invite us to 'Be still, and know that I am God,'" she explained (Ps 46:10). "That is at the heart of my prayer and at the heart of my relationship to Him as a consecrated virgin." Louise prays at every opportunity and shared, "I also make room for spiritual reading and reading of Scripture, and, of course, attendance at Mass as often as possible." She added, "Morning and Evening Prayer from the Liturgy of the Hours is part of my commitment."

PAUSE

Take some time to think about the single women you know. Is there something you can do to help them feel more included? If you are single, might you ponder if God is calling you to religious life or consecrated virginity?

ACT

Pray an extra Divine Mercy Chaplet or Rosary sometime soon specifically for single women.

A PRAYER OF MERCY

Dear Jesus, thank You for Your great love for me.
Please have mercy upon my soul.
I trust in You! I know I need to trust You more!
Mother Mary, help me, protect me, and guide me.
Saint Faustina, please pray for me.
Amen.

CHAPTER 15
Becoming a Godmother
or a Sponsor

*"Woman can only find herself
by giving love to others."*

— Saint John Paul II (MD, 30)

Being asked to be a godmother or a sponsor for someone receiving the Sacraments of Initiation is an honor and a privilege. A Catholic woman can certainly spiritually mother godchildren or Catholic brethren whom she's sponsored.

First, a quick word about Catholic Baptism. The *Catechism* states, "Baptism is the sacrament of faith.[45] But faith needs the community of believers. It is only within the faith of the Church that each of the faithful can believe. The faith required for Baptism is not a perfect and mature faith, but a beginning that is called to develop. The catechumen or the godparent is asked: 'What do you ask of God's Church?' The response is: 'Faith!'" (1253).

The Church teaches that the baptized person (often an infant) needs not just the parents' help, but also the godparents' help throughout their lives. The *Catechism* tells us, "For the grace of Baptism to unfold, the parents' help is important. So too is the role of the *godfather* and *godmother*, who must be firm believers, able and ready to help the newly baptized — child or adult — on the road of Christian life," and adds, "Their task is a truly ecclesial function (*officium*).[46] The whole ecclesial community bears some responsibility for the development and safeguarding of the grace given at Baptism" (1255, emphasis in original).

With regard to being a sponsor (usually for a Confirmation candidate), the Church teaches, "Candidates for Confirmation, as for Baptism, fittingly seek the spiritual help of a *sponsor*. To emphasize the unity of the two sacraments, it is appropriate that this be one of the baptismal godparents" (*Catechism*, 1311, emphasis in original). We learn from the *Code of Canon Law* that the primary responsibility of a sponsor is to provide guidance and prayerful support to the candidate. "Insofar as possible, there is to be a sponsor for the person to be confirmed; the sponsor is to take care that the confirmed person behaves as a true witness of Christ and faithfully fulfills the obligations inherent in this sacrament."[47]

A sponsor takes on the lifelong role of a spiritual parent who "brings the candidate to receive the sacrament, presents him to the minister for the anointing, and will later help him to fulfill his baptismal promises faithfully under the influence of the Holy Spirit."[48]

Being a godmother or sponsor is a big deal! My own godmother, Aunt Bertha, is such a treasure in my life. She is someone I would deeply admire even if she wasn't my relative or godmother!

Personally, I am blessed to be a sponsor and also a godmother to many godchildren. One of my godchildren came into my life in a very unexpected way when I heard of a teenaged girl with a little baby. Both were unwanted and had no place to call home. The teen's mother was mentally ill and had set fire to their New York City apartment. It was truly a miracle that this young woman had survived thus far.

Since I was very active in the pro-life movement, one of my friends told me about the unwed mother and child. To open my home to her, I had to be certified as a foster parent. I had never planned on doing this. It had never entered my mind. I was already a biological mother to two young children with another on the way. Yet God's plan unfolded in my life in a way I couldn't have imagined. I went ahead, applied, and received the certification to become an official foster mother.

Shortly thereafter, the young woman and her tiny baby were at my front door. My own 3-year-old daughter had given up her bedroom to accommodate the little family. It touched my heart. We all forged ahead together in my humble domestic church. I taught the girl (I'll call her Corina) mothering and basic housekeeping skills. We went to church together as a family. One day, I asked Corina if she would like to have her baby baptized in the Catholic Church. She was delighted that I'd asked. We made arrangements, and before long, little "Rebecca" was baptized and became a member of the Church.

When a woman takes on the role of godmother or sponsor, she can surely "find herself by giving love to others," as St. John Paul II said in the quote that begins this chapter.

A "Preacher's Kid" Surprises His Wife

Aly Tugaoen, a U.S. Army Reserve soldier married to a retired active-duty soldier, shared with me that her husband had grown up as a "preacher's kid." She said, "His father was a retired infantry soldier, but on the side, he was a Pentecostal minister." It was obvious to Aly that "the Christian faith was deeply ingrained into his character. It's one of the things I liked about him when we met."

However, Aly was serious about her own Catholic faith. So when she began dating AJ, she told him something that burned into her heart and of which she was absolutely sure.

"I told him that I was Catholic and that I would *never* change," she said. "So don't bother trying to convert me." Aly firmly believed in the Real Presence of Christ in the Eucharist — Body, Blood, Soul, and Divinity. "If that was a deal-breaker for him, then so be it." She was sticking with her Catholic faith! And AJ decided that he could live with it.

On the other hand, AJ made it very clear to Aly that he wasn't interested in becoming Catholic, so Aly "didn't push the issue." They fell in love and got married.

In the final years of AJ's active-duty service, they were stationed at Fort Bragg, North Carolina. Aly was deeply involved in the Catholic Women of the Chapel (CWOC) ministry through being an active-duty Army Reserve soldier. The couple agreed that both of their children would be baptized in the Catholic faith. AJ began attending Mass each Sunday with Aly and the children.

When it was time for AJ to retire from active duty, the family moved to their "forever home." As an Army Reserve soldier, Aly was mandated to attend military schools and training events. During a time when she had to be away for several months, AJ called. He told his wife that "he had been speaking to a local Catholic priest about converting to the Catholic faith." Needless to say, Aly said she was absolutely "*floored.*"

She told me, "This is not something we had ever discussed." She positively had to ask him what had transpired. She said, "When I asked what made him change his mind, he mentioned specifically that when we were stationed at Ft. Bragg all those years ago, he saw how every woman would step up to help one another, no matter what was going on in our own families and lives."

This is a powerful testament to how we Catholic women are supposed to live and the amazing example we can set. We may never know in this lifetime how our charitable acts have helped souls. We might focus on the people we are serving, hoping and praying that God's graces are working there, but fail to recognize that He is also working on the hearts of those who are observing!

Aly gave some examples of what had touched her husband's heart the most. She said that "whether it was a new mom and baby issue, deployment issue, or a medical issue," he saw the women rally around each other. He saw members of the local CWOC sit at church with a mom whose husband was deployed, taking places near her "so they could help wrangle rowdy kids in the pews."

AJ watched as women "banded together to create games that inspired our children to grow in faith." She continued,

"He saw us live out this Catholic faith in everything we did." And that drew him in. "He wanted to be a more integral part of that life." Aly shared what happened on a particular Divine Mercy Sunday.

"The tipping point was on Divine Mercy Sunday later that year," Aly recalled. "We went to Mass, prayed and sang the Chaplet in church, and then headed out to a late lunch with friends at a nearby Italian restaurant." Aly's husband ended up sitting next to his friend and one of the priests that concelebrated the Mass. It turned out that the friend and the priest were both converts to the faith. Without knowing what was on AJ's heart at that moment, "they alleviated his fears and reservations," Aly recounted.

Something truly amazing was about to unfold. Seemingly out of the blue, AJ asked Aly to be his sponsor for him as he came into the Catholic Church! Aly recalled, "I was surprised and touched when he stated he wanted me to be his sponsor." She added, "I don't know why I was surprised. The Holy Spirit works like that, right?" Graces were abounding on that Divine Mercy Sunday!

The next year, AJ was received fully into the Church. Aly will never forget that glorious day. The angels were surely rejoicing. Because of the way Divine Mercy Sunday had unfolded as the embers in AJ's heart stoked into flames, Aly now says, "Divine Mercy Sunday holds such a special place in my heart."

PAUSE

Take a moment to ponder your godchildren, people you have sponsored, or your own godmother. Are you in touch with any of them? Ask God to bless them in a special way.

Act

If it's possible, reach out to your godmother and let her know that you love her and are thankful that she's in your life (or pray for her soul if she has passed). Reach out to any significant people in your life that you haven't been in touch with. Pray for them, too.

A Prayer of Mercy

Dear Jesus, thank You for Your many gifts, most especially for the gift of my godmother.
Please bless her and every godmother.
Please have mercy upon my soul.
I trust in You!
Mother Mary, help me, protect me, and guide me.
Saint Faustina, please pray for me.
Amen.

CHAPTER 16
Hitting Rock Bottom

"So, I will boast all the more gladly of
my weaknesses, so that the power
of Christ may dwell in me."

— 2 Cor 12:9

We all struggle in some way. Even St. Paul struggled. In his Second Epistle to the Corinthians, he speaks about suffering from a "thorn" in the flesh, but he doesn't reveal what type of annoyance it was (2 Cor 12:7). Some have speculated that he had the stigmata. His "thorn" could have been an illness, failing eyesight, a form of persecution, the many scars from the beatings and imprisonment he had received for preaching the Gospel.

Whatever it was that caused St. Paul to struggle, he enlightens us about how to rise above it and accept God's grace. He said, "Three times I appealed to the Lord about this, that it would leave me, but he said to me, 'My grace is sufficient for you, for power is made perfect in weakness'" (2 Cor 12:8-9).

What was his solution?

He exclaimed, "So, I will boast all the more gladly of my weaknesses, so that the power of Christ may dwell in me. Therefore I am content with weaknesses, insults, hardships, persecutions, and calamities for the sake of Christ; for whenever I am weak, then I am strong" (2 Cor 12:9-10).

Saint Paul concluded that his "thorn" became a blessing when he finally realized that God had given it to him, meaning it for good. His thorn even became a source of strength for him. May God bless St. Paul for letting us in on his secret for dealing with the thorn in our own sides.

Do we boast of our weaknesses? Well, perhaps not publicly. But in our hearts? Can we admit our weaknesses and accept that God is the Divine Physician who gives us just what we need when we need it, so long as we welcome His help and are open to His Providence? Our thorn might be a temptation to a particular sin. It could be a suffering that we endure. Our lives as women are filled with misunderstandings and contradictions. Some of them pierce our hearts and become thorns in our sides.

Following St. Paul's advice can help us avoid hitting rock bottom or protect us from despair if we do crash. Jesus revealed to St. Faustina something very important about His graces: **"My daughter, do not pay so much attention to the vessel of grace as to the grace itself which I give you, because you are not always pleased with the vessel, and then the graces, too, become deficient"** (*Diary*, 1599).

Jesus continued, **"I want to guard you from that, and I want you never to pay attention to the vessel in which I send you My grace. Let all the attention of your soul be concentrated on responding to My grace as faithfully as possible"** (*Diary*, 1599). Meditating upon this teaching from Jesus can truly transform our outlooks and our souls!

Jesus provides experiences in our lives that can become powerful means of conversion both for our own hearts and the hearts of others. He also keeps us on our toes and keeps us humble. Let's take a look at another important lesson that Jesus taught His bride Faustina.

Jesus Unites Himself to Humble Souls

Saint Faustina recorded in her *Diary* (on February 2, 1938) that she was in total darkness though it was the "Feast of the Mother of God" (the Feast of the Purification of the

Blessed Virgin Mary, or Candlemas). She said the Lord had hidden Himself: "Not a single ray of light penetrates my soul." She was assailed with "frightful temptations" and begged for Jesus to help her. In deep pain, she wrote, "I am astounded that such torments could befall a soul. O hurricane, what are you doing to the boat of my heart?" She penned, "This storm has lasted the whole day and night" (1558).

Faustina spent the entire night "with Jesus in Gethsemane." With her pen, she articulated her profound pain: "From my breast there escaped one continuous moan." She added, "A natural dying will be much easier, because then one is in agony and will die; while here, one is in agony, but cannot die."

She sounds so dramatic. Yet I have no doubt that she was not exaggerating. She was allowed those sufferings, united as she was to our Lord. She cried out, "O Jesus, save me! I believe in You with all my heart." Our sister Faustina continued to relate how she had been formerly blessed to see the radiance of His face, but could no longer see Him. She made continual acts of faith. "I believe, I believe, and again I believe in You, Triune God, Father, Son, and Holy Spirit, and in all the truths which Your holy Church gives me to believe … ."

The young mystic was in absolute agony. Even after those fervent pleas, she explained, "But the darkness does not recede, and my spirit plunges into even greater agony." Stricken, she explained, "And at that moment, such terrible torment overwhelmed me that now I am amazed at myself that I did not breathe my last, but this was for only a brief instant" (*Diary*, 1558).

Then Jesus appeared to His bride. From His Heart issued forth the rays of Divine Mercy. Saint Faustina recalled that the two rays enveloped her and, in that moment, "[A]ll my torments vanished." Then Jesus spoke to her. **"My daughter,"** He said, **"know that of yourself you are just what you have gone through, and it is only by My grace that you are a participant of eternal life and all the gifts I lavish on you"** (*Diary*, 1559).

Faustina instantly received full knowledge of herself. She discerned, "Jesus is giving me a lesson in deep humility and, at the same time, one of total trust in Him." She added, "My heart is reduced to dust and ashes, and even if all people were to trample me under their feet, I would still consider that a favor."

Jesus told Faustina (and tells us all) that we are merely the sum of all our experiences without His grace. We absolutely need His grace to rise above all we have experienced and to continue to strive for holiness. Our experiences won't get us to heaven. Cooperating with God's grace will. We can do nothing without God.

Saint Faustina wrote, "I feel and am, in fact, very deeply permeated with the knowledge that I am nothing, so that real humiliations will be a refreshment for me" (*Diary*, 1559).

Can we say the same? Will we welcome humiliations? It's tough, but with God's grace, we can understand the need to be humble and open to His grace. Jesus told St. Faustina, **"My bride, you always please Me by your humility. The greatest misery does not stop Me from uniting Myself to a soul, but where there is pride, I am not there"** (*Diary*, 1563).

Are We Ever Alone?

Our sister Faustina helps us to understand that we are not alone in our struggles. So often we feel alone during dark times. Saint Faustina learned that for her to grow deeply in holiness, it was necessary that she experience some of the same things Jesus had experienced. After all, we know that if we are to be Jesus' followers, we need to deny ourselves, pick up our crosses, and follow Him (see Mt 16:24). I'll mention this repeatedly throughout this book since it is an important part of what it means to be His disciple. Though being a Christian is a difficult life in many respects, the rewards in Heaven are tremendous! Many of the saints have said that we can experience a foretaste of heavenly joys here on earth.

Saint Faustina shared in her *Diary*, "I have understood that at certain and most difficult moments I shall be alone, deserted by everyone, and that I must face all the storms and fight with all the strength of my soul, even with those from whom I expected to get help." However, the young mystic knew that, despite how she felt or would be treated, the reality was that Jesus would never leave her. She wrote, "But I am not alone, because Jesus is with me, and with Him I fear nothing. I am well aware of everything, and I know what God is demanding of me" (*Diary*, 746).

She was a victim soul and knew that she was destined to a life of suffering — that is, to be like her Lord and Savior Jesus Christ. She said, "Suffering, contempt, ridicule, persecution, and humiliation will be my constant lot. I know no other way. For sincere love — ingratitude; this is my path, marked out by the footprints of Jesus" (*Diary*, 746).

Regarding the difficulties of a suffering soul, St. Faustina stated, "Oh, if only the suffering soul knew how it is loved by God, it would die of joy and excess of happiness!" She added, "Someday, we will know the value of suffering, but then we will no longer be able to suffer. The present moment is ours" (*Diary*, 963).

Falling Into Despair

Women help other women. I'd like to share a true story told to me by a young female police officer. My friend shared with me about a young mother of three small children. It all happened one sunny afternoon when a jogger spotted this woman apparently sleeping or relaxing near a river. Jogging back later that day, he observed her again. However, the woman was in the exact same position he had seen her in much earlier.

He called 911.

The police officer told me how she ran like crazy through the woods to try to get to the woman in time, in case she was still alive. She was so determined to do all that she could to save that woman's life. The officer had with her the drug that could "reverse" the effects of the drugs that the woman had overdosed on in her attempt to commit suicide.

You know, with all the paraphernalia they carry, a police officer's gun belt weighs between 30 and 40 pounds — and she was running with all her might through thick brush and trees to get to a somewhat secluded location in the woods. The officer told me that as she ran towards the woman, she cried out loud, "You better be alive!"

Can you imagine?

Thank God the officer was able to save the young mother! I don't know further details, but I am sure that there is a long road ahead for this mother and family. Let's pray for her and others like her who have lost hope.

Saint John Paul II once said, "We are an Easter people and Alleluia is our song." We *really need* to be Easter people and bring that "Alleluia" with us wherever we go! John Paul didn't say it would be easy. He declared, "We are not looking for a shallow joy but rather a joy that comes from faith, that grows through unselfish love, that respects the 'fundamental duty of love of neighbour, without which it would be unbecoming to speak of Joy'. We realize that joy is demanding; it demands unselfishness; it demands a readiness to say with Mary: 'Be it done unto me according to thy word.'"[49]

You know, Mother Teresa told her sisters that if they didn't have *joy* in their hearts, they might as well pack up and go home! The poor didn't need their problems — they had enough of their own.

We should do all that we can to possess a holy hope and joy in our hearts so that we can impart them to those whom we meet along our journey through life.

Distractions and Temptations to Give Up

It might be human nature that causes us to cave in or give up completely when things get exhausting or dicey. In addition, our ancient foe, whom I call "you-know-who," absolutely loves to trip us and coerce us to give up. Truth be told, I don't want to give "old hairy legs" the dignity of space in this book. But bear with me, please. I'd like to make an important point that could be very helpful to your spiritual life.

Yes, life can be hard, especially for women — there's no arguing there — so we have to work hard, especially during tough times. When the going gets rough, it's not time to sit around, wallowing and eating Doritos or a tub of ice cream (or worse, I'm sorry to say, to do as the young mother who tried to take her own life)! We can't allow our present trial or tribulation to knock us down or take the wind out of our sails. "You-know-who" will have won the battle and will be doing a very evil happy dance if we give up on our call to holiness. We can't let that happen.

In Chapter 10, I mentioned Thomas á Kempis' good counsel in *The Imitation of Christ* about being alert so that we can nip temptations in the bud in order to thwart the evil one's wicked plans. We must stay alert, and not let him in! With God's help, we can do this!

Á Kempis helps us further:

> Someone has said very aptly: "Resist the beginnings; remedies come too late, when by long delay the evil has gained strength." First, a mere thought comes to mind, then strong imagination, followed by pleasure, evil delight, and consent. Thus, because he is not resisted in the beginning, Satan gains full entry. And the longer a man delays in resisting, so much the weaker does he become each day, while the strength of the enemy grows against him.[50]

When we feel upset or tormented; when our prayers seem as dry as the drifting sands of the Sahara Desert; when we are tempted to give up or give in to something that we shouldn't — that's when we must earnestly hold on to our faith and storm Heaven with our constant prayers. The old foe never sleeps and makes it his sick priority to drag us down to hell at his first opportunity.

How can he do this?

The Devil Tempts Us to Give Up Praying

It's simple — he tempts us to give up praying. It's impossible to fight the battle on our own. We shouldn't even entertain the thought — not for a moment. But he keeps us too busy with other things or causes the trials to seem overwhelming. With all that continuously bombards a woman's life, it's easy to succumb to the devil's temptations — those "pretty little packages" I mentioned in Chapter 9.

Sometimes, the temptation is in the form of something alluring to entertain ourselves with, or some kind of pleasure, such as too much wine, shopping, food, television, internet, or social media, or an inappropriate relationship — all of which can numb our conscience. At times, the temptation is that of fear. We can get so wrapped up in the fears we face that we do not pray as we should and then we stop trusting God. Because we have become engrossed with other things, we are not praying enough to enable us to stay on the straight and narrow path that leads to Heaven.

Thomas á Kempis reassures us, "We should not despair, therefore, when we are tempted, but pray to God the more fervently that He may see fit to help us, for according to the word of Paul, He will make issue with temptation that we may be able to bear it." The esteemed writer advises us, "Let us humble our souls under the hand of God in every trial and temptation for He will save and exalt the humble in spirit."[51] There's that word "humble" again. We need to strive to be humble! God helps the humble soul.

We can learn a life-transforming lesson from St. Faustina, who herself learned it from Jesus. I believe that this profound insight can carry us through life, and is really an eternal lifesaver!

Saint Faustina learned this truth during a Holy Hour on January 7, 1937. Faustina had ushered in the New Year with many holy resolutions. Just before this powerful experience, the young mystic had bidden good-bye to the old year.

She trusted Jesus to accompany her so that she could "go boldly and courageously into conflicts and battles." She professed, "In Your Name, I will accomplish everything and overcome everything. My God, Infinite Goodness, I beg of You, let Your infinite mercy accompany me always and in all things" (*Diary*, 859).

Faustina knew herself very well. She added, "As I enter this year, fear of life overwhelms me, but Jesus brings me out of this fear and lets me know what great glory this work of mercy will bring Him" (*Diary*, 859).

In bidding farewell to the old year and welcoming the new, Faustina made an important discovery about the spiritual life: "There are times in life when the soul finds comfort only in profound prayer. Would that souls knew how to persevere in prayer at such times. This is very important" (*Diary*, 860).

Eventually, the Lord would explain to her why.

Pray Longer!

Much happened to St. Faustina that first week of January 1937, which you can read about in the *Diary*. She went about her daily duties and was immersed in prayer. During the week, she had her first meeting connected with the painting of the Divine Mercy Image. She also received a visit from the Mother Superior of the Congregation and from an orphan girl who needed profound help and for whom Faustina suffered. She meditated upon Jesus' sufferings and "tried to comfort the Lord, by offering Him my love a thousand times over." She said that she felt within her soul a "great disgust for sin" (*Diary*, 866).

Saint Faustina experienced an even greater longing for her Spouse, Jesus: "My heart is steeped in continual bitterness, because I want to go to You, Lord, into the fullness of life." The young nun lamented that the world seemed like a "dreadful wilderness" (*Diary*, 867). She was profoundly thankful for Jesus in the Eucharist, but found herself longing for Him more deeply.

"I suffer because of my longing for You, O Lord. You have left me the Sacred Host, O Lord, but it enkindles in my soul an even greater longing for You, O my Creator and Eternal God!" (*Diary*, 867).

A couple of days later at her Holy Hour, wrote Faustina, "The Lord allowed me to taste His Passion." Can we even imagine? The mystic explained that she "shared in the bitterness of the suffering that filled His soul to overflowing"

(*Diary*, 872). It was during this profound time of suffering that Faustina came to understand a deep truth in the spiritual life.

"Jesus gave me to understand," she wrote, "how a soul should be faithful to prayer despite torments, dryness, and temptations; because [now here is the absolute clincher] oftentimes the realization of God's great plans depends mainly on such prayer" (*Diary*, 872).

Can we stop here a moment to really take this in?

Saint Faustina tells us, "If we do not persevere in such prayer, we frustrate what the Lord wanted to do through us or within us." We might now be thinking of the times that we gave up on prayer because it was too hard (we were too tired or just didn't feel like praying), not realizing that God needed that prayer to work some tremendous good in our life and in the lives of others. It's possible we might have thought that since He is God, after all, He doesn't really *need* our prayers. That thought had certainly crossed my mind years ago. But God's action in the world depends on our free will, on our choice to say yes to Him and allow Him to act freely. Why? Because He has such high regard for our free will.

We must not despair, but instead move forward knowing that we need to persevere in prayer throughout the rest of our lives. Saint Faustina encourages us, "Let every soul remember these words: 'And being in anguish, He prayed longer.' I always prolong such prayer as much as is in my power and in conformity with my duty" (*Diary*, 872).

Saint Faustina learned from Jesus' Passion, when He prayed in the Garden of Gethsemane and His sweat became like drops of blood. When Jesus suffered and felt abandoned, He prayed longer.

CRARD CRARD CRARD

PAUSE

How are you most easily distracted from God and prayer? Ponder the things in life that the evil one might use to take you away from God. Work on nipping those temptations in the bud, with our

Lord's help. Take a few moments to think about your prayer life and, if you can, make it a point to "pray longer" in the future. Our Lord will be right there with you in prayer.

ACT

Try to be more cognizant about the temptations in your life that cause you to want to give up praying, or the things that keep you so busy that you feel like you don't have enough time to pray. Make time for your Creator. Write it on your to-do list! Make it happen. Don't be afraid. Keep praying. Don't stop. Trust God!

A PRAYER OF MERCY

Jesus, You told St. Faustina not to pay attention to the vessel of grace, but rather to the grace that You gave her. You know that I am not always pleased with the vessel of Your grace, and then Your graces become deficient. You told St. Faustina that You wanted to guard her from that, and You told her, **"Let all the attention of your soul be concentrated on responding to My grace as faithfully as possible"** (*Diary*, 1599). Please, dear Jesus, help me, guard me. I want to be like You and pray longer. Jesus, please have mercy upon my soul. I trust in You!

Mother Mary, help me, protect me, and guide me.

Saint Faustina, please pray for me.

Amen.

CHAPTER 17
Returning to Faith

"Be sure to do everything for the glory of
God and the good of His people."[52]

— Mother Teresa

Most of us traverse some twisting roads in life, and at times, aimlessly wander crooked paths or stumble through darkness. My path was surely a crooked one. Nonetheless, God makes crooked lines straight! There are times when we might feel like we've been to hell and back, and we need to drop down to our knees at the foot of the Cross and beg God for forgiveness. He is waiting patiently there to rush in, scoop us up, and draw us close to His Heart — His blazing, passionate, Sacred Heart! At other times, we thank Him for bringing us out of some dark situation that was totally beyond our control.

The more we make room for God in our lives, the better off we and all those around us will be. Saint Faustina has much to teach us about prayer and union with God. She meditated upon the mystery of Divine Mercy and discovered that God was dwelling in her soul. She continuously contemplated our Lord wherever she was and spoke to Him often. We can do the same, no matter what path of life we tread.

How Might We Get Into Trouble?

We are talking about returning to faith in this chapter. However, it's good to consider what might have gotten us into trouble in the first place. Saint Faustina learned first-hand from the evil one about the kind of souls that are most vulnerable to his snares and temptations to sin.

One time, Faustina saw Satan hurrying about the convent. He was "looking for someone among the sisters, but he could find no one," wrote the young mystic. Faustina felt a sudden interior prompting to get information from the devil. She was inspired to "command him in the Name of God" to tell her what it was he was seeking among the sisters (*Diary*, 1127).

The devil confessed, "though unwillingly," Faustina attested. He admitted, "I am looking for idle souls." Sister Faustina asked him again to tell her "to which sisters in religious life he has the easiest access." Again, he said unwillingly, "To lazy and idle souls." Sister Faustina made a mental note of the fact that there were no idle sisters in the house. She wrote, "Let the toiling and tired souls rejoice" (*Diary*, 1127).

I just love St. Faustina's summation of her findings. Yes, let us rejoice and also keep this important lesson in mind, especially when temped to let our guard down or to become lackadaisical about our faith, our responsibilities, or our work. This does not mean we shouldn't seek the necessary rest that we need in our state of life and in situations of ill health. However, we need to be mindful of idleness.

Are we letting the devil in? I sure hope not! Are we engaging in frivolous or inappropriate pastimes? I sure hope not! Let's be on guard and aware. Let us examine our motives and our consciences. We need to ask ourselves if we are using our time wisely and if what we do is to serve God and others. This reminds me of something dear Mother Teresa once told me. She said, "Be sure to do everything for the glory of God and the good of His people." If we shape our lives in this way, we cannot go wrong.

Another way we might get lost in life is by listening to and falling for the prevailing culture that would rather not believe in the existence of hell and the consequences for sin. For example, one time I was giving a talk to a parish about the Rosary and the Blessed Mother. Lo and behold, the subject of hell came up. I discussed Our Lady of Fatima and the shepherd children's vision of hell on July 13, 1917. I also spoke about St. Faustina's testimony, recorded under obedience in her *Diary*, about the existence of hell. I'll also add here that in the past few years especially, I have been speaking about Our Lady of Fatima's messages, the existence of hell, the consequences of sin, and God's great mercy.

Well, during my talk, I noticed in my peripheral vision that a few people seated together were whispering. After my talk, a woman came up to me and thanked me profusely for bringing up the subject of hell. She told me that she knew three women in the audience (all in teaching roles in their parishes) who did not believe in the existence of hell. During my talk, she explained, she was nudging them and whispering, "You see! You see? It's true! Do you believe now?"

I was so surprised to hear about these women not believing in hell's existence. We need to pray that they and others will take heed before it is too late.

Let's turn our thoughts to a fascinating story told to me by a close friend.

Brought to Her Knees

I met my friend Ortrud Bianchi some years back when I was on a pilgrimage to the shrines of Canada, led by our mutual friend Fr. Brian Maxwell. We have stayed in touch. While writing this book, I reached out to Ortrud to ask if I could share some of her compelling story. Thankfully, she agreed.

The youngest of six children, Ortrud was born in the Czech Republic and spent most of her childhood in Germany. When she was 5 years old, her parents divorced. She shared with me, "Watching my mother's difficult life as a divorcée convinced me that I would remain single." Though she and her siblings received religious instruction and the Sacraments through their schooling, all religion was absent from their home life.

Ortrud's grandmother died abruptly when Ortrud was 16, and her mother traveled to Austria for the funeral. Her grandmother's death caused a great change in Ortrud's mother. My friend shared, "By the grace of God, she began to practice her Catholic faith with great fervor, making up for lost time."

But it wasn't just her mother's passing that caused Ortrud's mother to get back to Church. Amazingly, she had seen her father suffering in Purgatory! About 10 years after her father's death, Ortrud's mother had a vivid dream in which she saw her father in Purgatory enduring tremendous pain and torment. He looked at his daughter with an agonized gaze. Immediately, Ortrud's mother felt that she had to somehow relieve his pain. That's when she got serious about praying and fasting for her father and mother, as well as for all her children.

However, the children wanted no part of their mother's newfound religion.

After the funeral, Ortrud's mother stayed in Bavaria while Ortrud moved in with relatives and continued her studies in Germany. She visited her mother on every vacation. Ortrud shared, "I soon noticed that my mother was on a major mission to convert us children. The more she tried to convert us, the more our opposition grew." She added, "I finally made my mother promise not to mention religion to me anymore. Otherwise, I would discontinue my visits to her."

She said, "The next time I saw her, she kept silent about her faith in God." Ortrud was relieved that she didn't have to listen to preaching anymore or get into any arguments. However, her wise mother had been continuously praying for all of her children's salvation. She was also determined to get the word across one way or another! When it was time to say goodbye, she handed Ortrud a little pamphlet to take home. On the cover was a picture of Jesus.

"That was a dead giveaway to me that it was a religious pamphlet." She thought, "Therefore, it was boring and a waste of time to read." Ortrud took it from her mother's hands simply to keep the peace.

"Like Lightning!"

Months had passed and Easter vacation was fast approaching. Ortrud suddenly remembered the pamphlet. She knew what she had to do because "without fail, my mother's first question would be to ask me how I liked it." She surmised that the easiest solution would be to "read just one small page and then I would be off the hook." She figured it wouldn't "kill" her. She could then tell her mother she had read it.

"I was home alone and opened the pamphlet randomly." Ortrud quickly noticed that the text was from "the *Diary* of the Polish nun, Sr. [now St.] Faustina Kowalska." Immediately, her eyes fell on the text where, as Ortrud said, "Jesus explained to Faustina that His mercy was greater than any human or angelic mind could ever fathom." My friend explained what she read in detail to me. "Jesus invited every soul, no matter how sinful, to draw close to His merciful heart" (see *Diary*, 699).

"I couldn't sit!" she recalled. "The words hit me like lightning. Jesus loves me!" Many thoughts and questions flashed through her mind in what seemed like a millisecond. "Why be indifferent to the One who loves me more than I can ever imagine?" she thought to herself. Deep emotions of contrition flooded her soul.

"I felt a force that brought me to my knees. I began to cry, and I repeated over and over, 'Jesus, from now on I want to be your friend,'" she said. Ortrud shared with me that she had knelt there for two hours and repeated that cry to Jesus at least 100 times!

The following morning, Ortrud got up and dressed for Sunday Mass, to the amazement and disbelief of her relatives, who asked, "What are you doing? Where are you going?"

"I'm going to Sunday Mass and confession." That was the first time ever that she went on her own, and she has never missed a Sunday Mass since. She said, "I began to pray for all of the members of my family."

Life-Changing!

In the course of our long, holy gabfest, Ortrud would tell me, "All my life, I knew it was St. Faustina's writing that brought me to God." It was the Image of Divine Mercy that graced the cover of the little pamphlet.

"Boom!" she said, "my life was changed!" Before that moment, Ortrud had not been interested in anything religious — not one bit. She told me that at the time, her life "could have turned in a very bad way." She said, "God used St. Faustina's pamphlet and saved me. All it took was a couple of sentences!" (Well, it was a bit more than that, as Ortrud will explain soon.)

Ortrud shared that a jumble of thoughts were swirling round her brain: "He is all love — He is ready to forgive anyone anything! What could I possibly have against Him?"

She said the experience was like a "clear flash." It pierced her soul!

She thought, "Someone who is so, so loving — I only want to be His friend." To this day, Ortrud has no doubt that her mother's extreme sacrifices — day in and day out, spending entire days in prayer for her children, on her knees with all her heart — brought about "the graces received when I read that pamphlet. It was the fruit of her prayer and sacrifice."

She said, "It gave me courage. If my mother was able to, I could, too. It showed me the power of prayer. It gave me complete confidence: No matter what comes — prayer!"

Ortrud's life unfolded in amazing ways. I will share much more with you further along in this book. I'll quickly let you in on a secret, however. She ended up meeting and became influenced by a saint! But first, let's learn a bit more about the saint who is guiding us through this book — our sister St. Faustina — and her wise lessons.

God Worked in St. Faustina's Soul

"The interior of my soul," the humble mystic wrote, "is like a large and magnificent world in which God and I live. Except for God, no one is allowed there." At first, she struggled to find Him there. She wrote, "At the beginning of this life with God, I was dazzled and overcome with awe. His radiance blinded me, and I thought He was not in my heart; and yet those were the moments when God was working in my soul" (*Diary*, 582). This is something we can keep in mind ourselves as we go through times when we might mistakenly feel God's absence.

As her pen scratched across the pages of her *Diary*, St. Faustina knew that the sentiments she expressed would not be understood by everyone. Perhaps no one would understand certain parts. Nonetheless, she wrote, "Love was becoming purer and stronger, and the Lord brought my will into closest union with His own holy will." She continued, "No one will understand what I experience in that splendid palace of my soul where I abide constantly with my Beloved" (*Diary*, 582).

At another time, St. Faustina shared, "I am aware that You are dwelling in me, together with the Father and the Holy Spirit, or rather I am aware that it is I who am living in You, O incomprehensible God! ... O my God, I have come to know You within my heart, and I have loved You above all things that exist on earth or in heaven" (*Diary*, 478). Saint Faustina communed with God in the depths of her heart, which she referred to as a "living tabernacle" (*Diary*, 1302).

God Working in Our Souls

Life is truly an incredible journey. We work out our salvation in the nitty-gritty details of life. All along, Almighty God is working in our souls. As we return to the faith, we open our hearts to God's amazing mercy, His forgiveness, and His great love for us. Allow each day of your life to be a return to God — to an even deeper union with Him.

PAUSE

Take a few moments to ponder your direction in life. Examine your motives and your conscience. Do you nourish your faith? Are you using your time wisely? Do you strive to serve God and others?

ACT

God thirsts for your love. Thirst for His, too! As Mother Teresa preached, "Be sure to do everything for the glory of God and the good of His people."

A PRAYER OF MERCY

Dear Jesus, please help me to keep my eyes
on You. Please have mercy on my soul.
I trust in You! I want to trust You more.
Mother Mary, help me, protect me, and guide me.
Saint Faustina, please pray for me.
Amen.

CHAPTER 18
Called to Mission

"As Jesus was walking along, he saw a man
called Matthew sitting at the tax booth;
and he said to him, 'Follow me.'
And he got up and followed him."

— Mt 9:9

Every woman is called to a mission: to follow God's holy
will for her life. Her God-given gifts are a summons to
serve God and others. God calls us to mission throughout our
lives. As I mentioned in Chapter 7, St. Faustina heard a call
from God when she was only 7 years old. It grew in her heart
and eventually, by God's grace and amid much difficulty, she
became a nun.

Women can participate in more than one mission throughout their lives. God lays out the path. We endeavor to follow
it. Let us take a quick look at one of my dear saintly friends,
Mother Teresa. She answered the call from God to become a
nun, as a Sister of Loreto. She also served as a principal in a
Catholic high school for girls. Still, God had another calling
planned for the petite nun. He called her to found a religious
order, the Missionaries of Charity, in order to serve the poorest
of the poor and bring countless souls to Him.

We can certainly say that St. Faustina also embraced
more than one mission. She answered the call to the religious
life. In addition, she was given the tremendous mission of
propagating the Divine Mercy message and devotion through-

out the world, as well as indirectly founding another religious order (the Sisters of Merciful Jesus) and, in time, renewing the life and charism of the religious order of which she was a member (the Congregation of the Sisters of Our Lady of Mercy). The details of the order were given to her by Jesus before her death, but she was not to be part of that order in her lifetime. (But I think we can say that she *is* part of it from Heaven!)

How can we discover our God-given mission? It might be calmly revealed to us as life unfolds or become apparent in a more dramatic way. A major turning point of St. Faustina's life, as I mentioned earlier (see Chapter 7), came when she was at a dance with her sister at Venice Park. It was there, amid the music and hubbub of swirling dancers, that Helen encountered Jesus. Through experiences of "great torments," as she later recalled in her *Diary* (9), her life was redirected in ways she could never have imagined.

And her mission began at once!

We most likely won't experience that dramatic kind of encounter, with Jesus appearing to us all bloody and begging for our attention. Yet He certainly shows up in our lives in innumerable ways. We can undoubtedly take a lesson from our friend and mentor Faustina, who, when troubled and desperately wanting to know what to do, immediately sought help from Jesus in the Blessed Sacrament at church.

The Holy Spirit Guides Us

The Holy Spirit prompts us to live a more robust life of faith. He moves our hearts and opens our minds. Saint Faustina was in tune with the workings of the Holy Spirit and allowed Him to work in and through her. She often communed with the Blessed Trinity, and though she said she had trouble explaining the Trinity, she emphasized in her *Diary* how the Three Persons work together.

The young mystic also gave us teaching on being sensitive and docile to the Holy Spirit:

A noble and delicate soul, even the most simple, but one of delicate sensibilities, sees God in everything, finds Him everywhere, and knows how to find Him in even the most hidden things. It finds all things important, it highly appreciates all things, it thanks God for all things, it draws profit for the soul from all things, and it gives all glory to God. It places its trust in God and is not confused when the time of ordeals comes. It knows that God is always the best of Fathers and makes little of human opinion. It follows faithfully the faintest breath of the Holy Spirit; it rejoices in this Spiritual Guest and holds onto Him like a child to its mother. Where other souls come to a standstill and fear, this soul passes on without fear or difficulty (*Diary*, 148).

Mary Shows Us How

The Blessed Mother comes to our aid as well. Mary was the very first disciple to believe in the Good News, at the Annunciation. She was given a huge mission: being a co-redeemer along with her Son, Jesus.

Mary's soul magnifies the Lord! She exclaimed in her Magnificat, "My soul magnifies the Lord, and my spirit rejoices in God my Savior" (Lk 1:46-47). Mary turns everything to God. It has always been her sole purpose. She will always humbly lead us to her Son. We need to allow her to lead us to Divine Mercy and to her Son.

The great Marian saint Louis Marie de Montfort wrote of Mary, "She is *the echo of God* that says nothing, repeats nothing, but God. If you say 'Mary', she says 'God'. ... What Mary did then, she does daily now." He further explained, "When we praise her, love her, honour her or give anything to her, it is God who is praised, God who is loved, God who is glorified, and it is to God that we give, through Mary and in Mary."[53]

As we know, Mary was called to the mission of helping her older cousin Elizabeth. Mary knew what she needed to do and didn't waste time. The Archangel Gabriel had told

Mary, "And now, your relative Elizabeth in her old age has also conceived a son; and this is the sixth month for her who was said to be barren. For nothing will be impossible with God" (Lk 1:36–37). Though it would be an arduous 100-mile-long journey, Mary felt compelled to go straightaway to her older cousin's home to help, since Elizabeth was getting on in age. Mary must have been eager to share her joyful news with Elizabeth. So, after she addressed the angel, giving her wondrous *fiat* to God — "Here am I, the servant of the Lord; let it be with me according to your word" (Lk 1:38) — off she went! In a sense, perhaps it was the first Eucharistic procession — Mary bearing Jesus, fully present in her womb, Body and Blood, Soul and Divinity, with her to Elizabeth's home!

What can we learn from Mary's generous heart? Do we have a heart that desires to serve? Let's be like Mary, who "went with haste" (see Lk 1:39) to visit her older cousin Elizabeth as soon as she knew that Elizabeth was also expecting and could use her help.

Women Guard the Gate

I truly envision women as gatekeepers. We protect our families and loved ones from unwanted influences coming at us from a toxic world. We keep an eye on the comings and goings in our domestic churches. As gatekeepers, we can imitate St. Faustina, who took care of Jesus in those she met at the gate of the convent.

I absolutely love the story of what happened one dreary day when the young nun answered the gate for a shivering, hungry beggar and served him a hot mug of soup.

I discuss this at length in my book *52 Weeks with Saint Faustina*. I'll share a bit of it with you now:

> The stranger accepted the charitable meal from the sister's hands and consumed it right there by the gate. He seemed to enjoy it despite the inclement weather. Sister Faustina took the empty mug from the man's cold wet hands, and to her great surprise,

discovered that the poor man was actually Jesus Christ Himself! He then immediately vanished from her sight. Sister Faustina later reflected upon the encounter. She heard an interior voice: **"My daughter, the blessings of the poor who bless Me as they leave this gate have reached My ears. And your compassion, within the bounds of obedience, has pleased Me, and this is why I came down from My throne — to taste the fruits of your mercy"** (*Diary*, 1312). Can we even imagine this?[54]

We need to be attentive and courageous, and guard the gates in our life. In addition, we are called to be generous with our works of mercy.

Women Change the World

We are certainly all called to a unique mission, specific to us. Women share in the same femininity, but we are all unique in temperament, in our educational path, and in our upbringing. God uses all women — messy lives and all. Consider a few outstanding Catholic women: Mother Teresa, St. Faustina, and Mother Angelica. All three were very practical and got the work done. All three might not have been considered classroom prodigies. Yet God raises us up and grants each of us all the graces that we need to move forward in faith, hope, and love; to change our own hearts and help to transform the hearts of others; and to change the world!

Called to a special womanly mission as we are, let's not forget that God can use us in powerful ways, no matter our circumstances. Look at little St. Thérèse, who desired with all her heart to be a great missionary on every continent of the world! She also wanted to be a martyr. Where did God have her do her missionary work? Within the confines of the convent, behind the cloister gates. After deep soul-searching and research, St. Thérèse excitedly recognized her calling. She would be *love*!

Saint Thérèse recalled, "By chance the twelfth and thirteenth chapters of the first epistle to the Corinthians caught my attention, and in the first section I read that not everyone can be an apostle, prophet or teacher, that the Church is composed of a variety of members, and that the eye cannot be the hand."[55]

Yet she needed more: "Even with such an answer revealed before me, I was not satisfied and did not find peace." So the Little Flower continued to search the Scriptures, craving an answer. She wrote, "I found this encouraging theme: *Set your desires on the greater gifts. And I will show you the way which surpasses all others.* For the Apostle insists that the greater gifts are nothing at all without love and that this same love is surely the best path leading directly to God. At length I had found peace of mind."

Saint Thérèse then considered the Mystical Body of Christ, the Church. She stated, "I recognized myself in none of the members which St. Paul described, and what is more, I desired to distinguish myself more favorably within the whole body." She began to find the answer, or as she called it, the "hinge."

She explained, "Love appeared to me to be the hinge for my vocation. Indeed, I knew that the Church had a body composed of various members, but in this body the necessary and more noble member was not lacking; I knew that the Church had a heart and that such a heart appeared to be aflame with love. I knew that one love drove the members of the Church to action, that if this love were extinguished, the apostles would have proclaimed the Gospel no longer, the martyrs would have shed their blood no more."

Little Thérèse began to understand.

She wrote, "I saw and realized that love sets off the bounds of all vocations, that love is everything, that this same love embraces every time and every place. In one word, that love is everlasting."

She continued, "Then, nearly ecstatic with the supreme joy in my soul, I proclaimed: O Jesus, my love, at last I have found my calling: my call is love. Certainly I have found my proper place in the Church, and you gave me that very place, my God. In the heart of the Church, my mother, I will be love, and thus I will be all things, as my desire finds its direction."[56]

Women certainly change the world through God's love and mercy! Let us strive with all our hearts to embody the hinge virtue of love.

Follow the Saints and *Be* A Saint!

What is our particular mission in life? Sometimes we are deeply troubled by our mission in life or the effort required to discover it. I am reminded of what Jesus told His bride, St. Faustina.

One time when Faustina was reading about another saint, her heart immediately flooded with a deep desire that there should be a saint in her own religious congregation. She began to cry because there was no such saint, and asked Jesus why her congregation did not yet have a saint.

Jesus replied, **"Don't cry. You are that saint"** (*Diary*, 1650).

Isn't this amazing? We can only imagine the instant and immense joy that overflowed the young nun's heart. We can be deeply inspired by the lives of the saints, who take us by the hand and help us to move forward in faith. Let us follow the saints and aspire to be a saint!

PAUSE

Take time to thank God for all the blessings in your life. Ponder your path in life. Ponder your distinct mission within your family and your state of life.

ACT

Ask God to help you to become a saint! Work at it. Put in the time with your prayer life. Stay the course! Trust God. Change the world with God's love and mercy!

A Prayer of Mercy

"O Jesus, keep me in holy fear, so that I may not waste graces. Help me to be faithful to the inspirations of the Holy Spirit. Grant that my heart may burst for love of You, rather than I should neglect even one act of love for You" (*Diary*, 1557).

Jesus, please have mercy upon my soul.

I trust in You!

Mother Mary, help me, protect me, and guide me.

Saint Faustina, please pray for me.

Amen.

PART THREE
Autumn

"So let us not grow weary in doing what is right, for we will reap at harvest time, if we do not give up."

— Gal 6:9

Autumn's splendor stirs the heart. Where I live in the Northeast, in New England, as temperatures drop and we slip into our sweaters, we are blessed with marvelous bursts of autumn colors — vivid red, orange, and yellow. It's a good time for pondering our lives and trying to be extra quiet to hear the voice of God.

CHAPTER 19
Discovering My Gifts

"Through the insight which is so much
a part of your womanhood you enrich
the world's understanding and help to
make human relations more
honest and authentic."[57]

— Saint John Paul II

It would take a whole series of books to fully explain women's exquisite gifts, and how we might discover and use them for the glory of God and the good of His people. But I'll do my best to fit as much information into this chapter as possible!

God has gifted women with so many beautiful gifts to use in service to Him and our neighbors, but many women have yet to discover them, due to their difficult upbringing or the pain, suffering, and abuse they endured, or for many other reasons. Many women might have lost hope somewhere along the way. Perhaps there was no one in their life who taught them that they possessed these God-given gifts.

We can help them.

Let's take a quick look at some of the problems standing in the way of women discovering their God-given gifts.

Confusing, Mixed Messages

In women's search for happiness and contentment, women can inadvertently become entangled in things that take them away from God, *the* One who gifts women with His abiding peace — the very thing for which they are searching! This is a huge problem, especially because women are supposed to be raising the bar!

Unfortunately, for centuries many of us women have been struggling and confused over our identity, dignity, and gifts. We have all too often been relegated to the margins of society, used as sex objects, and considered to be inferior to men. Women have been bombarded by lopsided notions from this fallen world that we should conform to it rather than embrace our own feminine genius, God-given dignity, and gifts as beautiful daughters of God.

On top of all this, we know that women often struggle with perfectionism. (I discussed this in Chapter 10.) It's easy to become confused about *where* we stand in this world and *how* to stand.

Many women don't feel or receive support from others. Countless women don't know God's love. Some women even despair due to a myriad of trials. (In Chapter 16, I mentioned the example of the woman at the river.) I have counseled women who are on the brink of ending their lives, I'm sad to say, but I am thankful to God that I could help in some way: a word of encouragement, a promise of continual prayers, a shower of love, a warm hug! A listening ear is so important! When a woman needs professional help, we can lovingly recommend counseling.

Using our beautiful gifts, we women can be welcoming of others. We can ponder dear Faustina's encounters with all she met at the gate when she was assigned to be gatekeeper. She welcomed all and served them with love. I mentioned in detail one of her amazing encounters in our last chapter.

In addition to tangible help, such as the mug of soup Faustina gave to a beggar, a simple smile can go a long way in helping someone who is depressed or hurting. For instance, Mother Teresa encouraged people to smile. She said it was a way to peace. She also said we should smile at those whom we might not particularly like. "Peace begins with a smile," she said. "Smile five times a day at someone you don't really want to smile at at all — do it for peace."[58]

Saint Thérèse said something similar: "Without love, deeds, even the most brilliant, count as nothing."[59] We know from the biography of the saint of the "Little Way" that she used to smile often at a cranky old nun in her convent. Her warm, loving smiles eventually won the nun's heart over.

Women's Mission to Aid Mankind

On December 8, 1965, Pope St. Paul VI spoke about a woman's dignity and vocation when addressing women at the close of the Second Vatican Council. He gave to women "impregnated with the spirit of the Gospel" a distinct mission to aid mankind:

> And now it is to you that we address ourselves, women of all states — girls, wives, mothers and widows, to you also, consecrated virgins and women living alone — you constitute half of the immense human family. As you know, the Church is proud to have glorified and liberated woman, and in the course of the centuries, in diversity of characters, to have brought into relief her basic equality with man. But the hour is coming, in fact has come, when the vocation of woman is being achieved in its fullness, the hour in which woman acquires in the world an influence, an effect and a power never hitherto achieved. That is why, at this moment when the human race is under-going so deep a transformation, women impregnated with the spirit of the Gospel can do so much to aid mankind in not falling.[60]

Are we doing this? Are we up to the task?

Women Are Strong and Respond to Faith!

Are women the weaker sex? Let's take another look at Mother Teresa. She was very petite, and even a bit frail and sickly as she aged. Yet, with God's grace, this little woman changed the world. She was truly a powerhouse of faith, hope, and love! She opened our eyes to the truth that poverty is not only starving for a piece of bread or a drink of water. It also includes starving for love. The humble saint preached that the Western world, caught up in the lies of the culture of death and pleasing itself at all costs, is starved for love. We often fail to see or acknowledge the needs of others around us.

A tiny woman — yet so powerful with God's grace.

Saint Ambrose stated, "God, in the distribution of the gifts of His graces gives woman the first place."[61] Women were always the first to surround Jesus. They ministered to Him and became His followers. Who stayed with Jesus when the Apostles fled due to fear? The women stayed (and, of course, St. John).

Saint John Paul II said, "Christ speaks to women about the things of God, and they understand them; there is a true resonance of mind and heart, a response of faith" (*MD*, 15).

The pontiff pointed out that women were always there for Jesus. He wrote:

> From the beginning of Christ's mission, women show to him and to his mystery a special *sensitivity which is characteristic* of their *femininity*. It must also be said that this is especially confirmed in the Paschal Mystery, not only at the Cross but also at the dawn of the Resurrection. The women *are the first at the tomb*. They are the first to find it empty. They are the first to hear: "He is not here. *He has risen*, as he said" (*Mt* 28:6). They are the first to embrace his feet (cf. *Mt* 28:9). They are also the first to be called to announce this truth to the Apostles (cf. *Mt* 28:1-10; *Lk* 24:8-11). The Gospel of John (cf. also *Mk* 16: 9) emphasizes *the special role of Mary Magdalene*. She is

the first to meet the Risen Christ (*MD*, 16, emphasis in original).

Women Are Gifted!

As women, we are made in the image and likeness of God, Who saw fit that we should possess many exquisite gifts with which we serve others. Among our God-given gifts are generosity, receptivity, sensitivity, and maternity. Of course, today's culture confuses women's gift of receptivity with being a doormat. But that is not what being receptive means. We women are open to connecting and bonding with others. This darkened culture bombards us with lies to squash our gift of maternity. It doesn't take long to realize who is behind this: old hairy legs, our foe, who hates women, beginning with Eve in the Garden because she is a bearer of human life.

Human life itself is entrusted to women. Saint John Paul II stated, "*A woman is strong because of her awareness of this entrusting,* strong because of the fact that God 'entrusts the human being to her', always and in every way, even in the situations of social discrimination in which she may find herself. This awareness and this fundamental vocation speak to women of the dignity which they receive from God himself, and this makes them 'strong' and strengthens their vocation" (*MD*, 30, emphasis in original).

What a tremendous gift! We have to really let that sink in. You will see this amazing truth more than once in this book: The evil one hates women because we are life-bearers. We are spiritual mothers. Women bring forth life both physically and spiritually. Spiritually, we are mothers by being receptive and sensitive to the needs of others in our lives. We mother them! I am not talking about nagging or hounding others. I'm saying that we use our feminine gifts in a loving way to care for others.

Women need to be empowered as women. We should not be striving to be more like men in order to achieve the male definition of success. Trying to become something we are not makes us utterly miserable, and then we might be tempted to try to drink it away, medicate it away, or shop it away — and still, we will not be happy. We are certainly not meant to be like men by hiding our femininity.

We find our true happiness inside our authentic identity as feminine Catholic women. Mary, our Blessed Mother, is the perfect model of our feminine genius. We must come to recognize our own, unique feminine gifts, which show themselves in the distinctive ways each of us is called to serve those around us.

As we pray to our Lord and seek intercession and wisdom from His Blessed Mother, we will better understand our authentic femininity, our exceptional gifts, and our individual missions. I like what St. Edith Stein (1891-1942), a German Jewish philosopher and convert to Catholicism, expressed about a woman's soul being a shelter: "[W]oman's soul is ... fashioned to be a shelter in which other souls may unfold. Both spiritual companionship and spiritual motherliness are not limited to the physical spouse and mother relationships, but they extend to all people with whom woman comes into contact."[62]

When Haste Is A Good Thing

We women are blessed by God with generous hearts. When I ponder how we are lovingly present for others, my thoughts turn immediately to the Blessed Mother. As we've discussed in Chapter 17, Mary ran in haste to help her elderly cousin Elizabeth, who was pregnant with John the Baptist (see Lk 1:39). Of course, Mary was pregnant as well. Maybe she was still getting the hang of the gargantuan role entrusted to her: to be the Mother of God.

Yet rather than worry about her own pregnancy discomforts or the amazing miracle residing in her womb, Mary focused on providing service to another, and hurried to help Elizabeth for the remainder of her cousin's pregnancy.

When Mary arrived at Elizabeth's home, the two holy women embraced, and Elizabeth praised Mary for her faith. Mary humbly responded with her song of praise: the Magnificat (see Lk 1:46-55).

Contemplate Mary. She was indeed a faithful woman. She remained faithful to the care of her family, as well as totally faithful to her Son's mission, persevering through all her struggles and sorrow — all the way to the Cross and beyond. After Jesus' three-year public life and ministry, He was falsely accused, sold for 30 pieces of silver, scourged, spat upon, beaten mercilessly, mocked, crowned with thorns, and nailed to a wooden Cross.

While Jesus hung on the Cross, He called down to His disciple John, "Here is your mother" (Jn 19:27). He was also speaking to all of His disciples down to the end of time, telling us all that His own Mother Mary had become our Mother! He gifted us with our loving Mother Mary, full of compassion for us and totally attuned to the thoughts of God, completely imbued with the Word of God. Mary, who had become the New Eve, Mother of All the Living, at the Annunciation, was given to all of us as our spiritual mother by Jesus on the Cross, explicitly confirming and extending her role as the New Eve and Mother of All the Living.

Mary knows our sorrows and struggles. She has endured the same, and worse. Can we possibly imagine Mary's sorrow as she watched and suffered along with her Son at the foot of the Cross? Mary witnessed every drop of blood shed. She heard every sigh coming from her beloved Son's lips. She watched her Son breathe His very last breath. She is a Mother who knows deep suffering and certainly understands our struggles and pain, too.

Mary was indeed a prayerful woman. Her persevering and faithful prayers aided the beginnings of the Church. After Jesus had risen from the dead and ascended to Heaven, Mary was present with the Twelve Apostles who prayed together in the Upper Room for the coming of the Holy Spirit, Whose coming Jesus had promised and Who had already overshadowed Mary at the Annunciation. Saint Luke describes Pentecost in the Acts of the Apostles (see Acts 2).

Let's never be afraid to approach Mary with anything. I have no doubt that Mother Mary aided St. Faustina to run in haste with the message of Divine Mercy.

Mary awaits our greetings and conversations with her. She knows our hearts. She shows us how to really love and follow God's holy will. Mary shows us how to be spiritually beautiful for our Lord. We need to turn to Mary often, praying to emulate her virtues.

PAUSE

Ponder the fact that women possess exquisite God-given gifts and an amazing mission to aid mankind. Mother Mary is our dear teacher and intercessor.

ACT

Allow Mother Mary to show you how to run in haste to use your gifts and generous heart as you respond to faith.

A PRAYER OF MERCY

Dear Jesus, You endow me with a treasury of
exquisite gifts. Please help me to discover
them and use them for Your glory.
Jesus, please have mercy upon my soul.
I trust in You!
Mother Mary, help me, protect me, and guide me.
Saint Faustina, please pray for me.
Amen.

CHAPTER 20
God Sends Us Forth

"But thanks be to God, who in Christ always
leads us in triumphal procession, and through
us spreads in every place the fragrance that
comes from knowing him. For we are the
aroma of Christ to God among those
who are being saved and among
those who are perishing."

— 2 Cor 2:14-15

After reading about our beautiful gifts and Mother Mary's
exemplary example for us in the last chapter, perhaps you
can take some time to ponder how God might be sending you
forth to aid someone. Could it be your spouse, your child,
your fellow nun, your coworker, or your lonely neighbor?

Mother Teresa called these people "Jesus, in the distressing disguise of the poorest of the poor." She served Jesus in
everyone she met! She knew without a doubt that she needed
to receive Jesus sacramentally in the Eucharist in order to have
the strength to serve. It was the same for St. Faustina, who
united herself with Jesus in the Eucharist to receive all the
graces she needed to carry out her work.

God indeed sends us forth! He wants us to be a beautiful example of His love to all we meet. The stiff clerk at the
post office; the aloof grocery cashier covered with tattoos and

piercings; the harried delivery guy; the lonely neighbor; the homeless person; the irritable coworker; the guy who gives you the finger in the grocery store parking lot — they all need our prayers and loving responses. God sends us to love everyone with whom we ordinarily come in contact. Every one of them is a child of God. We need to pray for them!

Whether we realize it or not, and whether they even know we're Catholic or not, we represent the Church to them. When we are out and about, all kinds of conversations can ensue through which our faith is professed. I can tell you so many stories of inspirational conversations that have come to pass in the post office and other public places. I love it when God and our faith is discussed out loud in a government office.

Interesting conversations can unfold, but the joy of our simple smile or kind words when we are out doing our errands can be just the medicine someone needs.

We Are the Aroma of the Church!

We women are truly the aroma of the Church! But what does that mean? Well, I'm sure you've been to church on a feast day when incense, which causes billows of smoke to rise up from the censer and waft all throughout the building, is used. The intense aroma surrounds us and sometimes even makes us cough! But it's very ceremonial; it's holy — it helps draw us into the proper, prayerful frame of mind as our prayers ascend to God with the incense.

Saint Paul used the analogy of incense to illustrate who we are in the world: "But thanks be to God, who in Christ always leads us in triumphal procession, and through us spreads in every place the fragrance that comes from knowing him. For we are the aroma of Christ to God among those who are being saved and among those who are perishing" (2 Cor 2:15).

We, in essence, are holy incense to others — the "aroma of Christ." Through living a faithful Catholic life (through praying; following the commandments; frequenting the Sacraments, especially the Eucharist and Confession; and by both offering and accepting forgiveness), we, with God's grace, become that holy aroma, and with a feminine heart, we earnestly reach out to help others — our brothers and sisters who are in need — whether spiritually or physically.

Tears and the "Ripple of Reality"

Did you ever consider that your tears might be more than simply an emotion? When we were growing up, how many times did we hear someone tell us, "Don't cry"? Perhaps they were trying to comfort us. However, tears are very good as well as cleansing. Tears can help us move forward from our pain. We even see this in the Gospels.

When Jesus walked the earth, the women who followed Him accompanied our Lord in a much different way than men did. The women were with Jesus as the Apostles were, but the women *served* Jesus. According to Fr. Jose Tolentino Mendonça, who gave a spiritual meditation at the Vatican for Pope Francis and the Roman Curia, their reaction to Jesus was "profoundly evangelical."[63]

Mendonça said that women offer us a "ripple of reality that intervenes in order to shape faith. In this way it does not remain a prisoner — as often happens to our faith — rationalistic, lived mechanically according to doctrine or ritual." He added that it is because they are in touch with everyday life that they give "perfume to the faith." According to Fr. Mendonça, "the women in Luke's Gospel — the widow of Nain, the 'sinner,' the women of Jerusalem — also cry." He noted that "Saint Gregory (Nanzianzen) describes these tears as a baptism."

When we call to mind the image of the woman washing Jesus' feet with her tears, we see that this woman gave Jesus what the Pharisee "refused to give." It was this unheard-of hospitality that Jesus praised. Father Mendonça said it was "that thirst, expressed in tears!"[64]

This gives us women something to ponder. We can thirst for Jesus' love through tears. Let us take time to ponder our own prayers, our own tears, and our own thirst for Jesus. How often have I expressed my thoughts and feelings to Jesus through tears? One time, as a young teenager, I cried to Jesus with tears pouring from my eyes when I was held captive by a Vietnam veteran who had thrust a pistol into my hand and was trying to get me to pull the trigger to kill him! I was only 18 years old. Jesus came to my rescue!

Tears might brim in our eyes at times as we try to be strong. Jesus wants our tears. That is a prayer! God wants us to offer everything to Him in prayer, even our tears! Offer your feelings of pain and abandonment, and your tears.

Look at St. Faustina. She prayed and offered everything. Yes, she cried, too. She cried her heart out to God, often prostrating herself before Jesus in the Blessed Sacrament. Sometimes, her prayers were without words.

I very much like the phrase "ripple of reality" that Fr. Mendonça used in his talk. Women keep it real! We need to keep our feet firmly planted in reality through our prayers, so that Heaven is touching earth and earth is touching Heaven in our continual communion with God.

First and foremost, we find this communion with God at Holy Mass where we participate in the holy sacrifice of the Mass and partake of Jesus in the Eucharist. The Sacrament of Penance keeps us grounded and cleans our slate completely, making us new once again so that we need not fear our short-comings, but can instead give them to our Lord wholeheartedly and with contrite hearts, over and over again. That's because conversion of heart is not once in a lifetime, but should occur each day as we strive to move closer to God. We need the Sacraments to nourish our faith! We need to visit our dear Lord more often in Adoration, as well.

Our Example and Communion With God

We can be an attractive aroma of the faith, but we can also be a repulsive aroma if we're not steadfastly living our faith!

For instance, I know a woman who left the Church because she overheard some women gossiping in the parish office. We simply cannot be that bad example. On the contrary — we women absolutely need to be the attractive *aroma*, the perfume of the Church. Trust me when I say that people are watching. I can tell you so many stories of the power of a good example. I'll share just two.

One time, my husband and I ate out at a diner. Before eating, we bowed our heads, blessed ourselves with the Sign of the Cross, and quietly said grace. Immediately, I heard the people at the next booth first whisper about us praying, and then begin talking about a Rosary that their child had made at her faith formation class long ago. Suddenly, a story of faith began to unfold in that little diner because of the example of prayer. God only knows how their conversation might have continued once they left the diner and how it had impacted them, but my husband and I were sure to pray some extra prayers for them.

Another time, on a flight back to the United States from Rome some years ago, a young 20-something woman was very distressed about the powerful turbulence rocking the plane. I reached out, touched her arm, and offered her my Rosary with which I had been praying. She immediately drew it to her heart.

Next, I offered her a blessed Miraculous Medal, one that Mother Teresa had given to me. I sure hope that young lady still has it!

All through the long flight, I comforted the young woman with prayer and gentle words. She calmed down and was indeed thankful. What really surprised me, though, was when sometime later an elderly man from a couple of rows back reached forward to tap me on the arm. He asked me how I had done what I did. Not sure what he meant, I inquired. He wondered aloud how I had helped a complete stranger.

I simply told him, "God must have put a lot of love in my heart — I like to help people." He wiped away a few tears. I was so happy that I had gotten the word "God" into our little conversation!

Spiritual Kinship

Saint Faustina wrote in her *Diary* about the difficulty in describing her union with God, as well as her experiences with a few people she knew who were also united to God:

> It is a strange thing that although the soul which experiences this union with God cannot find words and expressions to describe it, nevertheless, when it meets a similar soul, the two understand each other extraordinarily well in regard to these matters, even though they speak but little with each other. A soul united with God in this way easily recognizes a similar soul, even if the latter has not revealed its interior [life] to it, but merely speaks in an ordinary way. It is a kind of spiritual kinship. Souls united with God in this way are few, fewer than we think (768).

We women can endeavor to seek God's will in all our relationships and friendships. We will hopefully be attracted to godly souls and discover a beautiful spiritual kinship with others. These special souls can become our sisters in Christ. Striving to stay connected with like-minded, faith-filled Catholics will help us on our own spiritual journeys, and we can be a blessing to them in turn.

With regard to spiritual gifts, our sister Faustina also wrote on the importance of moving our wills to follow the will of God and cooperate with His grace. She also pointed out what is more important than any gift: union of the soul with God. She learned this during a meditation when God gave her "an inner light and understanding as to what sanctity is and of what it consists" (*Diary*, 1107).

Specifically, she wrote, "Neither graces, nor revelations, nor raptures, nor gifts granted to a soul make it perfect, but rather the intimate union of the soul with God. These gifts are merely ornaments of the soul, but constitute neither its essence nor its perfection. My sanctity and perfection consist in the close union of my will with the will of God. God never violates our free will. It is up to us whether we want to receive God's grace or not. It is up to us whether we will cooperate with it or waste it" (*Diary*, 1107).

These are wise words to ponder in our hearts. Some folks believe that saints are canonized simply because they have seen apparitions or received supernatural gifts. That is not why they were declared saints. They were canonized because their lives were marked by heroic virtue. According to our friend Faustina, a soul has sanctity and perfection when she is in union with God.

Not by the Skin of Our Teeth!

We women can't merely aim to someday reach Heaven by the skin of our teeth. We absolutely need to be working hard on our salvation so that at the end of our lives, we don't just squeak by. Our goal needs to be that, through our loving witness and God's grace, we will bring countless souls with us to Heaven!

We must also remember that our Lord is not going to judge us on how much we have accomplished here on earth, but instead on how much we have loved! Remember, Jesus said, "Truly I tell you, just as you did it to one of the least of these who are members of my family, you did it to me" (Mt 25:40). We must ask ourselves: What *did* we do and *not* do for Jesus, that is, for the least of our brethren (see Mt 25:31-46)?

We women have a big job to do! But we can do it! We are made in the image and likeness of God!

PAUSE

Human life is entrusted to women. Take some time to ponder how God is calling you to use your exquisite feminine gifts to "go in haste" to aid someone — your spouse, your child, your fellow nun, your coworker, or your lonely neighbor.

ACT

Allow God to send you forth to be the magnificent aroma of our Church. Pray about ways in which you might serve His providential will.

A PRAYER OF MERCY

Dear Jesus, please grant to me an awareness of the beautiful gifts that You have bestowed upon me. Help me to be loving and courageous in using my gift to help others. Jesus, please have mercy upon my soul. I trust in You!
Mother Mary, help me, protect me, and guide me. Saint Faustina, please pray for me.
Amen.

CHAPTER 21
Devastating Breakup

"I have understood that at certain and most difficult moments I shall be alone, deserted by everyone, and that I must face all the storms and fight with all the strength of my soul, even with those from whom I expected to get help."

— Saint Faustina (*Diary*, 746)

Not everything fits into a nice neat little package, most especially our lives. Human nature is fallen, and sometimes it is not a pretty sight. In relationships, there might be times when we have to endure a devastating breakup. As terrible as it might be, that breakup could end up being for the good of everyone involved. It can free us from being trapped in something unhealthy.

While some relationship dissolutions are amicable, a breakup can occur when just one of the two in relationship suddenly hits a brick wall with a serious problem and cannot continue further. He or she calls it quits. The other might be left shattered.

When I was going through a terrible time of painful suffering due to an abusive husband, Mother Teresa encouraged me through a personal letter. In my case, the breakup was an absolute necessity since my husband had serious problems and was unwilling to get help.

I'll let you in on Mother's profound words. She told me, "I am sorry to hear of the sufferings you have to undergo. Jesus loves you and though He is the Lord of all — He cannot interfere with the gift of free will He has given to man."

The petite saint continued, "Jesus shares His love with you and shares His suffering and pain. He is a God of love and does not want His children to suffer, but when you accept your pain, suffering, death and resurrection, your pain becomes redemptive for yourself and for others."

Her words comforted my soul. In the same letter, she also thanked me for starting the lay Missionaries of Charity in my area, went on to say, "Be assured of my prayers," and continued with more amazing advice.

She wrote, "Christ calls us to be one with Him in love through unconditional surrender to His plan for us." And my saintly friend told me how we are to do it. "Let us allow Jesus to use us without consulting us by taking what He gives and giving what He takes." Mother Teresa wasn't implying that Jesus had caused the problem of abuse or that I should put up with the abuse. She was telling me that God had allowed me to go through it, shared His love, suffering, and pain with me — and that I could offer to Him my pain and suffering, and ask Him to redeem it so it would transform my own soul and the souls of others.

I believe that we can prayerfully ponder Mother's last line for hours. Again, she said, "Let us allow Jesus to use us without consulting us by taking what He gives and giving what He takes." We can surely take that teaching into our hearts, pausing to dwell on its meaning and endeavoring to apply it to our lives. Our Lord will surely grant the graces that we need to surrender ourselves in the way dear Mother Teresa has encouraged. Surrendering our lives in this way to our Lord will bring an abundance of abiding peace to our hearts.

Survival Mode

Stresses from trauma, changes, and loss can be utterly overwhelming. In response, sometimes we enter survival mode, focusing on just trying to get through the next 24 hours, or maybe just the next hour, because everything has become a mammoth chore. At the worst of times, daily activities become very difficult. We might not be able to see a way out of our mess. Experiencing a hurtful breakup can certainly thrust us into survival mode as we deal with intense emotions.

Survival mode can also happen when we are experiencing frightening things and trying to cope. It is usually short-term but varies from case to case. I have been in survival mode more than once. It's actually a natural mechanism that kicks in when something triggers the "fight-or-flight" response in us. Our instincts suddenly come into play. We can feel out of control when operating in survival mode.

Being in survival mode for the short term while dealing with stresses and changes might be helpful, but in the long run, we don't want to be just going through the motions in life and merely trying to survive — that's not really living. Excess fear in our lives can be devastating and crippling. Though we can't always help getting into a form of survival mode, we should endeavor to get out of it. You may need to simplify your life, even if only for a while.

An article in *Psychology Today* discussed how our emotions can both help us and disconnect us. The author, neuroscientist James Montgomery, stated, "In general, when we're in homeostasis [a state of physical and psychological balance] we tend to experience *positive* emotions and feelings, like joy or love, and when we're in survival mode, we tend to experience *negative* or distressing emotions and feelings" (emphasis in original).[65]

Montgomery continued, "The activation of a negative emotion like fear is precisely what throws our brains and bodies out of balance, into non-homeostasis or survival mode." Yet all emotions are important. He explained, "As unpleasant as some emotions can be, however, every type of negative emotion that we experience is evolutionarily designed to serve one overriding purpose: to help motivate behavior that will bring us back into homeostasis. Homeostasis is where our bodies and brains want us to be whenever possible."[66]

Many women are operating in survival mode. We need to help them if we can. If we are in this mode ourselves, we hopefully get out of it — the sooner the better. One reason that it is so important to surround ourselves with like-minded and faith-filled women — sisters in Christ — is so that we can be prayer warriors for one another. We fight for one another with love, attention, support, guidance, and prayer.

Meditating on Christ's Passion

Suffering can indeed be scary, but it's an unavoidable part of every human life. One time, Mother Teresa told me, "If we pray, it will be easy for us to accept suffering. In all our lives suffering has to come. Suffering is the sharing in the Passion of Christ ... ."[67]

Prayer is essential so that we can begin to share more deeply in the Passion of Christ. I highly recommend spending time with Jesus in the Blessed Sacrament where He will deeply stir your heart. It is there at the feet of Jesus in the Blessed Sacrament that my own heart was transformed.

In his apostolic letter *Salvifici Doloris* (*On the Christian Meaning of Human Suffering*; *SD*), St. John Paul II stated, "Suffering seems to belong to man's transcendence: it is one of those points in which man is in a certain sense 'destined' to go beyond himself, and he is called to this in a mysterious way" (*SD*, 2).[68] He explained that though we suffer in life, we live with great hope in the life that is to come. Specifically, he said, "As a result of Christ's salvific work, man exists on earth *with the hope* of eternal life and holiness" (*SD*, 15, emphasis in original). He explained the Good News: Jesus died for us, yes, but there will still be pain and suffering in life.

Jesus never hid the truth from us. He was always straight with us. He told us to deny ourselves, pick up our crosses, and follow Him if we wanted to be His disciples. I told you I would mention this important part of being our Lord's disciple more than once in this book!

Saint John Paul II pointed out, "And even though the victory over sin and death achieved by Christ in his Cross and Resurrection does not abolish temporal suffering from human life, nor free from suffering the whole historical dimension of human existence, it nevertheless *throws a new light* upon this dimension and upon every suffering: the light of salvation. This is the light of the Gospel, that is, of the Good News" (*SD*, 15, emphasis in original).

The pontiff underscored a huge consolation. He said, "It is especially consoling to note — and also accurate in accordance with the Gospel and history — that at the side of Christ, in the first and most exalted place, there is always his Mother through the exemplary testimony that she bears by *her whole life* to this particular Gospel of suffering" (*SD*, 25, emphasis in original).

Mary always stood by her Son. As a loving Mother and a co-redeemer with Jesus, she participated in His salvific suffering. She will also help us. In the same apostolic letter, St. John Paul II pointed out, "As a witness *to* her Son's Passion by her *presence,* and as a sharer in it by her *compassion,* Mary offered a unique contribution to the Gospel of suffering, by embodying in anticipation the expression of Saint Paul." He added, "She truly has a special title to be able to claim that she 'completes in her flesh' — as already in her heart — 'what is lacking in Christ's afflictions'" (*SD*, 25, emphasis in original).

We recall that St. Paul said, "I am now rejoicing in my sufferings for your sake, and in my flesh I am completing what is lacking in Christ's afflictions for the sake of his body, that is, the church" (Col 1:24). Saint John Paul II commented on this passage, saying, "The joy comes from the discovery of the meaning of suffering, and this discovery, even if it is most personally shared in by Paul of Tarsus who wrote these words, is at the same time valid for others." He goes on to explain how Paul's sufferings help us: "The Apostle shares his own discovery and rejoices in it because of all those whom it can help — just as it helped him — to understand the *salvific meaning of suffering*" (*SD*, 1, emphasis in original).

Saint Faustina Meditated on Jesus' Passion

The *Diary* of St. Faustina speaks a lot about Jesus' Passion and suffering. Jesus is very pleased when we meditate upon His Passion. Doing so can truly help us in facing our struggles, our pain, our fears, and every challenge we endure. In my own life, I believe that time spent with Jesus in the Blessed Sacrament or at home in my domestic church meditating on His Passion has helped my soul immensely.

Jesus told His bride Faustina, "**There is more merit to one hour of meditation on My sorrowful Passion than there is to a whole year of flagellation that draws blood; the contemplation of My painful wounds is of great profit to you, and it brings Me great joy**" (*Diary*, 369).

Another time, He told her, "**Remember My Passion, and if you do not believe My words, at least believe My wounds**" (*Diary*, 379). Jesus also revealed to St. Faustina, "**There are few souls who contemplate My Passion with true feeling; I give great graces to souls who meditate devoutly on My Passion**" (*Diary*, 737).

As mentioned in Chapter 13, Jesus told Faustina that He thirsted for souls and from the Cross asked her to join her sufferings to His Passion and offer them to God the Father for sinners (see *Diary*, 1032). This she did endlessly. Saint Faustina knew she had become a victim soul for God's Kingdom. She suffered greatly and offered it all lovingly to Jesus.

Let's ask ourselves an important question: Will we imitate St. Faustina, join our sufferings to Jesus' Passion, and offer them to the Heavenly Father for sinners? That doesn't mean we never seek to alleviate our sufferings. We are meant to offer up our truly unavoidable sufferings, those that cannot be relieved or healed, at least not right away. If any of our sufferings legitimately can be relieved or healed, we are called upon (out of proper love for ourselves as children of God) to remove those sufferings as best we can.

Our sister Faustina gives us stellar advice: "In the sufferings of soul or body, I try to keep silence, for then my spirit gains the strength that flows from the Passion of Jesus. I have ever before my eyes His sorrowful Face, abused and disfigured, His divine Heart pierced by our sins and especially by the ingratitude of chosen souls" (*Diary*, 487).

The Blessed Mother's words to St. Faustina can help us, too. On the Feast of Our Lady of Mercy, the Blessed Virgin told the young nun, *"Most pleasing to Me is that soul which faithfully carries out the will of God. ... Be courageous. Do not fear apparent obstacles, but fix your gaze upon the Passion of My Son, and in this way you will be victorious"* (*Diary*, 449).

It is immensely helpful for us to meditate upon Jesus' Passion so that we understand our own struggles, are able to offer them up to Jesus, and then ask that He make them redemptive. Mother Mary helps us. She stands with her children.

PAUSE

Ponder those whom you know (perhaps yourself included) who have experienced a devastating breakup. Are you able to reach out to them in some way to bring a spark of hope? Take time to sit or kneel in stillness to meditate upon Jesus' Passion.

ACT

Offer all of your sufferings lovingly to Jesus. Imitate our friend Faustina: Keep a spirit of silence and meditate upon "His sorrowful Face, abused and disfigured, His divine Heart pierced by our sins and especially by the ingratitude of chosen souls" (*Diary*, 487). Pray for those who are wounded

and in need of healing. Pray an extra Divine Mercy
Chaplet or Rosary for this intention.

A PRAYER OF MERCY

Dear Jesus, please teach me the beauty of silence
— of being with You and listening to You.
I desire to spend more time meditating upon Your
Passion. Please have mercy upon my soul.
I trust in You!
Mother Mary, help me, protect me, and guide me.
Saint Faustina, please pray for me.
Amen.

CHAPTER 22
Engagement, Courtship, and Marriage

"In all human love it must be realized that
every man promises a woman, and every
woman promises a man, that which
only God alone can give, namely,
perfect happiness."[69]

— Venerable Fulton J. Sheen

L ove within a courtship or marriage can be life-transforming. But I have to be honest: Being in a loving relationship also requires work. Just because we are in love and might be planning to walk down the aisle at some point does not mean that everything will be warm and fuzzy. Nor *should* our love relationship be always warm and fuzzy. Real love requires sacrifice. Mother Teresa often said that love hurts. Saint Faustina wrote, "True love is measured by the thermometer of suffering" (*Diary*, 343). Saint Francis de Sales wrote, "The state of marriage is one that requires more virtue and constancy than any other; it is a perpetual exercise in mortification."[70] In any healthy, normal courtship or marriage, there are times when either betrothed or spouse is going to carry crosses and be called on to make sacrifices for love of the other.

If you are serious about entering into a sacramental marriage with your fiancé or the man you are dating (courting), there is something you need to ponder. My dear sister, speaking as a wife who was abused and deserted, but am happily married now, I must be straight with you. Perhaps it can prevent future heartaches. I ask you: Will he lay down his life for you? I mean, really lay down his life? If he will, that is real love from a real man.

Laying down one's life requires dying to self and is accomplished in a myriad of ways. Saint Faustina wrote in her *Diary*, "I have learned that the greatest power is hidden in patience. I see that patience always leads to victory, although not immediately; but that victory will become manifest after many years. Patience is linked to meekness" (*Diary*, 1514).

Learning together in a new relationship can bring a few challenges. Sometimes we might feel irritated, exasperated, or annoyed. Someone might have ruffled our feathers. Perhaps it was our significant other! Could we be overtired? Are we taking care of ourselves properly and getting enough sleep? We discussed the need for holy self-care in Chapter 10. We need to be mindful of this. We will be better able to handle stresses and strains when we are cared for properly.

It's best to pause at times to examine our feelings, especially if they cause us to act out (or want to) in an inappropriate way, such as flying off the handle or spouting off at someone. Words and actions are difficult to take back once released. People might feel very hurt. If we are having trouble in this area, perhaps we need the virtue of patience.

Although St. Faustina told us that patience always leads to victory, it might be difficult to think of that happy outcome when we are chomping at the bit or feeling flushed in the face due to our fiancé's (or someone else's) words or actions. When we notice that we are fit to be tied, it is time to pray earnestly for the virtue of patience. In addition, we need to sit down and have a conversation with the other person. We can expect additional trials of patience when we are praying for patience! That's just the way it is. God allows us opportunities to prove ourselves. So don't lose hope — help is on the way. Pray for the graces that you need to bite your tongue and wait it out.

Patience is not achieved overnight, but victory will indeed come, St. Faustina reassures us!

Catholic Marriage

Truth be told, I'd have to write a whole book on this topic to cover it properly. However, I'll attempt to offer some valuable saintly advice, anecdotes, and Church teaching.

You might see yourself in the stories. You might even laugh at my confessions. It's good to laugh! I suspect as well that you'll be happy to be reminded that a husband does not lord it over his wife. Let's get to it.

I believe we should establish something right from the start. A Catholic wedding is not merely an event. It is a very powerful Sacrament in which a man and a woman commit their lives to one another in the presence of God and witnesses. They desire to become *one*. Many weddings these days are all about the event — usually flashy, themed events, sometimes very extravagant. Sadly, something (I mean, Some*one*!) important is missing from their plans. That would be God!

How is God included in the weddings that occur on beaches, at inns, backyards, and places other than churches? This is not to say that we cannot celebrate in these places after the wedding. We should give the young folks credit that they have decided to commit to one another as a husband and wife rather than just living with one another without a formal commitment. However, a Catholic wedding is so much more than saying "I do" amid a huge party.

It Takes Three

It actually takes three to get married — that is, according to Venerable Fulton J. Sheen. In his book *Three to Get Married*, he discusses the treasures of the Sacrament of Matrimony. He discusses the difference between sex and love, the three tensions of love, and underscores the fact that it takes three to make love.

The archbishop warns about promises we can't keep and what we should not expect. He wrote, "In all human love it must be realized that every man promises a woman, and every woman promises a man, that which only God alone can give, namely, perfect happiness."[71] We need to keep this in mind. We can't realistically expect our husband to be able to provide perfect happiness, nor will we be able to do so for him. Let's get that pressure off our shoulders right now.

Sheen continued, "One of the reasons why so many marriages are shipwrecked is because as the young couple leave the altar, they fail to realize that human feelings tire and the enthusiasm of the honeymoon is not the same as the more solid happiness of enduring human love."

He wrote, "One of the great trials of marriage is the absence of solitude. In the first moments of human love, one does not see the little hidden deformities which later on appear."[72]

Clearly, we need God in our marriages. We can't rely on feelings and enthusiasm; we need the "solid happiness of enduring human love." We need to give ourselves totally to our spouse. But there's much more, according to Sheen.

Sheen aptly wrote, "Without a sense of Absolute Love, which is stronger than the independent love of each for the other, there is a false duality, which ends in the absorption of the *I* into the *Thou* or the *Thou* into the *I*."[73]

Sheen also made clear, "If love were only mutual self-giving, it would end in exhaustion, or else become a flame in which both would be consumed. Mutual self-giving also implies self-recovery. The perfect example of this recovery, in which nothing is lost, is the Trinity, wherein Love circles back upon itself in an eternal consummation."[74]

We absolutely need God in our marriages.

Saint Faustina Eloped With Jesus!

I don't recommend eloping. But then again, St. Faustina eloped with Jesus, plain and simple! I discussed this in Chapter 7, but I mention it here because we are discussing marriage. Though St. Faustina was a professed religious nun, she still has much to teach a lay woman. That's why I set out to write this book for women of every state of life. The young mystic, through her obedience to writing the *Diary*, lets us in on her most intimate experiences of communion with Jesus and the amazing teachings that He gave her, experiences and teachings that were surely meant for the whole world, not simply for her. Yet sometimes, St. Faustina was at a loss for words to convey the indwelling of the Blessed Trinity in her heart and the precious insights taught to her by our dear Lord. Dissatisfied as she was with the inadequacy of words for the great mysteries she experienced, nonetheless, Faustina gave us an amazing entryway into her holy heart.

Saint Faustina wrote in her *Diary* that Jesus impressed upon her heart "the depth of His meekness and humility." He gave her to understand that "He clearly demanded the same of me," she stated. Faustina felt God's gaze in her soul. She explained how it made her feel: "This filled me with unspeakable love, but I understood that the Lord was looking with love on my virtues and my heroic efforts, and I knew that this was what was drawing God into my heart" (*Diary*, 758).

Through God's grace and teachings, Sr. Faustina was made to know that Jesus demanded more of her. She recorded this in her *Diary*: "[I] have come to understand that it is not enough for me to strive only for the ordinary virtues, but that I must try to exercise the heroic virtues." Then she gave an explanation: "Although exteriorly a thing may be quite ordinary, it is the different manner [in which it is carried out] that only the eye of God catches." Faustina continued, "O my Jesus, what I have written is just a pale shadow of what I understand in my soul; these are purely spiritual things, but in order to write something of what the Lord gives me to know, I must use words with which I am totally dissatisfied, because they do not express the reality."

Though St. Faustina thought her words were insufficient, we can surely understand the meaning of her expressions. Let us ponder what she wrote about seemingly ordinary things and how God sees our intentions and actions. Many "quite ordinary" things occur every day in a marriage, don't they?

Some things seem very ordinary, but carrying them out is another story. How many times might we do something a bit begrudgingly? Perhaps we don't want to admit it, but we are not always quick to help our spouse in a heroic manner.

As I write, I can think of an example in my own life. You might laugh. Are you ready for this? I will admit that I do not always want to cut my husband's toenails! I really don't mind if you laugh. It is a bit funny. My husband has a bad hip and can't bend very well to do it himself. Most times, I am more than happy to trim his toenails. But there have been times when it has been hard for me because of the pains that I endure to get into position to do it properly.

If I help my husband in any way without any inner (or outer!) grumbling or complaint, it is possible that I am practicing a heroic virtue, not simply an ordinary virtue. And if it "costs" me something to perform the loving action, as Mother Teresa would say, well, then, all the better. The cost might be inconvenience, a little ache or pain, a misunderstanding, and the like.

As I mentioned earlier when speaking about courtship, dear Mother Teresa often said that to love properly requires some kind of sacrifice. She said real love often "hurts." If we can perform these little sacrifices with love in our hearts rather than feeling put out, we will hopefully earn graces for our own soul and the soul of our husband. Let's do our best to imitate St. Faustina by striving to perform heroic virtues through heroic holy efforts and not just ordinary ones.

Trust me: God will supply ample opportunities!

Patience Is Required!

When we enter into sacramental marital union with our husband, no matter how much in love we might be, we will begin to see his warts, and he, ours. The tension or irritation might come about because of your husband's bad habits, or you may begin to notice something you didn't see before. As long as these things are just little idiosyncrasies and not serious problems, you will learn to work through them together. That said, these "little" things may seem huge as you try to work them out.

Possibly much more important than working out our differences is what we learn about ourselves through the process. One time I wrote an article for *Magnificat* magazine (June 2015) for the category "She Pondered These Things in her Heart" about marriage and family. I decided to convey something very real — not just a romantic kind of love story. Real love doesn't translate to simple bliss or merely "warm and fuzzy" feelings. Sure, we enjoy those moments, but marriage overall requires work. And, again, love sometimes hurts. We simply cannot rely solely on our feelings to forge ahead in our marriages. We will have to *choose* to love — to give — to surrender our hearts. Please don't get me wrong. We need to work at it. However, marital love is beautiful, amazing, and holy!

I titled my piece "Unexpected Discovery" because I think that is what discovery often is — unexpected. We can discover something we never realized about ourselves or our spouses as we go through the daily grind, the nitty-gritty details of life where we truly are working out our salvation. We can decide to work on getting rid of a vice and work towards cultivating a particular virtue once we open our hearts to God's amazing grace.

In my piece, I recalled what started out as a bit of a frustrating experience with my dear husband. I'll share it with you here because I think you might get a kick out of God's amazing humor and my unexpected discovery. Here goes:

> I used to think I was patient. That is until I married my husband. Joined in our sacramental covenant, I discovered something I might not have realized if my husband didn't possess his particular personality.
>
> Saint John Paul II proclaimed, "Marriage is an act of the will that signifies and involves a mutual gift which unites the spouses and binds them in their eternal souls, with whom they make up a sole family — a Domestic Church."

While navigating everyday household busy-ness, especially during challenges, we might forget that we reside in a "Domestic Church" and lose sight of our "mutual gift."

Pope Francis unambiguously states, "There are always arguments in marriages, and sometimes plates are thrown."

Feeling annoyed with my husband's teasing, I once reached for something nearby to pretend I'd hit him. It was a plaque inscribed, "Love is patient, love is kind."

I smiled.

Pope Francis reminds us, "Love is stronger than the moments in which we argue." I'm whole-heartedly convinced that God provides countless opportunities to ask for His grace to respond in love to the struggles and joys of home life.

Marriage and raising children is a vocation of love and discovery in which we work out our salvation through practicing the virtues, even heroic ones. Our responses (which don't include clobber-ing!) undeniably aid our loved ones in getting to heaven.[75]

So, while you might feel like clobbering your husband at times, the key thing is that you don't! Turn to God in prayer, get a hold of your feelings, and be sure to communicate it to your husband. Letting things fester will only make matters worse.

Also, make sure that your husband's faults haven't blinded you to your own. Wives can ask themselves, "Have I become a chronic nag? Am I so busy trying to fix him that I no longer notice the things in my life, habits, and character that need fixing, too — that he has to be patient with me about? Perhaps I am over-emotional at times. Perhaps I am annoy-ingly disorganized. Perhaps (due to various stresses and strains in my life) I am too quick to the trigger with him and the kids. Perhaps when we discuss things, I talk too much and listen too little. Perhaps I am so focused on bearing patiently with his bad habits that I too often overlook the daily sacrifices that he makes on behalf of me and our children (that is, if he is fundamentally a good husband who makes such sacrifices)." For centuries, the Church has recommended a regular examination of conscience to all the faithful — that is, an examination of our own conscience, not the conscience of our spouses!

If you talk to any happily married couple in a long-lasting marriage, they would tell you that their marriages had not been total bliss. They had endured many ups and downs and bumps in the road, at times feeling like it was useless to go on. What did they do? They hung in there. They discovered ways in which to work together in harmony. They sacrificed for the other, putting the other first. They practiced the virtues — even heroic ones! They communicated with one another. They worked it out with God's help.

Remember, your Catholic marriage is a Sacrament! There are many graces attached to a Sacrament, so call upon them, especially in rough times. Plead to God for the graces.

The Husband Does Not Lord It Over His Wife

Throughout the centuries, the implied submissive role of a wife to her husband has been a bone of contention. Saint Paul mentions this when addressing husbands and wives: "Wives, be subject to your husbands as you are to the Lord. For the husband is the head of the wife just as Christ is the head of the church, the body of which he is the Savior. Just as the church is subject to Christ, so also wives ought to be, in everything, to their husbands" (Eph 5:22-24). First of all, we need to keep in mind that St. Paul writes from his particular cultural context of life in the first-century Roman Empire, which was a hierarchical and patriarchal society.

I love how St. John Paul II explained this.

He wrote that St. Paul, "addressing husbands and wives ... recommends them to be 'subject to one another out of reverence for Christ' ([Eph] 5:21)." He continued, "Here it is a question of a relationship of a double dimension or degree: reciprocal and communitarian." He explained, "One clarifies and characterizes the other." He tells us from whence it comes. "The mutual relations of husband and wife should flow from their common relationship with Christ."[76]

Saint John Paul II went on to speak about where St. Paul is coming from. He wrote, "The author of the letter [St. Paul] speaks of 'reverence for Christ' ... [I]t is above all a case of respect for holiness, for the *sacrum*." And he tells us something that should put our hearts at ease. He explains that when St. Paul speaks of wives being submissive to their husbands, "the author does not intend to say that the husband is the lord of the wife and that the interpersonal pact proper to marriage is a pact of domination of the husband over the wife." He continued, "The husband and the wife are in fact 'subject to one another,' and are mutually subordinated to one another. The source of this mutual subjection is to be found in Christian *pietas*, and its expression is love." The pontiff explained, "Love makes the husband simultaneously subject to the wife, and thereby subject to the Lord himself, just as the wife to the husband."

Saint John Paul II told us that marriage requires a reciprocal donation of self. Specifically, he wrote, "The community or unity which they should establish through marriage is constituted by a reciprocal donation of self, which is also a mutual subjection." We find in Christ our model for this subjection, he said, "which, being reciprocal 'out of reverence for Christ,' confers on the conjugal union a profound and mature character." This model can "give rise to a new and precious 'fusion' of the bilateral relations and conduct."[77]

We Work Out Our Salvation Together

Let's talk about our holy work of choosing to love. It's much more than just learning to live with one another. We eventually become one, not just two people trying hard.

For all of the countless wonderful, blissful marital moments, there are certainly some challenges and growing pains that come with adjusting to living with each other, endeavoring to put the other first, and so on. Two people, a man and a woman, no matter how much in love they may be, will experience some discord at times. How many times are we willing to put ourselves after our spouse when it comes to conversations? How much are we willing to fully donate ourselves?

As I said before, at times, a disagreement might seem like it's the end of the world or that your problem is too big to fix. I assure you that this is most likely not the case. This, too, shall pass! Hang in there, dear sister in Christ! Please don't give up. Marriage is hard. It's all about two people coming together and trying to mesh. One is a man and one is a woman. What do we have in common, after all? I wish I could put a bunch of exclamation points here.

Kidding aside, really and truly, marriage takes work — a lot of work. Are we up to the task? It's actually holy work. With God's grace, we are certainly up to the task! We work out our salvation together right in the midst of disagreements *and* marital bliss!

I told you at the beginning of this book that it wasn't going to be about "fluff." I am committed to keeping it real for you. Please dear sister, don't become disheartened if you sometimes feel exasperated with your husband. We are all a work in progress! Saints are made within the details of life and in the give-and-take of marital "bliss"!

One woman who read my article "Unexpected Discovery" (mentioned above) wrote to me and let me know that she planned to tear out the page and frame it as a gift for her daughter and soon-to-be son-in-law. I think that is a very smart idea — to plant the seeds in advance that it's okay to have differences.

Yet, we need to work together! We need to choose love! We absolutely need to move our wills for the good of the other!

I love what Venerable Fulton J. Sheen said about the husband and wife growing, learning, and loving one another: "As life goes on, they become not two compatible beings who have learned to live together through self-suppression and patience, but one new and richer being, fused in the fires of God's love and tempered of the best of both."[78]

Let his words sink in.

He said, "One by one, the veils of life's mysteries have been lifted. The flesh, they found, was too precocious to reveal its own mystery; then came the mystery of the other's inner life, disclosed in the raising of young minds and hearts in the ways of God."[79]

We have to remember that we are all works in progress before our Lord. God grants us the graces to become united in Christ.

The Almighty helps us to truly discover and fall in love with one another's inner lives as we become one with each other in sacramental marriage. Amazingly, through the process, we ultimately help one another to get to Heaven!

PAUSE

Take a moment to ponder courtship and marriage. If you are engaged or married, are you striving to work out your salvation together with your betrothed or spouse?

ACT

Pray for marriages. Strive to practice the virtues in a more earnest way — to "catch the eye of God." You can do it with His amazing grace! Keep going!

A Prayer of Mercy

Jesus, help me to always put my husband before
myself in my loving actions towards him.
Help me to help him get to Heaven.
Jesus, please have mercy upon my soul.
I trust in You!
Mother Mary, help me, protect me, and guide me.
Saint Faustina, please pray for me.
Amen.

CHAPTER 23
Motherhood

"The quintessence of love is
sacrifice and suffering."

— Saint Faustina (*Diary*, 1103)

I'll share with you that I happen to despise clutter. I feel much more comfortable when things are neat and organized. However, don't think for a minute that my house is perfect. Far from it!

There is one thing, however, that I will not hesitate to "clutter" my home with: family photos! If you were to enter my home, you would see an array of family photos, old and new, gracing the table in my foyer. I can't help myself! I am a mom and grandma, after all!

Sometimes when I am standing there by the front door with my husband Dave, saying a few morning prayers before he leaves for work, the family photos catch my eye, and I remark to him that every life represented in those pictures is so unique and unrepeatable. If it weren't for my grandmother in that photo holding me as a baby, my mother (pictured in another photo and also holding me) wouldn't have been born and wouldn't have had me! I glance over the photos of my dear children and grandchildren smiling up at me, and my heart soars to great heights.

I suppose I should confess I have an entire wall in my dining room plastered with a patchwork of family photos. I can't seem to get enough! What an incredible blessing it has been to be a mother and grandmother!

This certainly does not mean that raising a family has always been a walk in the park. Every family will have challenges and struggles as they work out their salvation together in the midst of diaper changes, housekeeping, growing pains, and family dinners. An awful lot happens within the walls of our domestic churches, much more than meets the eye. Souls are nourished and consciences are formed right there in the heart of the home. Tenderness needs to be shown, as well as a whole lot of forgiveness doled out. Truly incredible stuff happens with our families.

We need to capture some of these tremendous blessings in photos! Don't keep those precious images online or only in photo albums. Frame them and put them all over your domestic church! Later on, you will reminisce and your heart will sing, like mine did the other morning when gazing upon my photos.

Children Are Miraculous Gifts!

In his apostolic exhortation *Familiaris Consortio* (*On the Role of the Christian Family in the Modern World*; *FC*), St. John Paul II professed, "When they become parents, spouses receive from God the gift of a new responsibility. Their parental love is called to become for the children the visible sign of the very love of God, 'from whom every family in heaven and on earth is named'" (*FC*, 14).[80]

I don't think that we will ever fully comprehend the gift of a child this side of Heaven. Still, we can clearly see what an incredible miracle it is to conceive a child and bring that life into the world. Saint John Paul II called this act of procreation "the greatest possible gift, the gift by which they become cooperators with God for giving life to a new human person." The child is "a living reflection of their love, a permanent sign of conjugal unity and a living and inseparable synthesis of their being a father and a mother" (*FC*, 14).

It's best to mention here that children are not our right. They are a gift to us. Not every couple will be able to conceive.

Perhaps those who can't conceive naturally might open their hearts and arms to adopt children.

When I became a mother for the first time, I was in total awe as I looked at the tiny babe that God had gifted to me. My firstborn, Justin, came into the world amid a bit of drama.

Certain tests I had undergone towards the end of my pregnancy were turning up results that caused my doctor to feel a great unease. He called me one afternoon just 10 days before my due date, bidding me to get to the hospital right away. I craned my neck to peer out the window behind me and observed that it was snowing pretty heavily.

"Now?" I asked him.

"Yes. Now. I'll meet you there. And, if further tests show distress, we will need to do an emergency Caesarean section."

Immediately, a lump formed in my throat. His forthright instruction was not the kind of message I wanted to hear that lazy afternoon. After all, I had gone through the classes to give birth naturally. *It can't be a Caesarean!* Fear had a hold of my heart. I said goodbye to my doctor and quickly dialed my mother as I slipped down to kneel at my bedside.

She picked up right away, and I spouted out what had transpired. I listened to her advice as I knelt there, silently calling on God. Looking back now as I write this, I am giving thanks to God that my mother was alive at the time to lovingly cheer me on.

I was still scared, knowing that, at barely 21 years old, I might have to go through a major surgery and then deal with the recovery while caring for a tiny newborn. I had to get up off my knees and rush to alert my husband. I wrapped a big wool poncho around me, grabbed my already-packed bag, and climbed up into our old truck. It would be a 45-minute ride on a good day. We braced ourselves for slippery roads.

Angels must have gotten us to the hospital in that blinding snowstorm. It was actually a blizzard, I'd learn later, one that shut down major highways in the Northeast and caused snowplow drivers to get off the dangerous roads. The governor closed down the state while I was in the hospital.

My doctor was right. I needed to get to the hospital as soon as possible. The fetal monitor revealed that my baby was in complete distress. His heartbeat was much too slow and weak.

I was wheeled into surgery. The spinal anesthesia needle was inserted near my spine, but it caused immediate shooting pain down my left leg. The medication was stopped, and a smelly mask was placed over my face. My mother's words were echoing in my mind as the anesthesia was about to take effect:

"You'll do anything to get your baby delivered safely."

Next thing I knew, I was being wheeled again — this time past the nursery. My gurney came to a screeching stop. I strained my anesthesia-fuzzy eyes to see a baby being held up by a nurse on the other side of the clear glass window. His legs were lanky, and he let out a soft howl.

He's my baby boy! I want to hold him.

That would have to wait. Off I went, wheeled down the hall and into the room that would be my new home for the next five days. Words simply can't describe a mother's feelings when she's holding her baby for the first time. An expectant mother becomes acquainted with her little one during its first nine months, as she rocks her little one with every move. But now she finally comes face to face with him and welcomes him permanently into her motherly heart.

Thigh-high snow with even higher drifts welcomed me home. Justin was bundled up tightly against my body as I slowly and carefully put one foot in front of the other, slogging up the long path that had been shoveled out for our arrival. I didn't want to drop my baby! We reached our little cabin door. I kicked off my snow-covered shoes on the screened porch, went inside, unwrapped my baby, and began to settle into my new life as a mom with my sweet little firstborn.

Memories of all the births and babyhoods of my five children are etched upon my heart. Through thick and thin, challenges and joys, I deeply cherished the vocation of motherhood.

Let's take a closer look at the fascinating vocation of motherhood. First, we'll ponder our Mother in Heaven.

Mother Mary in Our Mothering

A mother's love can never be completely explained or defined. However, we can ponder Mother Mary's life to get an idea of a mother's selfless love. When the Blessed Mother stood at the foot of the Cross, she suffered along with her Son as each drop of His blood was shed, as each of His last words were uttered, and as she heard His every gasp. Surely earnest prayers rose from her Immaculate Heart like aromatic incense.

Thirty-three years before that most sorrowful moment, Mary had cradled her Son in her own womb for nine months, rocking Him as she moved about. She would have held Him close to her breast as He suckled. Mary certainly knew every hair on her Son's head and counted His tiny fingers and toes numberless times as He fell asleep safely in her arms. Since the Angel Gabriel's greeting at the Annunciation, Mother and Son had been on a journey together like no other. They were and are coworkers in our salvation.

As the Blessed Mother took her Son's lifeless body into her arms after He was lowered from the Cross, her Immaculate Heart was breaking. Her Heart had already been pierced through with a sword of sorrow when she and St. Joseph had presented their Son, Jesus, in the Temple. Once again, that sword of sorrow surely must have been acutely felt.

Saint Faustina prayed to her Savior, "Jesus, You have given me to know and understand in what a soul's greatness consists: not in great deeds but in great love. Love has its worth, and it confers greatness on all our deeds. Although our actions are small and ordinary in themselves, because of love they become great and powerful before God" (*Diary*, 889).

Ordinary deeds with great love: This is the definition of a mother's life. Many of a mother's actions in caring for her children might seem small or insignificant. But the love that she puts into them is great indeed. Consider again the quote I used to begin this chapter: "The quintessence of love is sacrifice and suffering" (*Diary*, 1103). Love compels a mother to give of herself. A dedicated mother sacrifices her time and her interests for a season, as she is entrusted with the care of an innocent little person who is completely dependent upon her. A mother even gives up her shapely figure to shelter a baby for a long nine months.

The love between a mother and child is much more than heartwarming feelings, admiration of precious little dimples, or blissfully listening to enchanting baby coos. No doubt those sweet moments make mothers' hearts soar. But the love between a mother and her child is filled with ongoing, loving sacrifice. Though a dedicated mother will never have to go through what Mother Mary endured, we can learn so much from the Blessed Mother and then carry that wisdom into our mothering.

A Mother's Life Is a Prayer!

Years ago, I had the blessing of staying at a Missionaries of Charity convent in New York City and partaking in their prayer life. Father John A. Hardon, SJ (my spiritual director at the time), and Mother Teresa were there that weekend, too! Father Hardon was giving a retreat to the MC sisters, and he invited me to partake.

It was a wonderful, spiritually enriching weekend, during which I helped in the soup kitchen, which included making the meals and serving them to hungry gang-member guests who would show up in droves to get a hot meal. I remember vividly being told to heap up their plates because it might be their only meal that day.

Arrangements were made for me to sleep in the woman's shelter there at the convent. That was an amazing experience in itself! However, I will get to the point of my sharing this experience and how it relates to being a mother. And, by the way, I will mention that I was married and a mother at the time, and still partook in this unique opportunity to be there while Mother Teresa was visiting from Calcutta and when Fr. Hardon would be preaching all throughout. Also, I was pregnant at the time and didn't realize it! Talk about motherhood!

When the bell rings in the convent, it summons the sisters to the chapel to pray. While I was there, I experienced many prayer times in the chapel with the sisters, as well as Eucharistic Adoration. One time, when I was in the chapel alone, suddenly in walked Mother Teresa! She knelt down quietly nearby and prayed to our Eucharistic Lord, and I'm sure to Our Lady, too. Our hearts were mysteriously joined together in prayer.

The "bell" that rings in a mother's domestic church is the cry of her baby, her family hungry for dinner, her husband needing her time and attention, her child getting hurt and needing her care, her child spiking a fever, and on and on. That bell rings around the clock in a mother's life, right within the "chapel" of her home, her "domestic church."

At times, a mother might be concerned that she is losing time for prayer, for instance, when she has carved out a time to pray and in bursts a hungry child just waking up from a nap. But no prayer time is lost. God knows what is going on. Her contemplative prayer suddenly changed into an active form of prayer in lovingly caring for her child or others in need at that moment. A loving mother prays that her life can become a beautiful, living prayer. She continues to carve out the necessary time for prayer as best she can, but she learns that it is important to be flexible, totally open to God's holy will. God certainly wants us to take care of those He puts in our midst to love. It would be wrong to neglect their care because we think we have to continue our scheduled prayer.

Let's talk about how mothers are instrumental in creating a holy rhythm in their domestic churches. First, I must at least briefly mention how this church of the home gets established in the first place.

The Church of the Home

We spoke about Catholic marriage previously, but here we discuss it in relation to the family. Our Church teaches, "The family is, so to speak, the domestic church."[81] A domestic church starts with the Sacrament of Matrimony — a man and a woman become husband and wife. Saint John Paul II spoke of a Catholic couple's call to holiness within that Sacrament. He proclaimed, "In God's plan, all husbands and wives are called in marriage to holiness, and this lofty vocation is fulfilled to the extent that the human person is able to respond to God's command with serene confidence in God's grace and in his or her own will" (*FC*, 34).

In his encyclical *Evangelium Vitae* (*The Gospel of Life*), the pontiff called Catholic married couples to recognize their responsibilities. He said, "As the domestic church, the family is summoned to proclaim, celebrate and serve the Gospel of life. This is a responsibility which first concerns married couples, called to be givers of life, on the basis of an ever greater awareness of the meaning of procreation as a unique event which clearly reveals that human life is a gift received in order then to be given as a gift. In giving origin to a new life, parents recognize that the child, 'as the fruit of their mutual gift of love, is, in turn, a gift for both of them, a gift which flows from them.'"[82]

Jesus Himself was born into the heart of a family. His little domestic church consisted of His Mother, Mary; His foster father, St. Joseph; and Himself. Wherever the Holy Family set up their home — in the stable in Bethlehem for a time, in Egypt, or in Nazareth — their domestic church moved right along with them, simply because it was made up of their family. Down through the ages, as people were converted and became believers, "they desired that 'their whole household' should also be saved.[83] These families who became believers were islands of Christian life in an unbelieving world" (*Catechism*, 1655).

Today's Catholic families should also be good examples, or "islands of Christian life to an unbelieving world." Pope Benedict XVI said, "Every home can transform itself in a little church. Not only in the sense that in them must reign the typical Christian love made of altruism and of reciprocal care, but still more in the sense that the whole of family life, based on faith, is called to revolve around the singular lordship of Jesus Christ."[84]

Certainly, these are wonderful ideals to emulate. However, we know that not every Catholic family consists of a mother and a father. Today there are a great number of single-parent families in which mothers are raising their children alone. There is additional discussion on this in the "Single Motherhood" chapter. Also, grandparents are raising their grandchildren in many households.

We also know that not every Catholic husband and wife "mirrors the mystery of Christ's love for the Church, his bride," even in traditional families. Still, our Church summons Catholic families, in all their shapes and forms, to live in this virtuous way. Each domestic church can truly be a stable, loving, and holy environment for the family members to grow in faith together.

Again, we have discussed marriage in greater depth in the last chapter. However, I thought it would be wise to share this information here since we are talking about a mother's marvelous role within the church of the home.

Mothers Build Their Domestic Church

A mother, being the heart of her home, truly sets the tone for her family. She is instrumental in establishing the essential prayer foundation and family faith traditions in her domestic church.

Right in the heart of Christian homes, the family first learns about God and the need to pray and seek His will. The Church teaches that the parents are the first and foremost educators for their children. We mothers and fathers need to make sure that our children are taught properly.

One of our major jobs as a mother is getting the family together at the dinner table. Another important job: making sure that their hands are clasped in prayer, both together and by themselves. You will establish your family's prayer foundation and certainly help to form their consciences. Getting the family settled at the table for a meal or focused on prayer might not always be an easy feat. Competing distractions will pull at your children's attention, as well as their desire to do something else at that time.

Nonetheless, you set the schedule and can help to make eating together as a family a wonderful experience. Later on, the children will look back on those family meals as a secure haven and safe anchor in the storms of life. The family table is a sacred place where they grow as persons. Your conversations and teaching of the faith will nourish their souls now and stay with them into their futures.

Meals Together Transform Lives

While we know that eating is necessary for survival, enjoying a meal together is also transformative. Regular family dinners make a huge difference in everybody's lives. Try to unplug from unnecessary technology so that you can eat together in peace instead of being a slave to your devices. This way, you can spend more time enjoying one another's company. Eating together provides an opportunity to be with loved ones, de-stress, catch up on each person's news, enjoy meaningful conversations, improve family relationships, and pray and learn more about the faith together. The National Center on Addiction and Substance Abuse (CASA) at Columbia University stated that children who eat with their families five times a week or more are far less likely to abuse alcohol or drugs, or to become smokers. In addition, children who eat with their families achieve higher grades and report feeling closer to their parents than do children who eat less often with their parents.[85]

While we are at it, why not sometimes light a candle, play some soothing music, and use our good china, perhaps on a Sunday? When my mother was dying of cancer, she vowed she was going to take her good china out of the china cabinet and start using it. Sadly, my mother never had the opportunity. But we can certainly learn from my mother that we should not wait to make dinners special. We should celebrate life and family!

Moving on to getting the children's hands clasped in prayer, it's important to remember that a Catholic mom needs to set a schedule for prayer. We certainly need to be mindful that being part of a family requires flexibility, not regimentation. Still, if we don't carve out the time to pray, it might never happen!

I believe that there are four kinds of prayer for a mom to establish. They are:

1. her own prayer life
2. prayer with her husband
3. her family's prayer life
4. teaching individual prayer to each child.

A mom can pray on her own at times that she chooses, as well as hopefully continually living prayer as she raises her heart to God in love, praise, thanksgiving, and petition.

She should be sure to establish times to pray together with her husband. She should also make time for daily family prayer, by praying together a morning offering, mealtime prayers, the family Rosary, the Divine Mercy Chaplet, and evening prayer. Moms can seize the opportunity to pray together while all are seated at the table for a meal. She can fit in a little faith lesson. She has a captive audience, after all.

Finally, a mom can teach each child to be a prayerful person. I feel it's important to let the children know that they can pray at any time, no matter what! They can always pray silently from their hearts, no matter where they are or what those around them would prefer. Rules can't touch one's heart or soul. We need to move our wills to pray!

Mothers Need a Strong Faith

God desires that a mother possess a very strong faith. Faith, one of the three theological virtues that we are given at our Baptism, is meant to grow in our heart and soul throughout life. To mother our children well, we must work at strengthening this integral spiritual muscle of faith. We will certainly be flexing it quite a bit throughout the rearing of our children. I believe a heroic faith is required these days, and perhaps will be even more so in the future. Because of their unconditional love for their children, mothers are natural intercessors for their brood and someday for their grandchildren, as well. Be sure to do all that you can to strengthen your faith so that you will be ready at every circumstance to pray for your saints-in-the-making. It's possible that, later in life, our children or grandchildren might stray off the path, and our prayers will be needed to bring them back safely.

Naturally, you'll be praying for your children and grandchildren even when they are in the womb. Your prayers will rise from your maternal heart at every age and stage of their development after their birth. But there will be times when extra prayers are needed — when your fervent, loving prayers will be the absolute necessary anchor in your children and grandchildren's lives. God has appointed you as the heart of your home. You help to steer the ship. You are the safety net, the fervent flame of faith for the family.

Think that's too hard or impossible? You don't have to do it alone. You can count on help from Heaven.

Mother Mary's Loving Prayers

What would we do without a loving mother's prayers? Thank God for Mother Mary! She prays for us and guides us to pray like her — to stand beside our children — to pray with holy tears for their salvation. Mothering children is not just about taking care of their physical and emotional needs. It's about prayerfully escorting them to Heaven!

When Our Lady of Fatima appeared to the three shepherd children, Lúcia dos Santos and Francisco and Jacinta Marto, she was not all smiles. She was indeed filled with love, but her demeanor was that of utter concern for the salvation of the world. Sister Lúcia made note of this in her memoirs. During at least one of the apparitions, Our Lady had tears on her face. Another time, she appeared with her heart pierced with thorns. In October 1917, she appeared as Our Lady of Dolors. Mother Mary is always concerned for the salvation of our souls.

Sister Lúcia's younger cousins, Francisco and Jacinta, went home to Heaven at early ages. Sister Lúcia was left behind to propagate the message of Our Lady of Fatima. She was a professed nun in two congregations: First, she entered the Dorotheans, and then, with her superiors' permission, became a Carmelite nun. At one point, through correspondence between Sr. Lúcia and a cardinal, something quite incredible about the family and the future of the family was revealed.

In 1980, St. John Paul II appointed Cardinal Carlo Caffarra (Archbishop of Bologna) to plan and establish the Pontifical Institute for Studies on Marriage and Family. The cardinal wrote to Sr. Lúcia (through her bishop) to ask for prayers and received an unexpected letter from the Fatima visionary. In her letter, Sr. Lúcia gave both a warning and consolation.

She told the cardinal that "[t]he final battle between the Lord and the reign of Satan will be about marriage and the family. Don't be afraid," she added, because anyone who works for the sanctity of marriage and the family will always be fought and opposed in every way, "because this is the decisive issue." Sister Lúcia concluded, "However, Our Lady has already crushed its head."[86]

We are assured through Sr. Lúcia's words about the intrinsic value and the sanctity of the human family. The devil hates the family and seeks to destroy that which God has created. This should not make us tremble in our boots, but instead it should give us all the more reason to be on our guard so as to be ready to earnestly protect human life and the family, the domestic church. Let us not be afraid, but remember Sr. Lúcia's assurance: "Our Lady has already crushed its head." Let us mothers gain strength and courage from our faith!

Mothers Become Heroes to Their Children

This very morning, during a bit of housekeeping before I got into my book writing, I came across something beautiful. It was just two sheets of computer paper that had been inserted into a folder. They were labeled, "My Hero," and had been typed by my oldest daughter when she was a young teen. In her essay, she explained why I was her hero.

I had totally forgotten about her typed-up proclamation. Taking a break from my cleaning, I sat down and read her wonderful sentiments as a few uncontrollable tears made their way down my cheeks. What an unexpected gift it was to find her writing today! My heart was profoundly touched when I read her closing thoughts.

She wrote, "I admire her and want to follow in her footsteps so that one day I will be as good a mother to my children as she is to me."

My daughter grew up to be a wonderful mother to her two sweet sons, and I admire her! It's such an incredible gift to be the grandmother of her children and observe the way in which my daughter naturally mothers them. I could fill an entire book with beautiful memories and blessings that are woven throughout family life. I am sure that you can too, or that you will be able to someday. We certainly need to pause and thank God for His amazing gift of family life.

Kids Leaving the Nest

I have to admit that the hardest part of mothering for me has not been staying up at night taking care of little ones, losing sleep, breaking up sibling rivalry, or any of that. It's been watching them go out the front door and down the path to start life on their own. It tugs on my maternal heart big time. But we mothers absolutely have to let our children spread their wings! We earnestly hope and pray that the foundation that we have put down will be their comfort and steady anchor in life, no matter where they might stray. They need those roots — but also wings!

After they've left for college, marriage, or to launch their career, at times I have to hold back the tears at dinnertime when I see their empty chair. But I have to tell myself it's okay. Children moving out is part of life. We mothers are still deeply connected to our adult children. There will be times, dear sister, when your maternal heart will be ill at ease due to various circumstances. However, no matter how much we might wish to protect our adult children from harm or evil, we can only lovingly advise them if they are open to hear it, and we wear out our knees in fervent prayer. We must beg our Lord and our dear Mother in Heaven to protect our children. Yes, they've grown into adults, but they always need a mother's loving prayer. Many times those prayers are raised to God amid a flood of tears.

Kids Leaving the Church

Many faith-filled mothers lament the fact that their grown children have left the Church. It's important to remember that you are not alone. Countless caring mothers pray like St. Monica, begging God to bring their children back to the faith.

Every mother should take to heart the words spoken to St. Monica by her bishop. Saint Monica cried when begging the bishop to save her son Augustine's soul from the errant teaching in which he was wrapped up. Though Augustine was bright and gifted, he led a very sinful life and was ensnared in a religious cult.

The bishop assured St. Monica that, because of her prayerful tears, it was impossible for her son to perish.

It was true. Augustine would not be lost. It took about 15 years, but his mother's holy tears and continual intercessory prayers brought about his conversion. Saint Augustine was not only later canonized a saint in the Catholic Church, but was also made a Doctor of the Church!

Mothers' prayers are powerful! Let us not forget that.

In time, we mothers learn the "dance." Words sometimes fall on deaf ears. However, prayers never fail. We learn when it is appropriate to speak to our adult children and when it's best to remain silent and to continue to fervently pray. Prayer is always on a mother's lips and rising from her heart for her dear children. We mustn't forget the importance of our holy example, too.

PAUSE

Motherhood is a vocation of love! Take time to count your many blessings as a biological mother, a spiritual mother, and for the presence of any mother in your life. Ponder a happy memory.

ACT

Every life is sacred, unique, and unrepeatable. Thank God for the beautiful gift of motherhood and pray for mothers all over the world, especially those in need. Let us beseech Mother Mary and pray like St. John Paul II, who has said, "May Mary's thoughtful sensitivity, totally feminine and maternal, be the ideal mirror of all true femininity and motherhood!"[87]

A PRAYER OF MERCY

Dear Jesus, thank You for the amazing gift of a mother. Thank You for this wonderful vocation.
Jesus, please have mercy upon my soul.
I trust in You! I want to trust You more.
Mother Mary, help me, protect me, and guide me.
Saint Faustina, please pray for me.
Amen.

CHAPTER 24
Life Issues — Unplanned Pregnancy, Miscarriage, Abortion, and Infertility

"Human life is sacred because from its beginning it involves the creative action of God and it remains for ever in a special relationship with the Creator, who is its sole end. God alone is the Lord of life from its beginning until its end: no one can under any circumstance claim for himself the right directly to destroy an innocent human being."[88]

— *Catechism*, 2258 (emphasis in original)

Our dear Lord has given us the great and sacred gift of human life. As I mentioned in Chapter 19, women have been entrusted with this exquisite gift, not only as biological mothers, but as spiritual mothers. God made women with warm motherly hearts.

We will look at various life issues in this chapter, beginning with unplanned pregnancy.

Unplanned Pregnancy

We shouldn't expect that we will traverse the path of life without temptations knocking on our door. Thomas à Kempis points out, "So long as we live in this world we cannot escape suffering and temptation. Whence it is written in Job: 'The life of man upon earth is a warfare.'" He instructs, "Everyone, therefore, must guard against temptation and must watch in prayer lest the devil, who never sleeps but goes about seeking whom he may devour, find occasion to deceive him." He reminds us, "No one is so perfect or so holy but he is sometimes tempted; man cannot be altogether free from temptation."[89]

Since it is impossible to escape temptations in life, we might as well face the fact that we will indeed encounter them. Because of these temptations as well as our fallen human nature, some women will end up with unwanted pregnancies.

If you are faced with an unplanned pregnancy, no matter where you are in life, old hairy legs will work tirelessly to persuade you to feel defeated. He hates human life — plain and simple. The evil one will stop at nothing to convince you that you need to abort the unplanned child. He'll whisper in your ear that it's only a blob of tissue and other such lies. Don't listen to him. It's important to acknowledge that he will attack and to move on with faith and prayer. By doing so, you will simply recognize that there will most likely be struggles with doubt or discouragement.

Reach out for assistance, whether for someone to talk with or for tangible help (or both). If the Sacrament of Reconciliation is in order for you — don't hesitate to go. It's important to be honest with yourself and others, too. If you need help, ask for it. Don't try to be a martyr! You don't have to do this by yourself.

Hopefully, you will be able to enjoy that precious new life within you. If, due to circumstances beyond your control, you are not able to raise the child, the irreplaceable unique life, inside of you, please give your baby the gift of life outside of the womb. Please give your baby up for adoption. Rest assured that God can find a couple that is eager to adopt and lovingly raise your child. Abortion is never the answer to an unplanned pregnancy — never ever.

Saint Faustina's Remedy for Doubt

Saint Faustina noted in her *Diary* many times how she suffered from doubt and discouragement. She lets us know that there is certainly a remedy: our Lord! He strengthens our will when we prayerfully stay open to His graces. Saint Faustina wrote, "Although the temptations are strong, a whole wave of doubts beats against my soul, and discouragement stands by, ready to enter into the act. The Lord, however, strengthens my will, against which all attempts of the enemy are shattered as if against a rock." She said she could see that there were many actual graces granted to her by God. "[T]hese support me ceaselessly," she wrote. "I am very weak, and I attribute everything solely to the grace of God" (*Diary*, 1086).

Saint Faustina said, "I want to look upon everything, from the point of view that nothing happens without the will of God" (*Diary*, 1183). This is not to say that God planned that unplanned pregnancy. However, He will indeed be with you all the way. Call on Him. Trust Him.

Miscarriage

Miscarriage is the loss of an unborn human life. We need to do our best to trust that God is in control and has His reasons for that unborn child to go to Him so swiftly, before the parents have even had the chance to hold their baby. I personally have lost three babies to miscarriage. One was miscarried at 16 weeks. My heart goes out to every parent who has lost a baby through miscarriage or stillbirth. It is a pain like no other. We need to allow ourselves to mourn.

My heart holds vivid memories of waking up in a hospital room after a surgery to discover that there were two IVs in my arms rather than just the single one I had had when I was going into the surgery. I was confused, and would soon find out that I was in the process of getting a blood transfusion.

"Honey, you lost a lot of blood," the kind nurse told me when she saw that my eyes were open. "You will be staying overnight," she added.

"No, I can't stay over," I quickly shot back. "My little daughter won't understand where I am."

"Well, you'll need to talk to the doctor about that."

I didn't know then that I had almost died on the operating table. To be honest, there was a bit of trouble saving my life. However, I was not privy to this information at that time.

You see, my unborn baby's heart had stopped beating at 16 weeks in the womb. I learned that devastating fact soon after I started passing large clots of blood. My doctor told me to go to the hospital for an ultrasound. That's when I was told that my baby had no heartbeat. I was instructed to get a dilation and curettage (D and C) with suction right away because the pregnancy had been too far along to resolve without surgery.

How can they be absolutely sure that my baby had no heartbeat? I wondered. *It could be a mistake.* I felt like I couldn't take a chance. I knew that a D and C with suction would be an abortion if my baby was alive. I couldn't bear to think about it. I asked my doctor if I could have a bit of time. He told me I could go home, see how I felt, and call him first thing in the morning.

All night long, I was bent in half with horrendous labor pains and continued to pass huge clots of blood. I prayed, tightly gripping my Rosary beads, and waited for the morning to come. After a quick call to the doctor, I was off once again to the hospital. Another ultrasound was administered. Still no heartbeat.

With tears streaming down my face, I agreed to have the surgery. My doctor hurriedly arranged to have me prepared for immediate surgery. I observed tears in his eyes, too. His concern touched my heart. He was a compassionate doctor, indeed.

Blood plasma dripped down from the intravenous bag into the vein in my left arm, drop by clear drop, as I questioned the nurse about my staying overnight at the hospital. Before long, my doctor came into my room and listened to my pleas.

"I promise, I won't get out of bed." I told him. "I'll get some help — I promise!"

I knew full well that I'd have two children at home to care for and a husband who was not helpful. He is the one who would leave me on the side of the road a couple of weeks before I gave birth to our child (after the one I just lost). But that is another story for another time.

At that moment, all I could do was try my best to persuade my doctor to let me go home because I was so concerned for my children. I pestered him enough that he finally gave in and allowed me to go home. It would be after the blood transfusion if, and only if, I would promise to stay in bed for about two weeks. That was tough to hear, but I was extremely weak and had no other choice but to follow his orders and rely on others for help. He said he'd call me in the morning to see how I was doing.

The next day, my doctor called. During our conversation, a burning question needed answering: Why did my chest hurt so much with every single breath I drew in?

"You see, we had to quickly thrust a tube down your throat," he explained. "As soon as the anesthesia took effect, with your feet then in the stirrups, you hemorrhaged profusely."

What in the world was he saying? No one had told me this!

"Your blood pressure plummeted to almost nothing. We had to give you an injection and get another IV in, too — for a blood transfusion. We had to save your life," he explained. "You lost far too much blood."

Oh my God! I prayed interiorly and tried to take it in.

"If that had happened any place other than that operating room ... ." He paused. "Well, you wouldn't be here. There would be no way that your life could have been saved."

God's timing is impeccable.

May God bless the women from various churches who brought casseroles over to my modest apartment during my convalescence.

Over the years, as my life was so busy with caring for my family, at times as a single mother, and later on as the apostolate and book writing unfolded, I didn't have occasion to allow my thoughts to revisit that shocking conversation with my doctor.

However, there have been just a few times throughout my life (including right now as I write this) when I paused to ponder that very experience and felt moved to drop to my knees to give glory and profound thanks to God for saving me.

Bed Rest, Tears, and Prayers

Years later, I was placed on complete bed rest for my eighth pregnancy. I started passing blood at about 10 weeks. The doctor said I was having a miscarriage. I had had three previous miscarriages, and this pregnancy was not looking good. In addition to the bleeding, I had a heart condition. It had developed during the previous pregnancy. Unfortunately, the heart condition that came on due to the stress of this pregnancy was triple the problem, requiring triple the heart medication.

My doctor ordered me to lie down, rest, and get an ultrasound the following day. The test revealed a huge pool of blood in my uterus. Nothing could be done except for me to get off my feet and wait it out. I prayed that I wouldn't lose my baby. Still, my doctor (not the same doctor I mentioned above) was not hopeful — not at all! He even said, "I wish you would hurry up and have this miscarriage."

What?! I couldn't believe his sentiment. To give him the benefit of the doubt, he was probably trying to spare me additional suffering. However, I did not want to hear those words! I wanted to have *hope* in my heart, pray hard, and follow the doctor's orders, so that is what I did. I also got word to my friend in Calcutta, India — Mother Teresa. She prayed for my unborn baby and me. She sent to me a blessed Miraculous Medal and told me to put myself in the Blessed Mother's hands. "She has helped others," she wrote. "She will also help you."

Mother Teresa told me to pray a simple prayer to our Mother in Heaven: "Mary, Mother of Jesus, be Mother to me now." I most certainly prayed that prayer often, as well as the Rosary, and wore the Miraculous Medal that the diminutive saint had given to me. I am still wearing it now almost 30 years later. It got so worn that the top of the aluminum medal broke off. I placed it in a small clear locket that I wear day and night. I never want to lose it.

Well, I shouldn't keep you hanging. It was a very long pregnancy on bed rest amid tears, prayers, and concerns. But thanks be to God that it was long! My baby daughter survived! That precious daughter is almost 30 years old now as I write this. I named her after the Mother of God, as well as Mary's mother, St. Anne, and St. Catherine Labouré (the mystic who received the visions of the Miraculous Medal).

I should also tell you that a very interesting thing happened during that precarious pregnancy. It was something I never could have imagined: My books were conceived and born, too! God put tremendous inspirations on my heart when He kept me still. I wrote away on pieces of paper and in notebooks, and then stored them in a closet for *someday*. I knew that I had to focus on my growing family. At the proper time, God transformed the writings into books! And the inspiration keeps coming, thank God!

God brings much good out of our sufferings when we unite our wills to His. He has the perfect plan, and He knows when we need to be still and know that He is God!

How Can We Help?

How do we help a grieving mother, father, or ourselves when someone is suffering the loss of miscarriage? First things first! Acknowledge the loss. Give the parents a warm hug. Don't be afraid to offer condolences. After all, the baby lost in miscarriage was a real live baby, not merely a clump of cells, as this darkened world would have us believe. Some folks hesitate to say anything for fear of hurting them further. Be not afraid! We should let the grieving parents know that we care, we are sorry for their loss, and we will keep them in our prayers. This greatly helps them. Otherwise, they might suffer alone.

It's important never to say something such as, "Don't worry, you'll have another baby." Saying this does not acknowledge their loss — their tremendous sorrow. We can't predict the future. We don't know for sure that they will have another baby.

Stay in the present moment and offer warm words and love.

The United States Conference of Catholic Bishops has composed a prayer of blessing for miscarriage:

PRAYER OF BLESSING

From the United States Conference of Catholic Bishops
(after a miscarriage)
The leader says the prayer of blessing with hands joined.

Compassionate God,
soothe the hearts of N. and N.,
and grant that through the prayers of Mary,
who grieved by the Cross of her Son,
you may enlighten their faith,
give hope to their hearts,
and peace to their lives.
Lord, grant mercy to all the members of this family
and comfort them with the hope
that one day we will all live with you,
with your Son Jesus Christ, and the Holy Spirit,
forever and ever.
R/. Amen.

Or:

Lord, God of all creation,
we bless and thank you for your tender care.
Receive this life you created in love
and comfort your faithful people in their time of loss
with the assurance of your unfailing mercy.
Through Christ our Lord.
R/. Amen.[90]

Abortion and the "Mystery of Life"

The Church teaches, "Human life must be respected and protected absolutely from the moment of conception. From the first moment of his existence, a human being must be recognized as having the rights of a person — among which is the inviolable right of every innocent being to life"[91] (*Catechism*, 2270). This is an important truth that we must hold fast. The evil one would rather we deny the unborn's rights and even his or her existence!

Saint John Paul II said, "*You are called to stand up for life!* To respect and defend the mystery of life always and everywhere, including the lives of unborn babies," adding, "giving real help and encouragement to mothers in difficult situations." The pontiff succinctly stated, "You are called to work and pray against abortion."[92] He was not a stranger to the fact that women are bombarded with mixed messages and pressures from the world to end their pregnancies and gain supposed freedoms. Women with unplanned pregnancies need our prayers and concrete help.

Once a crusader for abortion, a man who had earned his living killing unborn babies (to the tune of 75,000 lives), Dr. Bernard Nathanson years ago said, "Fewer women would have abortions if wombs had windows!" He had presided over 60,000 abortions at the clinic he ran and knew without a doubt that actually seeing a live unborn baby would most definitely tug at hearts and souls. In addition to those 60,000 deaths, Nathanson took responsibility for 5,000 abortions he personally performed, and an additional 10,000 abortions performed by residents under his supervision.[93]

In the 1970s, Nathanson became a prominent opponent of abortion and said his change of heart and mind was not religious, but rather based on scientific facts and the principles of the rights, worth, and dignity of the human person. He narrated the anti-abortion film, "The Silent Scream."[94]

He would later be baptized a Catholic, after being drawn to the faith because of the Catholic Church's witness to the truth of the sacredness and inherent dignity of every single human life from conception until natural death.

Many a concerned Christian wonders if a baby dying without the Sacrament of Baptism will go to Heaven. The Vatican's International Theological Commission wrote:

> God does not demand the impossible of us. Furthermore, God's power is not restricted to the sacraments: '*Deus virtutem suam non alligavit sacramentis quin possit sine sacramentis effectum sacramentorum conferre*' (God did not bind His power to the sacraments, so as to be unable to bestow the sacramental effect without conferring the sacrament). God can therefore give the grace of Baptism without the sacrament being conferred, and this fact should particularly be recalled when the conferring of Baptism would be impossible. The need for the sacrament is not absolute. What is absolute is humanity's need for the *Ursakrament* which is Christ himself. All salvation comes from him and therefore, in some way, through the Church.[95]

You may recall that the traditional theory on the topic was that babies without Baptism would go to a place called limbo. They would not see the beatific vision, but they also would not be punished because they are innocent of all personal sin. However, the Church teaches that infants dying without Baptism are entrusted to God's mercy (see *Catechism*, 1261).

Let's take a quick look at the lengthy document, *The Hope of Salvation for Infants Who Die Without Being Baptized* (briefly excerpted above and below). The document states: "This theory [Limbo], elaborated by theologians beginning in the Middle Ages, never entered into the dogmatic definitions of the Magisterium, even if that same Magisterium did at times mention the theory in its ordinary teaching up until the Second Vatican Council." The theory of limbo is not mentioned in the *Catechism*, which "teaches that infants who die without baptism are entrusted by the Church to the mercy of God, as is shown in the specific funeral rite for such children," and reminds us that God desires salvation for all (see *Catechism*, 1261).

Further, the document states, "The conclusion of this study is that there are theological and liturgical reasons to hope that infants who die without baptism may be saved and brought into eternal happiness, even if there is not an explicit teaching on this question found in Revelation." In addition, it makes clear that the document's text cannot be used to "negate the necessity of baptism, nor to delay the conferral of the sacrament," but rather it gives reason for "hope that God will save these infants" when it is impossible to baptize them.[96]

How Can We Help?

How do we help women who have had an abortion, or someone who has helped in the abortion decision? We can be nonjudgmental. We do not live in someone else's shoes. We can choose to be loving towards women who are aching and grieving from the deep wounds that come from having aborted their own unborn baby. We can help steer them to practical assistance from organizations such as Rachel's Vineyard. We can certainly pray for them and let them know that we will keep them in our prayers. That can give great hope.

We should keep in mind that we live in a very challenging culture. Women are continually bombarded with misinformation, a heap of lies ultimately stemming from the evil one who hates human life. Some women have succumbed to the terrible act of abortion due to great fears. Only God truly knows their hearts. We should never judge anyone who has in any way partaken in the horrendous and senseless murder of the unborn. Instead, we can do our best to show our compassion and pray. We can help to educate others about the sanctity and dignity of every single human person — born and unborn.

I have vivid memories of kneeling on the pavement beside a car (to get on the level of the people inside) and speaking through the window to a young couple who were just about to go into an abortion facility to get an abortion. I had miraculously managed to get down into the side parking lot next to the abortuary that day when I was with a handful of pro-life Catholics who faithfully prayed and peacefully picketed in front of the abortion facility.

The couple were frightened, but felt they had no other choice but to go through with the appointment. God gave me the grace to offer kind words and to tell them that they should not kill an innocent baby. I told them about adoption, as well as an organization that would help them should they choose to keep their baby. The confusion and fear that I had seen in their eyes seemed to soften just a bit.

Soon, I had to move back to join the others before I was caught. From there, I peered down in the parking lot and could see the couple get out of their car and go into the building. My heart sank, but I prayed hard. Within minutes, they came out and got into their car. They drove up to me to tell me that they had changed their minds!

"We will somehow manage. We want to keep our baby!"

My heart soared! *Praise God!*

Let us heed St. John Paul II's encouragement: "Never tire of firmly speaking out in defence of life from its conception and do not be deterred from the commitment to defend the dignity of every human person with courageous determination. Christ is with you: be not afraid!"[97]

Infertility

We read in Scripture, "So do not worry about tomorrow, for tomorrow will bring worries of its own. Today's trouble is enough for today" (Mt 6:34). Infertility can be a huge cross to bear. Parents longing for a child might be upset with God or even themselves, not understanding why they can't conceive. They *do* worry about tomorrow. They want children to fill their homes.

Infertility could also be a blessing. It's possible that being infertile could open someone's heart to opening their arms to a very special person (or people) through the process of adoption.

A notion exists that we have a right to a child. But we don't. A husband and wife have marital relations, but that does not guarantee that a child will result. We can certainly pray for children, but we must also accept God's will. Using artificial means to conceive a child (in vitro fertilization, or IVF) is against Church teaching. One important reason for that is that we are not God. We do not create human life. We cooperate with God in the marital embrace to bring forth children, if that is His will. Another problem with IVF is that this process bypasses the marital act. Also, we should never dispose of human life, which is what happens in the process. Specifically, "In IVF, children are engendered through a technical process, subjected to 'quality control,' and eliminated if found 'defective.'"[98]

The Catholic Church has great compassion for those who suffer from infertility. Out of love for all human life and respect for the integrity of marital relations, however, the Church teaches that some means of trying to achieve pregnancy are not "licit." That is because "some of these means actually involve the taking of innocent human life, or treating human life as a means toward an end or a 'manufactured product.'" This means, "They do violence to the dignity of the human person."[99]

To learn more, and to see what means are licit, take a look at "Begotten Not Made: A Catholic View of Reproductive Technology" from the United States Conference of Catholic Bishops, written by Dr. John M. Haas, president of the National Catholic Bioethics Center, Boston, Massachusetts.

There is no denying the pain and suffering a women or couple might experience in not being able to conceive. Hopefully, they will prayerfully consider adopting.

Our sister Faustina wrote, "O Jesus, stretched out upon the cross, I implore You, give me the grace of doing faithfully the most holy will of Your Father, in all things, always and everywhere. And when this will of God will seem to me very harsh and difficult to fulfill, it is then I beg You, Jesus, may power and strength flow upon me from Your wounds, and may my lips keep repeating, 'Your will be done, O Lord.' ... O most compassionate Jesus, grant me the grace to forget myself that I may live totally for souls, helping You in the work of salvation, according to the most holy will of Your Father ... ." (*Diary*, 1265).

I'll share a story about how God is really present within the smallest of details of our lives.

A Divine Message in a Daisy

Have you looked at a daisy lately? I mean, closely? I just love the simplicity of daisies. I think of them as "happy" flowers. At one time, daisies were growing in my garden next to my front sidewalk. They are a perennial plant, but they didn't come up one year. I supposed it was because of the fierce winter we had before that particular spring. With each snowstorm, every time my husband shoveled the sidewalk, he piled up lots of snow right over that spot. *My poor daisies!* I thought. It was no great wonder that the daisies didn't show their heads that year. Even so, rather jubilantly surprised, I was able to enjoy watching them open their petals and bloom the following year.

What can we learn from a simple and humble flower? Saint Thérèse reminds us: "Our Lord's love shines out just as much through a little soul who yields completely to His Grace as it does through the greatest ... Just as the sun shines equally on the cedar and the little flower, so the Divine Sun shines equally on everyone, great and small. Everything is ordered for their good, just as in nature the seasons are so ordered that the smallest daisy comes to bloom at its appointed time."[100]

One summer day, walking past the daisies, my husband plucked one from the garden, turned to me, and held it out.

"This is for you!" he said.

I took it from his hand and thanked him. But I must confess that it was half-hearted, because I was sort of "complaining" that he should have picked it with a longer stem! Geesh — I have a lot of nerve! I quickly caught myself and thanked him again — with much more sincerity — and even with a thankful kiss for his little impromptu surprise gift. I brought the little flower inside, dropped it into a tiny glass vase of water, and placed it on the table.

The next morning, we sat down to enjoy a simple breakfast together. We prayed our grace before meals and a few quick morning prayers, and then we talked about the day ahead between spoonfuls of yogurt and granola.

Before long, my husband rose from his seat and cleared his plate. I asked if he could please sit down again — just for a few minutes. I pleaded, actually. I had wanted him to read a morning prayer and Psalm while I finished my breakfast. (I am a slow eater and he is fast!) I hadn't yet read the little reading and the Psalm, but I felt deeply inspired to have my husband read it.

Dave was in a bit of a rush that morning, but to my delight, he sat down again. I slid my prayer book in front of him, pointing to the passages. We blessed ourselves with the Sign of the Cross, and then Dave began to read:

> Lord God, you have made heaven and earth by your great might, with your outstretched arm, nothing is impossible to you (Jer 32:17).

> Our glory is to mirror back in loving praise to the God who made us the beauty we glimpse dimly in all that comes from his hand.

> Praise the Lord from the earth,
> sea creatures and all oceans,
> fire and hail, snow and mist,
> stormy winds that obey his word;
> all mountains and hills,
> all fruit trees and cedars,
> beasts, wild and tame,
> reptiles and birds on the wing;
> all earth's kings and peoples,
> earth's princes and rulers;
> young men and maidens,
> old men together with children.

Let them praise the name of the Lord
for he alone is exalted.
The splendor of his name
reaches beyond heaven and earth.
He exalts the strength of his people.
He is the praise of all saints,
of the sons of Israel,
of the people to whom he comes close (Ps 148).[101]

As Dave was reading, I was listening and praying, and
then I found myself gazing at the short-stemmed daisy, which,
by the way, happened to be right in front of my face.

God Reveals Himself Within the Details of Our Lives

As I leaned in a bit closer, I suddenly discovered something that, to me, was entirely unexpected. Staring at the
modest little gift my husband had given to me the previous
day, I was truly amazed at the most perfect, yet petite and
intricate pattern on that simple yellow and white flower.

I don't think I had ever looked that closely before. But
my sweet daisy was "speaking" to me during the reading and
the Psalm, which was all about mirroring back "in loving praise
to the God who made us the beauty we glimpse dimly in all
that comes from his hand."

God certainly cares about all the details of His creation. So
I have no doubt that He takes care of every detail of our lives.

We can ponder: *If God can create such incredible and
intricate beauty in one simple daisy, just think of the beauty He
wants to make of our hearts and souls!*

We finished our prayer together, blessing ourselves with the
Sign of the Cross, and Dave headed to the other room. Before
I dove into some preparations for our upcoming barbecue, I
decided to step outside to pause a moment beside the daisies in
my garden where I could give thanks and praise to God.

There had been a gentle rain earlier that morning. Some
of the raindrops were clinging to the daisy petals, which was

another reminder to me of how God takes care of the details. My thoughts immediately turned to one of my very favorite Bible passages:

> Therefore I tell you, do not worry about your life, what you will eat or what you will drink, or about your body, what you will wear. Is not life more than food, and the body more than clothing? Look at the birds of the air; they neither sow nor reap nor gather into barns, and yet your heavenly Father feeds them. Are you not of more value than they? And can any of you by worrying add a single hour to your span of life? And why do you worry about clothing? Consider the lilies of the field, how they grow; they neither toil nor spin, yet I tell you, even Solomon in all his glory was not clothed like one of these. But if God so clothes the grass of the field, which is alive today and tomorrow is thrown into the oven, will he not much more clothe you — you of little faith? Therefore do not worry, saying, 'What will we eat?' or 'What will we drink?' or 'What will we wear?' For it is the Gentiles who strive for all these things; and indeed your heavenly Father knows that you need all these things. But strive first for the kingdom of God and his righteousness, and all these things will be given to you as well.
>
> So do not worry about tomorrow, for tomorrow will bring worries of its own. Today's trouble is enough for today (Mt 6:25-34).

God is waiting for us in all the details of our lives. Will we meet Him there? Will we take time to pause, reflect, see the beauty of His creation, and strive to understand His loving messages to us?

Let us endeavor to live within all the present moments of our days — the tough ones and the joyful ones. Amazing graces are in store for us. We need to allow God to make a beautiful creation of our hearts and souls — right in the here and now of our lives! We can start by striving to become more attentive to His whispers to our souls and respond with love to His many graces.

PAUSE

Every single life matters. Take a moment to ponder the intrinsic value of human life. What can you do to protect it and to help others to recognize the true gift that life is?

ACT

Pray for an end to abortion and euthanasia. Pray for the infertile. Ask God to use you to help others. Don't ever give up. God loves you!

A PRAYER OF MERCY

"God of unfathomable mercy, embrace the whole world and pour Yourself out upon us through the merciful Heart of Jesus" (*Diary*, 1183).
Dear Jesus, please have mercy upon anyone who has helped to procure an abortion. Please also heal their hearts and souls. Allow me to be a vessel of love and hope to others who have miscarried, are infertile, and in need of consolation.
Please also have mercy on my soul.
I trust in You!
Mother Mary, help me, protect me, and guide me.
Saint Faustina, please pray for me.
Amen.

CHAPTER 25

Single Motherhood

"Love begins by taking care of the closest ones — the ones at home."[102]

— Mother Teresa

There are some women who choose to raise children without a partner. However, for the most part, single mothers are single because they lost their spouse due to his passing, or they are divorced or separated from him (or from the biological father). Some mothers feel single even though they are married because their husband does not support them in mothering the children or teaching the faith to them. Therefore, they are pretty much on their own in the nurturing and teaching department.

As I've mentioned before, I became a single mother when my then-husband suddenly pulled our car over to the side of the road, looked at me, and exclaimed, "I'm leaving!" He got out of the car, stuck out his thumb, and hitchhiked away. Just like that, I became a single mother. I had two children and another in the womb. I was about to give birth in just a couple of weeks.

So, I got behind the wheel (in more ways than one), and I drove on. There's so much more to the story, but I won't get into it right now. I'll tell you, however, that it was tough — very tough. Many times I wasn't sure how I'd feed my children or keep our humble abode warm enough in our harsh New

England winters. The furnace broke down, and the landlord refused to come out to fix it. I had to put hats on my little ones' heads and bundle them up — inside of the apartment! The wind rushed through cracks in the old, worn windows. And the old furnace was unreliable. I continued to pray to God for better days.

Without letting the kids know, when they were at school, I'd pick up a "takeout" meal once or twice a week from the local soup kitchen. The meal usually consisted of tomato soup and grilled cheese sandwiches. I didn't want my kids to feel embarrassed that I'd received their food from a soup kitchen. It was hard enough for them that their father had left so abruptly.

One day, there was a knock at the door. It was a representative from the welfare department showing up to do a surprise inspection of my apartment. She said they suspected I was living with a man and, if so, they would terminate my benefits immediately.

I really wanted to scream. *Why should I be violated like this just because they suspected something?* The baby was now awake from her rudely interrupted nap, and I was thoroughly flustered. I kept my cool, but felt ill at ease as she stuck her nose here and there and rummaged through my personal items. Even worse, I felt I was being falsely accused of something I would never do.

Plain and simple, I did not want that stranger in my home! As the inspection proceeded, something came over me. I couldn't help myself. I stretched out my hand and passionately pointed to the picture of the Sacred Heart of Jesus hanging on my living room wall.

"That's the man I live with!"

I sincerely hope that my declaration of faith might have touched the woman in some way. I will probably never know, but thankfully, she left a few minutes later, and there were no more surprise inspections after that. The officials sent a letter to me, concluding that I was abiding completely by all of their rules. And thank God, after I got back on my feet, I no longer required the assistance.

A Silver Lining

A few years later, when I was still a single mother with small children, I received a very unexpected birthday gift that would make my heart swell and my knees buckle. At that time, my children and I lived in a modest apartment with rowdy, noisy neighbors, and we struggled financially. My greatest joy was watching my children blossom and grow, and being their mom, an integral part of their lives.

On my birthday that year, about one month before Christmas, my children baked a cake for me and created sweet birthday cards with markers and crayons. It had suddenly grown cold, as it usually does in my neck of the woods in Connecticut. But, though the winds blew outside our apartment and snowflakes were already making an appearance, the warmth of love inside our home was palpable.

I expressed my thanks to my children as we ate dinner that night of my birthday. The three of them sang a birthday song to me, and I hid the hot tears that welled up in my eyes. The tears were joyful tears, yet I was thoroughly aware that I had been mothering in a way I hadn't planned. Nonetheless, my children's love made up for every single pain and worry. The birthday celebration they gave me brought much joy to my heart.

I tucked everyone into bed that night after our prayers. Later, I went into my bedroom to settle down for the night and discovered an envelope on top of my bureau. The word "Mom" was neatly scrawled across it. I couldn't open it quickly enough. However, seeing the contents caused my knees to buckle. I had to sit down on the edge of my bed. With a quick sigh, I read the note inside.

It began, "Mom, you can use this money for Christmas presents ... ." It was signed by my eldest daughter. Tears fell and hit the bed, and I drew the note to my heart. I took a closer look at the contents of the envelope and discovered 100 dollars in small bills. It was every bit of my daughter's babysitting money. She had been saving it for quite some time.

Her unexpected and generous gift that evening was so selfless. She did not expect any credit on Christmas morning for secretly gifting me the means with which to buy Christmas gifts for my children. My heart was full.

After I got my tears under control, I quietly walked into my daughter's bedroom and thanked her. I gave her a big hug and let her know how I deeply appreciated her selfless and generous surprise gift.

After all these years, I still have that envelope and note.

I often share personal experiences in my books and talks in an effort to inspire others to deeper faith, hope, and love. I believe that hearing stories of faith can inspire folks to do their part to push beyond their own comfort zones to help others. Single mothers are so important in their children's lives, yet they often lack the support they need to hold their heads up high and be the mothers that they should be.

Unfortunately, some single mothers have been deserted, abused, or wounded in some way. In addition, they might be grieving the loss of their husband or the death of their marriage. We should do what we can to help them. Even a warm smile or a caring word can lift their spirits.

A Cry for Help

With "Susan's" permission, I share this story. It happened a few years ago when a woman got in touch with me by email. She was extremely concerned for her friend and had high hopes that I could do something to help her — somehow. I didn't quite know what she expected of me, and I read further.

The woman said she had attended an event in Connecticut where she had heard me speak. She also had read my memoir *The Kiss of Jesus* and went on to explain the reason for her email.

She wrote, "My reason for getting in touch with you, is that I have a dear friend named 'Susan' [I have changed her name] who lives in Connecticut … A year and two days ago, Susan's husband left her, with 3 young children. It is a very long story."

"After having read your book, I should have sent one to 'Susan,' but to date have not. I had asked her to contact you, however, she is on the verge of a nervous breakdown, and I told her I would email you, in hopes you could be of some comfort to her."

My heart skipped a beat as I read about a perfect stranger on the verge of a breakdown. "I am thanking you dear Donna-Marie in advance for any words you might offer to me and/or 'Susan.'"

Wow. Learning of this tragic, urgent situation suddenly became a mammoth weight on my shoulders. I stopped reading to say a prayer for the woman and her children, and then put my fingers to my keyboard to respond to the email. I also knew that I should reach out to Susan right away through another email. The woman who had contacted me had also given me Susan's email address. Soon after I sent the email, I heard back from Susan.

Susan opened up to me in emails. She seemed to trust that she could be honest with me. She said, "I am exhausted and depressed beyond what I ever thought I could be … ." She explained the intense problems with her abusive ex-husband. There were many. Immediately, my own intense court battle came to my mind.

She continued, "I am a mess, I am tired and overworked. I breakdown at least 5 times a day. I am so sad all the time and cannot imagine ever feeling happy again." Then she explained, "I am a religious person and do not believe in divorce and feel very alone and stigmatized. I will never love or trust again — the pain is unbearable."

My heart felt troubled as I read her next line.

"I have lost my will to live. I would never hurt myself because my children need me but I sure wish God would just take me. Please help in any way possible … ."

There was a profound ache in my heart as I read her words. *That poor woman*, I thought. *What can I do?* I wanted to help her in any way that I could. We continued to email back and forth over a week's time. Each time I wrote, I prayed that my simple, yet earnest words could reach her heart. I wanted her to know that I cared. I reminded her that God loved her very much and would get her through this.

Suddenly, her emails stopped. I didn't hear from her for a while. My life was so busy with tending to family matters, numerous tight writing deadlines, and migraines, too, but I continued to pray for her.

Then one day, I *knew* that I had to send Susan another email to check on her and let her know that I was thinking of her and praying for her. I'm so glad that I acted on that inspiration to get in touch with her, because she wrote back to say that she was not doing well at all.

I suggested that we meet someplace. Would she want to do that? I didn't even know how meeting her could help, but I had to trust God.

She said, "Yes!" We set a time and place. I put my work aside and carved out some time. Susan seemed to be in such a dark place. I had absolutely no idea what I could possibly say that would help her. I did know that God would figure it out for me. He needed my open heart, and He would do the rest.

I grabbed up some blessed Miraculous Medals, St. Benedict medals (which bear a full exorcism blessing), and a copy of my memoir for her and her three children, and headed out the door. I prayed the Rosary on the way.

All the while, I was still totally unclear about what I would say to Susan. What could I possibly say or do to help untangle the messy events in this woman's life and relieve the intense pain she endured?

I had absolutely no clue. However, I didn't worry about it. I would simply rely on God's grace to intervene. I was to show up with a loving heart, and God would do the work. I trusted in His love, mercy, and grace.

Daisies, Daisies Everywhere — and a Rebirth!

I arrived at the library and waited outside, checking out each vehicle that pulled up to see if it could be Susan and her children. I decided to stand outside my car and wait. After about 10 minutes, a woman came out of the library and asked if I was "Donna O'Boyle." After I confirmed that I was, she told me that Susan had called and said she was caught up in traffic and would be a bit late. I was relieved to learn that she hadn't backed out of our little get-together.

When Susan and her children arrived, one of the first things she told me was that she had bought a bouquet of daisies for me but didn't have time to stop back at her home to get them after her appointments, due to heavy traffic that morning.

Daisies? *Really? Aww!* It turns out she had read my blog post about daisies (similar to my story in the last chapter) and felt inspired to gift daisies to me.

What a sweet gesture on her part, I thought! Of course, it didn't matter that she didn't bring them. Her heartfelt intention was more than enough. We chatted away at the library while her three small children played at our feet. Time and time again, we paused our conversation, pulling a new book or DVD off a nearby shelf to show the kids at each query and interruption.

Lively kids and all, Susan and I covered an awful lot of territory in that two-and-a-half hours together. Before leaving the library, I gave Susan the blessed medals and the autographed copy of my memoir.

We parted with tight hugs outside the library alongside Susan's vehicle. I told her that I loved her. It just popped out. God's love is powerful like that. She immediately expressed the same to me.

God is so good to arrange this kind of meeting. It might seem totally serendipitous, but truth be told, He had it planned all along. I am constantly in awe of God's amazing work. He's always mindful of even the tiniest of details.

Susan said she'd meet me at Sunday Mass at my parish in just a few days. Meanwhile, we had just exchanged phone numbers and would stay in touch by email or texting.

I woke up the next morning to find a heartfelt email from Susan. In it she told me that our conversation had helped her in ways she couldn't express adequately. She said she was helped more than I would ever know. She felt dramatically changed because of it, and thanked me profusely.

Miraculously, Susan was happy again! She had not felt even a smidge of happiness in over a year — which is so hard to imagine. I can't begin to express how my heart felt to read her words and to know that, by God's grace, my reaching out to her had helped her so much.

In another email, she wrote, "I have been thinking of you tonight. All day your kind words and smile went through my head. You have given me so much." She confessed, "I had been in such a dark place for a year that I could not give like I wanted. You do not know how much you have helped me by allowing me to let go so I could be myself again." And then, the clincher! She wrote, "I feel like I had a rebirth … ."

Wow! I immediately got down on my knees and gave thanks to God. He had profoundly touched Susan's heart! I felt immensely humbled and blessed that He'd used His lowly servant to help this woman. God was showing me once again that He wants us all to push beyond our comfort zones to help others, and to trust Him that He will always come through to do the work. He will give us the words. We need to trust Him!

Susan shared something else that immensely pierced my heart. She said, "I cannot begin to tell you how much you helped me. I woke up today happy for the first time in a year." Immediately, my heart began singing praises to God. Susan recalled, "I was outside with my children today and we have daisies all over my hill. I just did not notice the flowers as I was so sad." She continued, "And daisies — What a sign! Now I get to bring you two bunches of flowers!"

She was happy! She was truly happy! It was the first time in a year! Can you imagine — and daisies? You see, a daisy is such a simple — dare I say, a *humble* — flower, but if you look very closely, you will see such amazing intricate details. Daisies have become a sort of theme for Susan and me.

Because she knew I was fond of daisies, she had decided to bring a bouquet to me upon meeting. And, wouldn't you know — daisies had been all around her, but she was too depressed and sorrowful even to notice them. Imagine her utter delight upon seeing them! In a sort of rebirth, Susan's eyes were literally opened and able to see God's beautiful creation, and she was able to experience His love for her.

God is certainly all about the details of e-v-e-r-y-t-h-i-n-g. My heart rejoiced!

God Opens the Way

On Sunday evening, just a few days after we had met at the library, I looked forward to seeing Susan and her children at Mass at my parish. When my husband and I arrived at Mass that evening, my heart immediately sank. The parking lot was barricaded off due to new pavement. The parking lot project was supposed to have been finished before then, and I grew concerned because I hadn't warned Susan about it when I gave her directions to the church.

We drove to the back entrance and were able to get in that way. I prayed that Susan would find the way in and not be discouraged or turned away by the barricades. I had to trust God that He would lead the way.

Imagine my delight when, after the final blessing and hymn at Mass, I turned to walk down the aisle and spotted Susan and her three sweet children coming out of a pew. Two of them were holding *daisies*! It took my breath away! Susan's little daughter held the bouquet of daisies. A small round vase filled with daisies that had been plucked from Susan's backyard was held proudly by one of Susan's sons.

Lots of hugs were shared all around, and the children gifted the daisies to me. Holding his gift carefully with both hands, Susan's little son looked straight up into my eyes and said, "I picked these all by myself and put them in this vase!"

As he handed them to me, he was sure to remind me once again that they were picked and arranged all by himself.

Tears came to my eyes as I peered down at that glowing, smiling face and those sweet daisies, all arranged as only a little boy could. God's abiding love deeply permeated my heart and soul as sweet children gifted me daisies and hugs. Our hearts are profoundly touched by God's love in so many ways when we seek to reach out to help His children.

Is God asking you to push beyond your comfort zone to bring love and peace to others? Mother Teresa, who modeled herself after St. Thérèse, was all about doing small things with great love. Christ's love through us — even in small things — never fails to work miracles in human hearts.

Susan and I stayed in touch and got together on many other occasions. After a while, Susan moved away and in with her father to help him during his last chapter of life. Because she was busy as a single mom, and now a caregiver to her dad, we seldom got in touch. I felt that God had done His work and she had moved on to her new life.

Yet every time I laid eyes on a daisy, I couldn't help but think of Susan and her sweet children, and I'd whisper up a prayer for them.

Please say a prayer for continued strength for Susan and her children, as well as for all of the other hurting and wounded people and single mothers out there who are craving Christ's love.

PAUSE

Take a moment to thank God for the many blessings in your life. Think of a way that you could possibly help a single mother.

ACT

You are never alone. Reach out to those who feel alone or who might need help. God will supply the graces! God loves us all!

A PRAYER OF MERCY

Dear Jesus, I am thankful for my life and
all the blessings You have given to me. Help me
to be more attentive to the needs around me.
Jesus, please have mercy upon my soul.
I trust in You!
Mother Mary, help me, protect me, and guide me.
Saint Faustina, please pray for me.
Amen.

CHAPTER 26
Entering a Religious Vocation

"It seemed to me that I had stepped into the life of Paradise. A single prayer was bursting forth from my heart, one of thanksgiving."

— Saint Faustina (*Diary*, 17)

Saint Faustina couldn't have been happier than she was to finally enter religious life. She had set her heart upon a religious vocation ever since she felt our Lord call her to it at the tender age of 7. Though it was a struggle to get there — having had to "elope" with God because of her parents' refusal to let her go — when she finally crossed over that threshold into the convent, Faustina was ecstatic. In the quote above, we see through her words that she felt as if she had stepped into Paradise.

Still, Sr. Faustina would learn early on that what was required of her was much more than meets the eye. And the young nun wholeheartedly embraced it. I'll let her tell you about it.

"It was four days after my perpetual vows. I was trying to make a Holy Hour," she recalled in her *Diary*. "It was the first Thursday of the month" (*Diary*, 252).

She wrote, "As soon as I entered the chapel, God's presence enveloped me. I was distinctly aware that the Lord was near me. After a moment, I saw the Lord, all covered with wounds." That was when Jesus would tell His bride, **"Look at**

whom you have espoused." Faustina understood the meaning of these words. She answered the Lord, "Jesus, I love You
more when I see You wounded and crushed with suffering like
this than if I saw You in majesty."

Jesus asked her, **"Why?"** and she answered, "Great majesty terrifies me, little nothing that I am, and Your wounds
draw me to Your Heart and tell me of Your great love for me."

After her conversation with Jesus, all was silent. She wrote,
"I fixed my gaze upon His sacred wounds and felt happy to
suffer with Him. I suffered, and yet I did not suffer, because I
felt happy to know the depth of His love, and the hour passed
like a minute" (*Diary*, 252).

From the outside, religious life might seem like a bed of
roses. The truth is that there is much to be endured, as is the
case with every vocation when one is serious about a call to
holiness. All throughout her *Diary*, the young mystic humbly
speaks about the trials of religious life and how God uses those
sufferings for His greater glory, the conversion of sinners, and
as a way in which fervent souls can climb the spiritual ladder to
be closer to union with Him.

Pius XII explained how a vocation may be discovered
through God's Providence excluding other choices. He stated:

> When one thinks upon the maidens and the women
> who voluntarily renounce marriage in order to
> consecrate themselves to a higher life of contem-
> plation, of sacrifice, and of charity, a luminous word
> comes immediately to the lips: vocation! ... This
> vocation, this call of love, makes itself felt in very
> diverse manners ... But also the young Christian
> woman, remaining unmarried in spite of herself,
> who nevertheless trusts in the providence of the
> heavenly Father, recognizes in the vicissitudes of life
> the voice of the Master: "*Magister adest et vocat te*"
> (John 11:28); It is the master, and he is calling you!
> She responds, she renounces the beloved dream of
> her adolescence and her youth: to have a faithful

companion in life, to form a family! And in the impossibility of marriage she recognizes her vocation; then, with a broken but submissive heart, she also gives her whole self to more noble and diverse good works.[103]

Every woman who is called to the religious life has her very own unique story perfectly suited for her own soul. Some are called early in life, some later. Numerous women feel called to religious life, try it out, and realize that God is calling them to another vocation. Was their time in the convent wasted? I think not. On everyone's journey through life, there are twists and turns in the road as well as doors that close. The important thing is that we always seek God's holy will, remain in the state of grace, and keep praying.

I'd like to share an enthralling love story about a woman's promise to God to enter the convent. Her journey involves wild horses, a stranger on a bench, a mother's prayers, Jesus, Our Lady, St. Faustina, St. Padre Pio, and more.

Let's jump in!

A Woman's Promise to Enter Religious Life

"Jesus, if I am going to make it out of here alive, I'll go into the convent!" This was the earnest cry of a 21-year-old woman all alone in the wilderness in the Bavarian Mountains.

The day had started out perfectly fine as Ortrud set out hiking in the mountains to meet up with the Scout leader whom she would assist as a volunteer at an Austrian mountain camp. But she couldn't find the campgrounds. Somehow, she missed them and kept on walking.

She said that the sky was amazingly clear so high on the mountain. She felt she could just reach up and touch the millions of stars! But that delightful notion quickly melted away in the face of the ever-present fact that she was totally alone and it was getting colder by the minute. She began to worry, since there were not enough clothes in her backpack to keep her warm.

And then the wild horses attacked. Two wild horses came galloping at full speed towards her, attacking her, knocking her down. The horses wouldn't leave her alone, and she couldn't get away. Ortrud prayed every prayer she knew over and over. She also exercised her body for hours throughout the afternoon and night, stretching and wiggling her toes (trying her best not to draw the horses' attention) to try to keep from freezing to death. In the wee hours of the morning, Ortrud started her escape, inching away from the horses until she was safely on the other side of a fence where she could then speedily trek a great distance downhill to find civilization. When she finally did, she was welcomed with great amazement and nursed back to health and warmth. The camp staff told her that some of the most seasoned hikers had perished in those hills.

Seeking Saintly Wisdom

Having survived that terrifying experience, Ortrud, who had come to know St. Padre Pio and had become Padre Pio's spiritual daughter, wanted desperately to ask him if she should indeed enter the convent. She had made a promise to Jesus, after all.

By now, you must surely recognize my friend's name. This is the same Ortrud who made an appearance earlier in "Returning to the Faith" (Chapter 17) with her compelling life transformation at the age of 16 due to the tremendous power of God's unfathomable mercy, as well as the sacrificial prayers of her mother. And now, at 21 years of age, she wanted to be certain about her "call" to religious life. As soon as she finished volunteering at the camp, Ortrud was off to San Giovanni Rotondo to consult with the saint!

I'll back up now to fill you in on how this woman came to know Padre Pio in the first place. You see, Ortrud's mother had been informed by a friend about a holy monk, Padre Pio, who could read hearts, had the stigmata, bilocated, and lived in San Giovanni Rotondo, Italy. Through her mother's arrangements, Ortrud's brother and his fiancé would be married by him. This would be the first time Ortrud would lay eyes on the saint.

Ortrud shared, "As we traveled to Padre Pio's monastery, I became more and more excited at the thought of seeing a saint."

In the Presence of a Saint

"Our first experience was to be present for the opening of the church doors at 4:50 a.m. for Padre Pio's 5 a.m. Mass," Ortrud said, and she described the chaotic scene. "People started to push and shove," she recalled, "causing my brother-in-law to lose his shoe. Another person's glasses flew off." It was sheer bedlam. She had never witnessed such a scene. "Inside the church, people were racing down the middle aisle and jumping over the pews. It was like a sports event."

Padre Pio entered the sanctuary. All eyes were on the saint. Ortrud observed, "He looked old, weak, and even sickly. I could tell that he was suffering and I felt sorry for him." Though happy to be there, she thought, "It would be better for him to have some bed rest rather than to be surrounded by people who seemed more devoted to him than to Jesus and Mary." Feeling puzzled, she thought, *Why do these people bother Padre Pio, trying to talk to him and touch him?* She said, "Don't they know that we have Jesus in the Blessed Sacrament? We don't have to run after a person!"

Ortrud kept her eyes focused on the saint. She watched intently as he celebrated Mass. "Nothing extraordinary happened." She was expecting "holiness to be radiating from him." She wanted goosebumps, but there were no goosebumps. "Nothing happened inside of me." Ortrud decided that there was no need for her to ever return to San Giovanni Rotondo again. Once was enough.

On the Road Again and Again!

Prayers and persistence do pay off. A couple of years later, Ortrud's persistent and prayerful mother persuaded Ortrud to make a pilgrimage with her and a friend to see Padre Pio. It would be an awfully long trip — 230 miles on back roads in an old car, but after some discussion, they set off together. Their journey took some major twists and turns. Their 1949 Volkswagen broke down twice. Hitchhiking and sign language were required to negotiate the car repairs to get on the road again.

Still, they reached their destination at the monastery right on time — 5 a.m.! Ortrud said, "My mother was overjoyed and made a solemn proclamation, 'Isn't God good? We have arrived on time for Holy Mass!'" After Mass, providentially, they met a German woman in front of the church who knew how to get tickets to go to Confession to Padre Pio, as well as tickets to enter the sacristy where he would pass after the morning confessions.

Ortrud's mother obtained tickets, and the next morning they were ushered into the old sacristy along with about 15 other women. Ortrud shared, "It was no big deal for me. This time around I knew better than to expect anything." She said, "I knew that Padre Pio was just a human being," adding, "Yes, he might be a saint, but I felt it was selfish to bother him the way the people did." She figured she would go along to appease her mother.

Suddenly, the door opened. There stood Padre Pio. "We all knelt down for his blessing as he passed in front of each person." He stopped in front of Ortrud's mother, looked at her and blessed her. He approached Ortrud.

"Then he placed his hand on my head." Ortrud was not expecting anything. Yet, she recalled, "My whole body felt that touch. It felt like electricity going through my body and at the same time my soul was touched." Words suddenly eluded her, but words were not necessary, for she "knew that something had taken place." Immediately, she was certain that "a strong bond, a deep spiritual relationship between Padre Pio and myself had been established. He had become my spiritual father and I had become his adopted spiritual daughter. I ran outside the church and started to cry."

Back home in Austria, Ortrud could not stop talking about the saint she had just come to know through a deeply spiritual connection. So, just three weeks after her return home from San Giovanni Rotondo, she was on the road again to see the modern-day mystic, this time with her two sisters, brother, brother-in-law, and of course, her mother. They would stay for several weeks.

It was pure happiness for Ortrud. She shared, "I finally realized that the people who came to the monastery to see Padre Pio were not selfish like I had first thought. They were there for the same reason that I was there." She believed "Padre Pio was taking us closer to Jesus." She said, "Just looking at Padre Pio made you want to love Jesus more. He was like a magnet, drawing people closer and closer to God." And Ortrud couldn't get enough of him, so much so that when it was time for her family's departure home to Austria, she refused to go back.

"As a religious education teacher, I still had three weeks of vacation left and I wanted to stay as long as possible," she explained. Her family didn't understand her need to stay and tried to reason with her. They came up with some pretty good arguments. "You don't know the Italian language. You don't have money for a hotel. You don't have money for the train ticket back to Austria. You do not even have enough money for food!"

She Dug Her Heels In

Ortrud told them, "I am 21 years old, and I can make my own decisions." She shared, "I loved Padre Pio like all those crazy Italian women, and all I cared about was to be near him."

After seeing her family off, she went back to the church to pray. "When I was near Padre Pio, all of my earthly desires seemed to disappear. Being close to him was like being on a retreat." During the afternoon she began to inquire about lodging, but she couldn't afford what was available.

"I asked the German lady who had befriended me if she knew of a place I could stay overnight, but she did not know of anything."

That evening after the Benediction service, the church doors were locked and Ortrud made her way across the plaza. *What now? Where do I sleep?* She had no money for a hotel, and sleeping out in the open air under the stars made her nervous. She'd heard about snakes and wild stray dogs roaming the area.

Ortrud offered up a quick prayer for help. Right away, a young man who had been sitting on a bench under a tree got up and headed towards Ortrud.

"We talked for a few minutes, and I informed him that I had to be on my way, for I had to find a place to stay for the night." The man asked Ortrud to wait on the bench, and he would be back soon. She was tired, and the bench did seem very inviting. Ortrud sat and waited. Fifteen minutes later, the man returned.

"Come, follow me," he said. "I found a place for you to stay." He led her down a hill to the first house across from the monastery, into the house and down the stairs. The man opened the door to a furnished room with three beds. Pointing to the bed on the right, he said, "This one is yours. It is 50 cents a night." Ortrud thanked him, and he left.

Soon, there was a knock at the door. It was the young man again. He handed Ortrud two paper bags, smiled, and said, "This is for you. Good night."

"Inside the bags were two delicious sandwiches, an apple and a pear. My mind was racing. How did he know that I had not eaten a meal that day?" The next morning, an Italian lady staying at the same residence invited Ortrud to a little room and served her pasta, bread, and wine.

"*Mangia, mangia*," she said. Ortrud didn't need much encouragement; she was hungry.

She ran into the young man again later that day. Ortrud would learn that her helpful new friend was an American who was studying medicine in Rome. He had some free time before his school opened and felt inspired to spend it in San Giovanni Rotondo to be near Padre Pio.

Ortrud's delightful days in San Giovanni Rotondo, receiving Padre Pio's blessings near the sacristy and little daily wave from his window, would soon be over. It was almost time to go back home to Austria, and Ortrud didn't know how she would make the 1,000-mile trip.

The Plot Thickens!

One day Ortrud met a woman from Austria named Adelinde. They hit it off quickly, and the woman asked Ortrud to pray for Padre Pio to send her a traveling companion for her drive to Austria, for she was nervous to go alone. Well, Ortrud smiled and told Adelinde that her prayer was answered, "and that she was looking at her traveling companion." On top of that, Ortrud shared, "The idea popped into my mind that it would be great to have a man in the car, in case we had a flat tire." They agreed, and the kind American was offered a free ride to Rome.

"Leaving San Giovanni Rotondo the following week was extremely painful to me. The thought of returning soon was the only thing that made it bearable," she shared. The three traveled to Rome, and once in Rome, Adelinde excused herself to take care of some business. Waiting in the car, Ortrud suggested to the American that they pray the Rosary together.

"I led the first part of the Hail Mary in German and he answered in English." Three Mysteries into the Rosary, Ortrud could sense something had happened, but didn't know what it was.

Adelinde came back and they proceeded to the hotel to drop off the American. Ortrud said she "felt a hand on my right shoulder. It was the American." But it was a supernatural feeling. She shared, "The strange thing was that it did not feel like a human hand. I experienced the exact same powerful feeling in my body as when Padre Pio put his hand on my head." Before leaving the car, he handed her a piece of paper with his name and address, and asked for hers. His name was Germain.

Several days after Ortrud was home in Austria, the doorbell rang. "When I opened the door, there stood the American." She was dumbfounded, but at the same time wanted to introduce him to her mother. For the life of her, she could not remember his name.

Just three weeks later, he showed up again. "[His] traveling such a long distance to see me alarmed me, so I had a talk with him. I began by saying, 'I am not interested in any close relationships. I am very happy being single, and I want to remain single. I don't want to divide my love for Jesus. I like to go to church whenever I please and pray.'" She added, "I love being a religious education teacher. I would never want to take the chance of getting married. These days people make promises and later it is a different story."

Germain listened carefully, paused a moment, and then responded to each point she had made. He said to her, "You are very happy to be single, but it is also possible to be happy as a married person. You should never divide your love for Jesus. Neither would I. Rather, we would help each other to love Jesus more and more. And I would never be unfaithful to you. You have my word."

Quickly, she told herself, "Ortrud, stick to your principles. Don't give in. Don't get weak!" However, she shared, "I could feel my heart softening just a bit." Even so, she asked, "Why are we discussing marriage? I don't even know you and you don't know me."

"I know you well enough," Germain said, "that I would like to ask you to marry me. When we were sitting in the car and you asked me to pray the Rosary with you, you were the first girl that ever asked me to pray the Rosary. I knew then that I wanted you to be my wife." It turns out that at one point early on, Germain had literally bumped into Ortrud in the crowded church. Ever after, he had kept his eyes on the young woman who spent so much time in church. Hence sitting on the bench!

Off to See the Saint Again!

The next day, Germain took a train to San Giovanni Rotondo to see Padre Pio. In Confession, he told Padre Pio that he had met a girl that he wanted to marry, but that she was not sure about him. Ortrud told me, "Padre Pio, a man of few words, advised him, 'Marry her and prepare well for your marriage.'"

"Germain heard what he wanted to hear, but I still needed my own sign," Ortrud recalled.

So Ortrud set off to San Giovanni Rotondo at Christmastime. Germain was there with her. "I wanted to ask Padre Pio about marrying Germain." She was praying for the right opportunity. She said, "One day I happened to have an excellent position in the front row of a crowded sacristy. There were many other women there as well." She knew that "Padre Pio would be passing within two feet of me and at that time."

Brother Joseph Pius, a Capuchin who lived at the monastery, suddenly approached Ortrud and motioned for her to follow him. She was nervous about this idea. "I told him that I was in an excellent spot to talk to Padre Pio, but he insisted that I go with him." Not very thrilled to give up her place in the front row, she followed Br. Joseph Pius anyway.

The Door is Unlocked

Through the big church they went. The Capuchin unlocked the door to the monastery and instructed Ortrud to wait in the middle of a long hallway. A few minutes later he reappeared, this time with Germain, whom he had found in the upstairs hallway waiting with the men for Padre Pio to pass by. "He told Germain to stand next to me and then he left without any explanation." They had no time to figure out who had arranged this interesting happening because within seconds, another door opened.

There was Padre Pio, aided by two friars! They entered through the doorway. "Knowing that Padre Pio could see into the souls of people, my first reaction was to look down towards the floor and avoid eye contact," Ortrud remembered. Yet she couldn't help herself. She explained, "Instead, I looked straight into his beautiful brown eyes the entire time he was walking slowly towards us."

"When he reached us, he stopped." First, he put his hand on Germain's head, "then on my head," my friend said, "and with one blessing, he blessed us both together." Ortrud shared, "No words were spoken, no angel appeared, but I received my sign." She said, "I knew at that moment that Germain and I were meant to be together and to marry."

Ortrud was not meant to remain single or to enter religious life as a nun, but by God's amazing grace and mercy, her life would unfold in ways she could never have imagined. Stick with me, and I'll tell you the rest of the story!

Blessed Rings and Holy Promises

Every vacation, Ortrud would travel to see her saint. On August 15, 1967, Germain and Ortrud were officially engaged. "Germain had an engagement ring made for me from a gold Miraculous Medal surrounded by tiny pearls," she said. Padre Pio kept the ring in his room for many days and blessed it in time for their engagement.

The couple was wed on the Feast of the Assumption, August 15, 1968, in the church of Our Lady of Grace where Padre Pio had received the stigmata, celebrated Mass for most of his life, and heard daily confessions.

Due to poor health, Padre Pio no longer performed weddings, but he was taken in his wheelchair to meet the couple before their wedding ceremony began. On the day of their wedding, Padre Pio approached them. Germain thanked their friend, the mystic, for everything. Padre Pio blessed their wedding rings and gave them his blessing.

"Then he tapped me three times on my head. I felt as though he had opened a valve inside of me, for I felt a happiness that was indescribable." By the end of the day, Ortrud was saying to herself, "God has to take this feeling away for I feel my heart is ready to burst with joy."

Brother Joseph Pius and Fr. Ermelindo Di Capua surprised Germain and Ortrud at the wedding reception with their presence. Brother Joseph Pius made an announcement to the newlyweds: "Germain and Ortrud, I hope you will enjoy this wedding gift from Padre Pio. Because he is often sick, he no longer signs pictures or cards," he said. "Instead, we sign them for him." The brother explained further, "I asked him what I should write on the back of this picture of Our Lady of Grace, and Padre Pio answered me, 'Give me the picture and let me sign it myself.'"

Padre Pio wrote, "*Maria vi tenga stretta nel sua amore,*" which is, "May the Virgin Mary hold you tightly in her love." The bride and groom decided to forgo a lavish honeymoon and instead stayed for several weeks at the place they loved more than anywhere else in the world — San Giovanni Rotondo.

Bidding Farewell to Her Saint

One month later, they were saddened to hear that their beloved Padre Pio had died. They quickly set out to San Giovanni Rotondo to attend the funeral.

"As I stood at his coffin, I prayed, 'Padre Pio, please bless our marriage with a child,'" she said. Nine months later, their first son was born. Ortrud remarked, "It is said that our prayers are often answered in a more abundant way than what we ask. We were blessed with eight beautiful children, the last being twins." Their twins were born on the Feast of Our Lady of Grace, the patroness of San Giovanni Rotondo.

"Padre Pio didn't just bring us together," Ortrud stated. "He has taken care of us ever since. His fatherly care and love has been with us for almost 40 years of married life."

Needless to say, that lost 21-year-old woman who made that promise to Jesus to enter the convent did not enter religious life as a nun. She got married! God had another plan for her and her future family. Saint Padre Pio guided them all the way! They never really did bid "farewell," because he is still with them, leading them, guiding them.

The saints are our great intercessors. Don't forget to call upon them!

The Story Has Not Ended

Our stories are never over. They continue to unfold. In my friend Ortrud's case, as I mentioned, she didn't enter the convent, but two of her daughters did! One is a Sister of Life and one a Missionaries of Charity sister.

Our lives can seem so mysterious. Our dreams and plans appear to take on a life of their own! But God always has a plan! As it turned out, Ortrud had more than one saint in her life! Along the way, she met Mother Teresa, who arranged for Ortrud and her family to take care of lepers in Yemen and Ethiopia. Yet Ortrud didn't end up in the mission she so passionately desired. As they were about to depart for the trip, a war broke out, and the plan was immediately halted. Ortrud smiles anyway because now, years later, her daughter, Sr. Mareja, MC, is doing the work of a missionary!

Another beautiful part of the story is how the couple were blessed with unexpected twins in the end. Ortrud knew that if she had another girl, she would love to name her Gertrude, because of St. Gertrude's love for the Sacred Heart. One time in the Adoration chapel, as Ortrud was pregnant with the twins, she said out loud, "Gertrude for the Love of the Sacred Heart and Faustina for the Mercy of the Sacred Heart." Quickly she thought, *What am I saying? I don't even know if I have two girls!*

She indeed had two girls, and when it was time to give birth, Ortrud wanted the first baby to be born to be named Gertrude and the second to be Faustina.

Divine Mercy All Over Again!

Gertrude and Faustina made their First Holy Communions on Divine Mercy Sunday at the National Shrine of The Divine Mercy in Stockbridge, Massachusetts. There, they met the sister of the late Fr. Seraphim Michalenko, MIC (then-rector of the Shrine and vice-postulator for North America for St. Faustina's cause for canonization). Her name was Sr. Sophia Michalenko, CMGT, and she took a liking to 7-year-old Faustina Bianchi. Sister Sophia had never come across a girl with that name in America.

Through Divine Providence, about 20 years later, they would unexpectedly meet again, this time at a retreat. Sister Sophia remembered Faustina, saying she recognized her eyes! Sister Sophia said, "I always wondered what happened to that little Faustina." At this meeting, Faustina was a postulant in the Sisters of Life religious order, and was just two weeks shy of getting her habit and a new name.

When Sr. Sophia found this out early in their conversation, she told Faustina, "Don't you dare change your name!" She also handed the 26-year-old postulant a copy of her book, *The Life of Faustina Kowalska*. However, as nice as that sounded from Sr. Sophia, in religious life, you ordinarily have to give up your birth name and are given a new one. Still, Sr. Sophia's strong encouragement about hanging on to her meaningful name sure didn't hurt.

Later, when it came time to meet with her Mother Superior, Faustina humbly and courageously suggested that "Faustina" be considered along with "Mary" and "Maria." Of course, she mentioned "Faustina" after the other two suggestions. Her Mother Superior quickly told the young postulant that her name would be "Sr. Faustina Maria Pia, SV."

Ortrud was overjoyed when she heard the news. She told me that she had made a secret pilgrimage to the Divine Mercy Shrine and, with tears running down her cheeks, she had poured her heart out. "Please, St. Faustina, don't let her change her name!" Ortrud felt that her daughter's name was meant for her whole life — that beautiful holy name that had come to Ortrud mysteriously yet distinctly as she knelt in the presence of Jesus in the Blessed Sacrament, pregnant with her twins.

As she spoke with me, Ortrud reflected, "It's like a continuation. The Mercy of God came into my life in the most powerful way," she said, "and she [her daughter Sr. Faustina] is now telling people about God's mercy!"

You might recall that Sr. Faustina Maria Pia's mother, Ortrud, was the 16-year-old (in Chapter 17) kneeling on her living room floor and crying out, "Jesus, from now on I want to be your friend" after being pierced through when reading the words from Faustina's *Diary* printed in the pamphlet that her mother had given to her.

"God's plans are different from ours," Ortrud noted. "You look back at it — He had a plan all along!"

We each have an exquisite story. If we look closely, we might see the gorgeous golden threads of grace woven throughout. If you have trouble seeing them, perhaps you are looking at the wrong side of the tapestry. Maybe you are just looking at the tangled threads and the knots. Turn it over. You'll see God's masterpiece!

As Providence would have it, Ortrud's daughter Sr. Faustina Maria Pia, so connected to Jesus' Divine Mercy, ended up writing a beautiful prayer. It's called the "Litany of Trust." You will see it below. By the way, the little pamphlet containing that litany (given to me by Ortrud years ago) just "happened" to fall out of my bookcase when I was writing this chapter.

In writing the Litany, she set out to dispel two huge lies from the evil one. One is "God, You're not good," and the other is "I'm not good." Sister Faustina told me, "It's so precious to God that we trust Him." She shared, "It was a real grace for my own heart to write the Litany," and added, "Trust is something so longed for by God."

We must remember that Jesus told St. Faustina that the vessel that pours His amazing love and grace into us is *trust*. We have to trust God!

Pause

Take some time to ponder lessons from the saints. Think of St. Padre Pio, St. Faustina, and others. Ponder your trust or lack of trust in our Lord.

Act

Persevere — God's plan might be different from ours, but it's always better! Trust Him!

Litany of Trust

Composed by Sr. Faustina Maria Pia, SV.

In this prayer, we ask Jesus to deliver us from the things that hold us bound, and we place our trust in His promises.

From the belief that I have to earn Your love,
Deliver me, Jesus.

From the fear that I am unlovable,   *Deliver me, Jesus.*

From the false security that I have what it takes,
Deliver me, Jesus.

From the fear that trusting You will leave me more destitute,
Deliver me, Jesus.

From all suspicion of Your words and promises,
Deliver me, Jesus.

From the rebellion against childlike dependency on You,
Deliver me, Jesus.

From refusals and reluctances in accepting Your will,
Deliver me, Jesus.

From anxiety about the future,   *Deliver me, Jesus.*

From resentment or excessive preoccupation with the past,
Deliver me, Jesus.

From restless self-seeking in the present moment,
Deliver me, Jesus.

From disbelief in Your love and presence,
Deliver me, Jesus.

From the fear of being asked to give more than I have,
Deliver me, Jesus.

From the belief that my life has no meaning or worth,
Deliver me, Jesus.

From the fear of what love demands,   *Deliver me, Jesus.*

From discouragement,   *Deliver me, Jesus.*

That You are continually holding me, sustaining me, loving me,
             Jesus, I trust in You.

That Your love goes deeper than my sins and failings and
 transforms me,   *Jesus, I trust in You.*

That not knowing what tomorrow brings is an invitation
 to lean on You,   *Jesus, I trust in You.*

That You are with me in my suffering, *Jesus, I trust in You.*

That my suffering, united to Your own, will bear fruit in this
 life and the next,   *Jesus, I trust in You.*

That You will not leave me orphan, that You are present in
 Your Church,   *Jesus, I trust in You.*

That Your plan is better than anything else,
             Jesus, I trust in You.

That You always hear me and in Your goodness always
 respond to me,   *Jesus, I trust in You.*

That You give me the grace to accept forgiveness and to
 forgive others,   *Jesus, I trust in You.*

That You give me all the strength
 I need for what is asked,   *Jesus, I trust in You.*

That my life is a gift,   *Jesus, I trust in You.*

That You will teach me to trust You, *Jesus, I trust in You.*

That You are my Lord and my God, *Jesus, I trust in You.*

That I am Your beloved one,   *Jesus, I trust in You.*[104]

Here is the link to see Sr. Faustina Maria Pia, SV, on YouTube praying the Litany of Trust and explaining its purpose: https://youtu.be/tKbOi92_UNE.

A PRAYER OF MERCY

Jesus, Your ways are not my ways, but I deeply
desire Your ways — Your plan for my life.
Please have mercy upon my soul. I trust in You!
Mother Mary, help me, protect me, and guide me.
Saint Faustina, please pray for me.
Amen.

CHAPTER 27

Losing a Loved One and Widowhood

"As a deer longs for flowing streams,
so my soul longs for you, O God."

— Ps 42:1

Can we imagine seeing Jesus' empty tomb? It might cause someone's heart to jump or lead them to question their faith, since being empty meant the tomb was missing Jesus. We can't see Him. *Where is Jesus?* Our hearts can be troubled. But the empty tomb means something great: Jesus is raised up! Jesus conquered death, and He gives us life!

Jesus' Resurrection is a great mystery. We accept and believe on faith, inspired and supported by the evidence of the eyewitness testimony of those who saw and ate and drank with Him after He rose from the dead (see Acts 1:3; 2:32; 10:39-41; 1 Cor 15:1-19). His Resurrection and victory over death gives us great hope. Whatever "tomb" we are in, Jesus can reach in and give us life. We can receive the fullness of life by the gift of faith given us at our Baptism. That gift is meant to grow in our hearts.

Our lives are pierced through with sufferings and losses. Along the way, we will most likely lose a loved one to death, either tragically or peacefully. Though we mourn the losses and miss our loved ones, we know that they have entered into eternal life. Death is in fact our entrance into eternal life. It is not to be feared, for it is a part of our journey. We have to pass through it in order to reach our eternal reward.

That said, we must get our lives in order and be ready. In addition, as Christians, we are called to help others get ready, too.

Death is Our Coronation

As hard as it might be to grapple with the death of someone we know, or even with our own upcoming death, Mother Teresa called death our "coronation." When my sister Barbara was dying of leukemia, I asked the Missionaries of Charity sisters to pray for her, and I hopped on the first plane I could take to Texas. You see, my sister had beat cancer, but was then afflicted with devastating leukemia. Her doctor gave her a few short months to live. I wanted to see her and also to be of help if I could.

The MC sister I spoke with delivered some powerful words over the phone and in a letter that she quickly got off to me that also contained a relic of Mother Teresa. The very kind sister told me that she and the other sisters would be praying for Barbara and our family. She told me how Mother Teresa viewed death: "Death is nothing except going back to God, where He is and where we belong," Mother Teresa said, adding, "Death is the most decisive moment in human life. It is like our coronation: to die in peace with God."

I couldn't help but think about the thousands upon thousands of dying people that the petite nun had baptized before they closed their eyes on this life.

When I arrived at my sister's home, at Barbara's request, I placed a special blessed Miraculous Medal that I'd brought to her on the chain that she wore around her neck. I had previously placed the medal on St. John Paul II's tomb and Mother Teresa's bed when I visited Rome. I believed that powerful graces could be obtained through it with Mother Mary's intercession.

My sister and I conversed between her many naps. When she slept, I quietly prayed the Rosary and the Divine Mercy Chaplet. Much of the time, I had to repeat my prayer or start over when I lost my place. I had trouble concentrating. However, I knew that God didn't mind if I couldn't get it just right because He is a God of Love and understood that I was distraught. His concern was where my heart was, not necessarily my mind.

Mother Teresa had said, "When the time comes and we cannot pray, it is very simple — let Jesus pray in us to the Father in the silence of our hearts. If we cannot speak, He will speak. If we cannot pray, He will pray. So let us give Him our inability and our nothingness."[105] This is advice that will come in handy for each and every one of us.

It was intensely sorrowful for me to lose my sister, having to watch her suffer and wither away in her last days. However, I also felt much peace knowing that Barbara was on her way home to Heaven. My spiritual mother's words rang loudly in my ears: "Death is nothing except going back to God, where He is and where we belong." Amazingly, Mother Teresa had helped me, even after her death, to endure the loss of my sister.

Praying for the Dying and Deceased

We have a responsibility to pray for the dying and the deceased. Jesus asks this of us. His holy Mother asks us. This subject will be discussed at length in our final chapter, but we will touch upon it here. While we most likely won't be visited by deceased souls (as was Faustina), we can still pray for those who are dying and for the Holy Souls in Purgatory. Our Lady of Fatima requested these prayers.

One time, the soul of a deceased sister appeared to Sr. Faustina to ask her for a day of fasting and for Faustina to offer her spiritual exercises for the late sister's soul. Saint Faustina told the soul that she would and offered everything the following day for that soul in Purgatory.

Saint Faustina suffered for that soul. She recorded in her *Diary*, "During Holy Mass, I had a brief experience of her torment. I experienced such intense hunger for God that I seemed to be dying of the desire to become united with Him." She wrote, "This lasted only a short time, but I understood what the longing of the souls in purgatory was like" (*Diary*, 1186). She explained what happened next. "Immediately after Holy Mass, I asked Mother Superior's permission to fast, but I did not receive it because of my illness. When I entered the chapel, I heard these words: 'If you had fasted, Sister, I would not have gotten relief until the evening, but for the sake of your obedience, which prevented you from fasting, I obtained this relief at once.' Obedience has great power. After these words I heard: 'May God reward you'" (*Diary*, 1187).

We need to be generous *and* obedient souls!

Loss Through Suicide

It is very difficult for someone to talk about the loss of a loved one through suicide. Their hearts are pierced through. I know a few families who have experienced the sudden and dreadful loss of their child, spouse, or other family member. On top of that, some folks are crippled with a sense of guilt. Could they have done something or said something that would have prevented the tragedy? In almost every case, the answer would be, "No." We won't know this side of Heaven the extent of the suicide victim's terrible and perhaps unrelenting pain, or the troubles that caused them to carry out their fateful choice.

The *Catechism* teaches:

> Grave psychological disturbances, anguish, or grave fear of hardship, suffering, or torture can diminish the responsibility of the one committing suicide. We should not despair of the eternal salvation of persons who have taken their own lives. By ways known to him alone, God can provide the opportunity for salutary repentance. The Church prays for persons who have taken their own lives (2282-2283).

Father Chris Alar, MIC, director of the Association of Marian Helpers, cowrote an excellent book on the subject with

Br. Jason M. Lewis, MIC, titled *After Suicide: There's Hope for Them and for You*. In this book, Fr. Chris shares about a life-transforming conversation he had with his confessor that gave him much hope about his own grandmother's suicide.

Father Chris also talks about the importance of our prayers for the dying and deceased. He uses the example of St. Faustina discovering that her "entreaties" on behalf of the dying "open the floodgates of Jesus' Divine Mercy to such a degree that His grace is 'always victorious' when she intercedes for them." He notes that according to Faustina, our intercession can move souls to turn to God in their final moments and accept His forgiveness.[106]

Of course, there's so much more discussed in the book. Hopefully you will get a chance to read it!

Saint Faustina discussed suicide in her *Diary*. She wrote, "Once, I took upon myself a terrible temptation which one of our students in the house at Warsaw was going through. It was the temptation of suicide." Saint Faustina suffered long and hard to help save the girl. She wrote, "For seven days I suffered; and after the seven days Jesus granted her the grace which was being asked, and then my suffering also ceased. It was a great suffering. I often take upon myself the torments of our students. Jesus permits me to do this, and so do my confessors" (192).

At another time, the humble mystic pointed out that we should not presume to judge those who appear to be dying without any outward sign of repentance — which would include persons who have committed suicide — for we do not know their situations, nor do we know if they turned to God or not. She wrote in her *Diary:*

> God's mercy sometimes touches the sinner at the last moment in a wondrous and mysterious way. Outwardly, it seems as if everything were lost, but it is not so. The soul, illumined by a ray of God's powerful final grace, turns to God in the last moment with such a power of love that, in an

instant, it receives from God forgiveness of sin and punishment, while outwardly it shows no sign either of repentance or of contrition, because souls [at that stage] no longer react to external things. Oh, how beyond comprehension is God's mercy! ... Although a person is at the point of death, the merciful God gives the soul that interior vivid moment, so that if the soul is willing, it has the possibility of returning to God (1698).

In addition, we can be comforted knowing that Jesus does not tire of calling to despairing souls. Faustina recorded in her *Diary* (1486) that Jesus visited a despairing soul steeped in darkness three times to save it from the fires of hell. Jesus never rejects a contrite heart. He is merciful — He forgives!

How to Forgive God and Your Dead Brother

Even knowing all that, we might still wonder where God's mercy is when someone we love is suddenly taken through suicide. One time, I met a young woman discerning religious life (I'll call her "Laura") who'd lost her brother through suicide. She shared very intimately with me about her deep pain and loss, and how she tries to cope. I pray that her words and insights will be helpful to you.

Laura told me, "Losing my brother was one of the hardest things in my life, leaving me in deep bewilderment. It kind of knocked me off my high horse and grounded me in reality." She said it was "the reality of suffering and of the Cross, and of the truth that this life is not forever." At first, Laura could not accept her brother's death and was not able to grieve.

She shared, "I wasn't able to grieve Thomas' death right away. I was perhaps numb to the pain and didn't want to face it. It was too much to handle. I personally think I ran from the pain."

In the long run, her brother's death changed Laura's perspective. She shared, "It made me view people differently,

too, and really come to terms with God's mercy in a new way."
She felt that she had to discover God's mercy specifically as a
survival tactic.

"Because the nature of Thomas' death was so traumatic
since he died by suicide, the need to find God's mercy in all of
this has almost been necessary to stay alive." She shared, "In
fact, the only time I am able to find peace in it all is to remember that God still loves Thomas and I, and His goodness has
not changed because of his death."

Grief That Brings You to Your Knees

Needless to say, the death of a loved one is life-changing.
Laura felt "like an atomic bomb went off" in her life, an experience many of us have shared. She said, "Suddenly, I had been
thrown off kilter and had no idea what just took place. There
I was in the middle of a storm trying to regroup and figure it
all out."

Laura said, "Losing Thomas brought me to my knees. It
humbled me. It taught me how short life is and how precious
it is." She also realized how much she loved her brother. Her
brother's death deeply stirred something in Laura. She said,
"It made me need to face my own issues. I guess you might say
that his suicide was the catalyst needed to begin the process of
a deep cleaning of my own soul."

It was an arduous journey for Laura as she dealt with
intense pain and anger. She was determined to put one foot in
front of the other, even as she was groping about in survival
mode. She shared, "Honestly, up until then, I thought I was
holy and perfect — self-sufficient — such an illusion distanced
me from my very real and wounded humanity — so much in
need of God's love and mercy." She added, "Thomas' suicide
made me come face-to-face with my weakness and frailty, as
well as that of my family."

In time, Laura realized what she had to do to survive.

Her Heart Opened

"I had to rely on God and His merciful love more than ever. It was the only thing I could cling to," she explained. "See, when I feel so dark inside, it's hard to find life and light, so I go to the Cross and I remind God that this is the Tree of Life. I beg God from the depths of my grief to give me life when on the inside all I feel is death."

I'm reminded of dear Faustina and how she meditated on Jesus' Passion and death on the Cross — how she clung to Him and trusted in His mercy and love. Through her intense pain, Laura's heart opened. "Losing Thomas opened a space in my heart to love others. It created a space that could now embrace others." As hard as it was for her, she began to feel that she could "be more compassionate to others and love those who are emotionally troubled." Going through her own grief process, Laura began to "find it easier to sympathize and be with people in their pain."

Yet it has not been effortless, and the process continues. Laura shared, "The frustrating part about losing Thomas has been dealing with the emotions that come with it." For one thing, she tries not to hate herself. "There's a lot of anger and hatred towards him and my family and even myself, and sometimes God, too." She added, "There's much unforgiveness at times and despair."

She deals with anxiety, too. She shared, "Sometimes the darkness of his suicide would seem to overcome me, and it was very hard to come out of it [panic] and enter into the light of God's mercy." She continued, "Sometimes, facing Thomas' suicide makes me enter into darkness and there seems to be no way out. I have found that only when I believe in God's love and mercy for Thomas and me and my family, only then do I find the strength to move forward and to love again and to be at *peace*."

Coping

Laura shared how she tries to cope with her brother's sudden death. She said, "Sometimes the best thing is to cry and to talk to Thomas or write him a letter." She said, "Going to God with the pain is the most healing, especially to the wounds of Jesus or to His mercy."

Laura journals to "put a framework to all" her emotions "and to make them make sense." She said it helps her to learn where her anger is coming from. Laura works with therapists, participates in bereavement groups, and talks with her friends and others. She said she wasn't ready to share so much after Thomas' passing, but with time, it became easier. Laura said, "Visiting Thomas' grave has been helpful. It allows me to be close to him. I have found that talking with my family about Thomas has been most helpful." Laura also expresses herself through art or music. She said, "Using art or music to express my emotions has been a healthy outlet to the built-up emotion." She maintains "a simple prayer life," which she finds is indispensable.

Laura said, "I feel that with my grief, it has not been the novenas and Rosaries that have helped me, but the simple childlike presence I try to have before God." She shared, "Sometimes my prayer is just crying and letting God hold me." She added that her prayers are "simple, real, and vulnerable." She recognizes that everyone's prayer life is different, but she has to keep hers simple in order to function and cope.

"For me," she explained, "it has been very hard to keep up with the prayer routine I had prior to his death. I find it so hard to pray a Rosary, and if I pray one with a group, I get so distracted." She added, "Sometimes just sitting with Mary and asking her to be my Mother is the greatest help."

"It is also okay to remind oneself once in a while," Laura added, "to take it easy and to be gentle with oneself, almost talking to oneself as if one were a little child who just got hurt and needs gentle words spoken to them instead of words of anger and harsh correction." She advises, "Be gentle with yourself and please lower the expectations. It will not help in the healing if you act otherwise and will only make things worse."

"I would also suggest," she said, "that if you know someone who lost a loved one, you can talk with them. Sometimes a listening ear is all that is needed. It keeps one from feeling alone."

Laura said, "Though it has been through much pain over the past few years, I feel a lot closer to God in all this and a lot closer to the true version of myself."

When We Need Solace

Jesus told His bride Faustina, **"Lay your head on My shoulder, rest and regain your strength. I am always with you"** (*Diary*, 498). We all need a strong, loving shoulder to cry upon or simply to lean on. We should feel encouraged by Jesus' words to our sister Faustina and endeavor to lay our heads upon Jesus' mighty shoulder in our prayers and to commune with Him. When things are sad, lonely, or somehow out of control, we can turn to Jesus for strength and rest.

We might even meditate upon Jesus carrying His Cross on the holy shoulder that promises us rest and strength, and endeavor to place our heads upon His shoulder in our prayers.

Becoming a Widow

Saint Faustina wrote in her *Diary*, "Everything begins with Your mercy and ends with Your mercy" (1506). God is certainly merciful to the widow. In the Bible, we read, "A father to the fatherless, a defender of widows, is God in His holy dwelling" (Ps 68:5).

Jesus cared for His widowed mother, Mary. When He was giving up His life on the Cross, He made sure that she would be cared for. He gave the world the eminent gift of His mother:

> Meanwhile, standing near the cross of Jesus were his mother, and his mother's sister, Mary the wife of Clopas, and Mary Magdalene. When Jesus saw his mother and the disciple whom he loved standing

beside her, he said to his mother, "Woman, here is your son." Then he said to the disciple, "Here is your mother." And from that hour the disciple took her into his own home (Jn 19:25-27).

The Bible mentions 11 widows (in both the New and Old Testaments). In Scripture, we find that widows are the subject of miracles. Becoming a widow is not a vocation that most women will desire. However, it is a reality that many women will face and live out.

My dear friend and sister in Christ Mariola told me that she is still sorrowful over her husband's sudden death. She shared with me that, after his death, there is just one time she feels united to her husband: When she receives Holy Communion, that powerful Sacrament of the presence of the Lord's Body, she feels connected to him. It brings her to tears, as I have witnessed when I've been with her at Holy Mass.

Jesus Has Opened the Gates of Heaven

When we are feeling the loss of our loved ones who have gone before us, let us remember that Jesus has risen and is with us! By His Cross and Resurrection, He has opened the gates of Heaven for us and for all. He gives us great hope with regard to our deceased loved ones. Jesus continues to knock on the door of our heart. Let us welcome Him in! Let us continue to beseech Him with intercessory prayers for our deceased loved ones.

In addition, Jesus lets us know that He needs our prayers for the dying. We will discuss the dying in more depth in Chapter 34, but for now, I'd like to share with you Jesus' words. They urge us on to be more generous and selfless with our prayers for the souls who most need them.

Jesus told Faustina:

Pray as much as you can for the dying. By your entreaties, obtain for them trust in My mercy, because they have most need of trust, and have

it the least. **Be assured that the grace of eternal salvation for certain souls in their final moment depends on your prayer. You know the whole abyss of My mercy, so draw upon it for yourself and especially for poor sinners. Sooner would heaven and earth turn into nothingness than would My mercy not embrace a trusting soul** (*Diary*, 1777).

Mary's Sorrowful Heart

As we face sorrow and loss in our own life, let us meditate on the sorrows of Our Lady, and ask her assistance with our own:

Facing rejection from dear St. Joseph and possible death by stoning; taken away from your home late in pregnancy; rejected again when searching for a birthplace for the Savior of the world, you bore such sorrows in the earliest days of the Incarnation. A sword of sorrow pierced your heart when your baby was presented in the Temple. Later on, you found yourself frantically searching for your Child. Throughout His life on earth, you were feeling the sting of rejection when your Son was unwelcome by others. Finally, you had to watch as He suffered on Calvary a cruel death on the Cross. He then lay dead in your arms. Mary, you know. Pray for me, please. Amen.[107]

PAUSE

Take a few moments to give great thanks to God for your very life and for all of the blessings in it.

Act

God loves you! Rest your head on Jesus' holy shoulder often. In your own way, reach out to any widows and others that you know who have lost loved ones. They might be hiding their tears and could truly benefit from loving gestures. Continue to pray for those in need and spread Divine Mercy to all!

A Prayer of Mercy

Dear Jesus, our hearts can be easily troubled.
Yet we need to remember that Your empty tomb
means something great! You were raised up!
You have conquered death and You give us life!
Please, dear Lord, have mercy upon my soul.
I trust in You!
Mother Mary, help me, protect me, and guide me.
Saint Faustina, please pray for me.
Amen.

PART FOUR
Winter

"O Eternal Love, You command
Your Sacred Image to be painted
And reveal to us the inconceivable
fount of mercy,
You bless whoever approaches Your rays,
And a soul all black will turn into snow."

— Saint Faustina (*Diary*, 1)

Winter can be fierce where I live in Connecticut. Knowing ahead of time that it will be frigid helps lessen the anxiety over winter's approach and prods one to prepare, gathering warm essentials — just as being prepared with God's grace and trust in His mercy and love can strengthen us in the spiritual life for battles to come so that we may endure in faith, hope, and love.

CHAPTER 28

Facing My Fears

"In difficult moments, I will fix my gaze upon
the silent Heart of Jesus, stretched upon
the Cross, and from the exploding flames of
His merciful Heart, will flow down upon me
power and strength to keep fighting."

— Saint Faustina (*Diary*, 906)

At times, we might think that Jesus is asleep! He can seem
totally unaware of the stormy sea of troubles raging all
around us. Because of the storm and His seeming absence, we
can become frightened. What is missing from our hearts when
we fear? Is it faith? Is it hope? Is it love? Is it all three? How do
we face our fears?

Fear can certainly drive away our faith. It can bind us in
chains. It can smother us! Much of the time, when we fall into
fear, it is our lack of trusting God out of fear of the unknown.
Do you remember what happened to St. Peter? Jesus had been
up on the mountain praying. Out on the water, caught in a
storm, the disciples saw a strange figure out walking on the
rough waters and became terrified. Making His way towards
them and knowing of their fear, Jesus said, "Take heart, it is I;
do not be afraid" (Mt 14:27).

At first, Peter was courageous. Peter called out to the
figure, "Lord, if it is you, command me to come to you on the

water" (Mt 14:28). Peter seemed ready to risk his life in the storm, but he also wanted to know who the figure was. When Jesus called to Peter, he got out of the boat and began walking towards Jesus. The wind howled with a vengeance. As soon as Peter took his eyes off of Jesus and focused on the storm, he sank. He had not trusted Jesus, but only his own inabilities. He gave in to fear. Even so, Jesus' strong arm swiftly hoisted Peter up from the water (see Mt 14:29-31). It is what Jesus does for us, too. He wants us to trust Him with our fears and our lives.

He will always hoist us up!

Jesus asked Peter, "You of little faith, why did you doubt?" I am sure that He can ask us the same question many times a day. When they got back into the boat, the winds immediately died down completely. The fishermen began to worship Jesus after seeing Him walk on water, save Peter, and calm the sea. They said, "Truly you are the Son of God" (Mt 14:31-33).

Why Are We Afraid? Have We No Faith?

On March 27, 2020, just before Holy Week and during the writing of this book, Pope Francis walked out alone into St. Peter's Square through a steady drizzle of rain. Why was he alone? Well, during the course of Lent 2020, a deadly, novel strain of coronavirus called COVID-19 (which had originated in Wuhan, China), spread out of control and frightened the living daylights out of most of the world. It was indeed an anomalous and devastating time. The world changed dramatically. It seemed as if it all happened overnight. Many businesses were shut down. Whole countries shut down, for that matter. Holy Mass was suspended in many parts of the world for a very long period of time. The world stood still.

Pope Francis was about to deliver an important message and a powerful blessing called the *Urbi et Orbi* (meaning "to the city [of Rome] and to the world") during a time of worldwide pandemic. He read a passage from the Gospel and gave a moving homily. I believe it is fitting to mention it here in a chapter that speaks about facing our fears.

The Pope opened with a description of how the pandemic had insidiously changed our lives. "Thick darkness has gathered over our squares, our streets and our cities; it has taken over our lives, filling everything with a deafening silence and a distressing void, that stops everything as it passes by; we feel it in the air, we notice in people's gestures, their glances give them away." He explained our troubled hearts. "We find ourselves afraid and lost. Like the disciples in the Gospel we were caught off guard by an unexpected, turbulent storm."[108]

"We have realized that we are on the same boat, all of us fragile and disoriented, but at the same time important and needed, all of us called to row together, each of us in need of comforting the other." He continued, "On this boat ... are all of us. Just like those disciples, who spoke anxiously with one voice, saying 'We are perishing' (v. 38), so we too have realized that we cannot go on thinking of ourselves, but only together can we do this."

What was up with Jesus' attitude? Did He care? Pope Francis said, "While his disciples are quite naturally alarmed and desperate, he is in the stern, in the part of the boat that sinks first." Apparently Jesus was not concerned, and He slept soundly, trusting the Father. The pontiff pointed out that it was "the only time in the Gospels we see Jesus sleeping."

What happens next? "When he wakes up, after calming the wind and the waters, he turns to the disciples in a reproaching voice: 'Why are you afraid? Have you no faith?' (v. 40)."

Does Jesus Care About Us?

The disciples had not stopped believing in Jesus. In their distress, they *did* call upon Him. So where is their lack of faith? Pope Francis explained that it was in the *way* they called upon Him: "'Teacher, do you not care if we perish?' (v. 38)." The pontiff explained how that phrase hurts. "One of the things that hurts us and our families most when we hear it said is: 'Do you not care about me?' It is a phrase that wounds and unleashes storms in our hearts. It would have shaken Jesus too. Because he, more than anyone, cares about us."

The pontiff underscored our absolute need for God and for salvation. He said, "Faith begins when we realise we are in need of salvation. We are not self-sufficient; by ourselves we flounder: we need the Lord, like ancient navigators needed the stars." He encouraged us, "Let us invite Jesus into the boats of our lives. Let us hand over our fears to him so that he can conquer them."

He went on to say, "Like the disciples, we will experience that with him on board there will be no shipwreck. ... He brings serenity into our storms, because with God life never dies."

Saved by His Cross

Hanging on to what I will call the "holy hope" that comes through our Easter faith is so important. It all boils down to the gift that our Lord gave us from His Cross. In his blessing, Pope Francis explained, "The Lord awakens so as to reawaken and revive our Easter faith. We have an anchor: by his cross we have been saved. We have a rudder: by his cross we have been redeemed. We have a hope: by his cross we have been healed and embraced so that nothing and no one can separate us from his redeeming love." Pope Francis continued, "The Lord asks us from his cross to rediscover the life that awaits us, to look towards those who look to us, to strengthen, recognize and foster the grace that lives within us. Let us not quench the wavering flame (cf. *Is* 42:3) that never falters, and let us allow hope to be rekindled."[109]

Saint Faustina often felt alone in her sufferings. Ridiculed as often as she was by her fellow nuns, as well as enduring terrible dark nights in the spiritual life, she still knew wholeheartedly that she was called to suffer for the salvation of souls. Her suffering was holy since it was enveloped in God's grace and was within His will. Her suffering became redemptive and helped to convert souls when she offered it lovingly to God.

Saint Faustina boldly proclaimed a heroic desire and decision. "O Jesus, today my soul is as though darkened by suffering. Not a single ray of light. The storm is raging, and Jesus is asleep." What does the humble mystic do? Because of her faith and trust in God, she decides not to "wake" Jesus for help. Her desire and decision is heroic. "O my Master, I will not wake You; I will not interrupt Your sweet sleep. I believe that You fortify me without my knowing it" *(Diary,* 195).

The saint-in-the-making continued her praise: "Throughout the long hours I adore You, O living Bread, amidst the great drought in my soul. O Jesus, pure Love, I do not need consolations; I am nourished by Your will, O Mighty One! Your will is the goal of my existence." Faustina's sensitive, holy heart sensed the need for her prayers for the world. "It seems to me that the whole world serves me and depends on me. You, O Lord, understand my soul with all its aspirations" (*Diary,* 195).

There will be plenty of times in our lives when we feel inclined to quickly rouse Jesus — to wake Him from His "slumber" because the darkness surrounds us and our little boat is being thrashed about in the stormy sea. Other times, with God's grace, we will be able to courageously face our fears and cling to our faith — digging even deeper into our faith and trusting God. He will steady our boat and calm the raging storm. Our Lord will gently pull us into His loving arms — right up against His Sacred Heart.

Our Response to Fear

There might not ever be a way to completely escape from the fears in our lives. At times, fear seems to be lurking around every corner. The key question, though, is how we will respond. Will it be with the gift of faith? In my own life, I know that there were times when I was bound in unrelenting chains of fear because of various devastating situations that I had had to endure. I ended up in survival mode at times, just trying my best, praying, and waiting to get through to the other side of the ordeal. It was truly God's grace that got me through each time. I believe I am much stronger because of those trials.

As I wrote my memoir, *The Kiss of Jesus,* I began to see threads of God's grace woven all throughout my life. I want to let you know that God is truly with us in the dark corners of our lives, including all throughout our doubts, struggles, and fears. God is not sleeping!

When we are fearful, let us push beyond our comfort zones, and with God's grace, trust Him with all our hearts. Let us meditate on Jesus' Passion and Cross when navigating the rough seas of this world, and let us gaze upon the pierced side of Jesus, opened for us on the Cross. From His Sacred Heart and through His pierced side gushed Blood and Water as a fount of Divine Mercy for us. Let us cling to this.

Saint Faustina Sought Mother Mary When Paralyzed With Fear

Before we move on, I'd like to encourage you to try to always remember that our dear Blessed Mother is forever willing to help us through our fears. Let's not forget that Mary's help is like none other!

To whom did St. Faustina turn when, at 19 years old, she felt a rush of panic fill her heart as she sat down on the seat of the train headed for Warsaw setting out on her mission (the mammoth scope of which was not yet revealed to her)? This was right after Jesus had appeared to Helen at the dance, summoning her to follow Him in a dramatic way. The reality of what she was doing immediately set in, and she worried about her parents being upset.

Upon reaching Warsaw, when Helen walked down the metal steps of the train to the platform below, she felt a terrifying dagger of fear pierce her entirely. People were headed out of the train scurrying like ants in every direction, and Helen was at a total loss about where she should go in a city of a million people. Becoming paralyzed with fear, Helen earnestly turned her heart to her Mother in Heaven.

"Mary, lead me, guide me" was her simple, albeit fervent plea (*Diary*, 11).

Helen felt the answer rise from her innermost being. She recalled in her *Diary*, "I heard these words within me telling me to leave the town and go to a certain nearby village where I would find a safe lodging for the night. I did so and found, in fact, everything was just as the Mother of God told me" (*Diary*, 11). Mary most certainly guided her daughter every inch of the way. Our friend, the young nun-to-be, would confidently follow Mary's loving, holy guidance.

This began her amazing and courageous journey. As we know, from this point, Helen, with God's grace and encouragement from her mother in Heaven, continued to knock on convent doors until one finally opened to her.

Let us remember that we also have help in the Holy Spirit. Fear is a natural part of life. Even the apostles were afraid at times. However, after Pentecost, filled with the Holy Spirit, they left their fears in the dust and trusted God more fully. We, too, need to pray to the Holy Spirit often for courage, guidance, and enlightenment.

It's important to remember that the virtue of courage is not the absence of fear. Rather, it is continuing to trust in God and doing the right thing despite our fears. Even Jesus felt afraid in the Garden of Gethsemane of the heavy weight of the Cross He was soon to bear — yet He was committed to doing His Father's will, even if the cup could not be taken from Him.

Take some time to ponder your fears or an area in which you are struggling. Is it possible to share them with a spiritual director or priest in Confession? Can you pray to the Holy Spirit and Mary, Mother of Mercy, for guidance, help, and courage?

However, there is one fear that we might wish we possessed more fully. Saint Faustina wrote in her *Diary* that after each time she conversed with Jesus, she felt her soul was strengthened, and she was given great courage. At those times, she wrote, "I do not fear anything in the world, but fear only lest I make Jesus sad" (*Diary*, 610).

PAUSE

Take a moment to ponder your faith or lack thereof. Can you pray for an increase in the gift of faith? Turn to Jesus and Mary often.

ACT

God is not sleeping! He is here with us. Be not afraid.

A PRAYER OF MERCY

"Lord, may you bless the world, give health to our bodies and comfort our hearts. You ask us not to be afraid. Yet our faith is weak and we are fearful. But you, Lord, will not leave us at the mercy of the storm. Tell us again: 'Do not be afraid' (*Mt* 28:5). And we, together with Peter, 'cast all our anxieties onto you, for you care about us' (cf. 1 *Pet* 5:7)."[110]

Dear Jesus, please have mercy upon my soul.

Please increase my faith!

I trust in You!

Mother Mary, help me, protect me, and guide me.

Saint Faustina, please pray for me.

Amen.

CHAPTER 29
Spiritual Motherhood

"Let us pray that we women realize
the reason of existence is to love and
be loved and through this love become
an instrument of peace."[111]

— Saint Teresa of Calcutta

I love what Venerable Fulton J. Sheen communicated about how women take care of life. He said, "The man is the guardian of nature, but a woman is the custodian of life. Therefore in whatever she does, she has to have some occasion to be kind and merciful to others."[112] In other words, every woman by nature is called to be a mother. Everyone needs a mother. Ultimately, the Virgin Mary is a mother to us all.

We women fill such an important role as *spiritual mothers* to those around us, even if we are not biological or adoptive mothers — and not just for our own family members.

Spiritual Mothers Find Where the Shoe Pinches

Women have been called and gifted by God to look out for others — to love, protect, and nurture them, whether it is within their own families or simply in general. I've been known to give advice or try to help someone in need and punctuate it by saying, "It's the mom in me!"

Saint Edith Stein once remarked that women help others because they are attentive to the needs of others. Specifically, she said, "If the factory worker or the office employee would only pay attention to the spirits of the persons who work with her in the same room, she would prevail upon trouble-laden hearts to be opened to her through a friendly word, a sympathetic question; she will find out where the shoe is pinching and will be able to provide relief." She added, "Everywhere the need exists for maternal sympathy and help, and thus we are able to recapitulate in the one word 'motherliness' that which we have developed as the characteristic value of woman."[113]

She goes on to stress that our spiritual motherhood to others must not stop in our own families. She says, "The motherliness must be that which does not remain within the narrow circle of blood relations or of personal friends; but in accordance with the model of the Mother of Mercy, it must have its root in universal divine love for all who are there, belabored and burdened."[114]

This is precisely what we women are called to do. It's innate. God gives us generous hearts to take care of our world. The need is certainly plentiful. As I write this chapter, I am reminded of a time when I became a spiritual mother on the spur of the moment to a complete stranger in an airport.

Her name was April, and she was a single mother. I actually discovered her on the floor of the airport. She was rummaging through her baggage and yelling at her two small children, one a tiny tot in a stroller. I couldn't just walk by. I felt a need to help. As I got closer, I instantly recognized the little family because they had been on my first flight that day. I bent down to get at the young woman's level and asked if I could help, quickly adding that I had been on her last flight, in an attempt to alleviate her fears about some crazy person approaching her. I figured I'd establish that connection with her. It turned out that April was convinced she had left her cellphone on the plane, which had already left the terminal. I helped her to find her phone, which was in her bag all along.

Nevertheless, throughout our initial conversation, April was very agitated and seemed to be taking it out on her two young girls. That was what had initially drawn my attention to the situation. I thought if I could lend my hand somehow, if she would trust me, that I could perhaps dispel the chaos a bit and help her to calm down so that the children would be safe.

What ended up happening was so much better than I could have imagined. Initially, however, things were not pretty.

Expressing herself through some cussing and yelling, April was having trouble breathing and had to take a few puffs on her inhaler. I spoke to her calmly, and by God's amazing grace, I was able to ask her if I could give her a hug. Time stood still while the people around us rushed back and forth to make their flights. April looked up through misty eyes, nodded her head, and said, "Yes."

I gently threw my arms around her and held her a moment. Her tears let loose with heaving sighs. She meshed her petite body into mine. April caught her breath, exhaled, and revealed her pain to me, a complete stranger, but joined with her through God's grace.

"I'm going through a divorce and I have to get these kids to their father in California," she burst out. More tears, and then April disclosed the profound cause of the excruciating pain she was enduring. "My mom and my stepmom abandoned me!"

She just blurted it out. Poor April: She sobbed and melted a bit more into my embrace. I knew then how much she needed that mother's hug. And then I did what I often do: I pulled a blessed Miraculous Medal from my pocket and held it up. The words just came out of me. I said, "Here is your Mother," pointing to Mary on the medal. "She will help you mother your children."

She let out a deep sigh. "Oh! And I am Catholic!" It was as if that proclamation came from deep within her heart. Perhaps the *Catholic* in her had been buried for a while. I don't know. God does. I do know for certain that God allowed me to be a spiritual mother to this stranger at the airport. I could have easily walked by April and her children. I was supposed to be headed in another direction, but God surely had me pay attention and pause to see if I could help. In addition, I believe that Mother Mary profoundly touched April's heart through her blessed sacramental, the Miraculous Medal.

Did I get up out of bed that morning with the thought that I was going to look for someone in my travels — a total stranger — and give them a hug? No, this was absolutely not on my mind as I rushed off to the airport to take the two flights to get to my speaking engagement. I had prayed the Morning Offering as I do every day, and asked God to use me as He willed. I then prayed my Rosary and other prayers throughout my first flight before I met April.

To this day, I am deeply grateful that I didn't walk right past April and her girls. Thank the good Lord, because that little "chance" encounter could have been the spark that would help to ignite the embers of faith in April's heart. Let us pray for April and all the others in our world who are hurting and in need of help. Let us pray for God's grace to be a bright beacon of hope in their lives. God will set up the opportunities for us women to spiritually mother others. We need to trust God, to pray, and to act.

Let's now shift our focus a bit to again ponder our dear Mother in Heaven and see how we can learn from her humility and loving service to be a spiritual mother.

The Blessed Mother Washed Dishes and Swept Floors

Our Lady, whom we should revere and honor as the great Mother of God and Queen of Heaven, often profoundly practiced the virtue of humility. She set an example for us women who are searching for direction. We know that when Mary was pregnant with Jesus, she went "with haste" to visit and help her older cousin St. Elizabeth (see Lk 1:39). At Elizabeth's home, Mary was quick to pick up the dish cloth or the broom and get busy helping. If St. Elizabeth objected, her holy cousin Mary would look for opportunities to perform humble acts of service at times when it would go unnoticed. This is according to Venerable Mary of Agreda (1602-1665), who wrote much about the Mother of God in her book *The Mystical City of God*.

Mary continually consoled, strengthened, and enlivened St. Elizabeth all throughout her stay with her. She spoke to her about heavenly things, always comporting herself with great humility. Venerable Mary of Agreda wrote, "Whenever She could find an occasion, She swept the house of her relative, and always her oratory at regular times; and with the servants She washed the dishes, and performed other acts of profound humility."[115]

The venerable author explained how Mary's actions were not only loving and helpful but also an example to us about the need to humble ourselves. She wrote, "Let no one think it strange that I particularize in these small matters; for the greatness of our Queen has made them of importance for our instruction and in order that knowing of them, our pride may vanish and our vileness may come to shame." She continued, "When saint Elisabeth learnt of the humble services, performed by the Mother of piety, she was deeply moved and tried to prevent them; and therefore the heavenly Lady concealed them from her cousin wherever it was possible."[116] Mother Mary's holy life and example illustrate to us the great need for humility.

As St. Faustina penned in her *Diary*, "The floodgates of heaven are open to a humble soul." She wrote that she finally understood why there are so few saints. I'll allow dear Faustina to explain. Here she reveals the key to holiness and happiness. Her words will surely help us on our search through life:

> O humility, lovely flower, I see how few souls possess you. Is it because you are so beautiful and at the same time so difficult to attain? O yes, it is both the one and the other. Even God takes great pleasure in her. The floodgates of heaven are open to a humble soul, and a sea of graces flows down upon her. O how beautiful is a humble soul! From

her heart, as from a censer, rises a varied and most pleasing fragrance which breaks through the skies and reaches God himself, filling His Most Sacred Heart with joy. God refuses nothing to such a soul; she is all-powerful and influences the destiny of the whole world. God raises such a soul up to His very throne, and the more she humbles herself, the more God stoops down to her, pursuing her with His graces and accompanying her at every moment with His omnipotence. Such a soul is most deeply united with God. O humility, strike deep roots in my whole being. O Virgin most pure, but also most humble, help me to attain deep humility. Now I understand why there are so few saints; it is because so few souls are deeply humble (*Diary*, 1306).

Spiritual Motherhood Changes Many Hearts

Father Benedict Groeschel, CFR, used to tell the story of being scared out of his wits the day he came face-to-face with the "Wicked Witch"! The friar began his story by telling about a kind Sister of Charity named Sr. Teresa Maria, his second-grade teacher when he was still known by his baptismal name, Robert Peter Groeschel. She was a tiny woman whose radiance and gestures of joy and peace touched young Robert's heart in a huge way.

When Fr. Benedict was in the second grade, he became extremely curious about what Sr. Teresa Maria did after school. Every day, he observed her coming out of the convent carrying a tray of food and heading down a run-down street to then disappear into a tenement house. Each time, he imagined all kinds of reasons for her secret trips.

One day, the lad's curiosity got the best of him. He decided to follow her. Because of this decision, Robert would be dramatically transformed.

He trailed behind the unassuming nun on a mission from a distance. He felt like he was a detective about to solve a mystery. It was going along fine until she disappeared once again. After a moment's quandary, Robert had an idea. He had a dime in his pocket, so he decided to walk into Giuseppe's Barbershop and get a haircut, whether he needed it or not. He hopped in the chair and began his rapid-fire interrogation. Giuseppe let the cat out of the bag. He told the boy that Sister took care of an ill, elderly woman who lived on the top floor.

Robert was still curious.

He went to the back of the building, climbed up the old stairs that doubled as the fire escape, shoved a milk box under the window, and peered inside. He didn't see the sister. Instead, just inches away, the old woman was staring straight at him! Young Robert firmly believed that she was the "Wicked Witch" from the "Snow White and the Seven Dwarfs" movie! He jumped off the milk box and ran down the stairs as fast as his legs would carry him!

Upon reaching the church, Robert finally caught his breath. He instinctively dropped down on his knees. He felt safe now beneath the sweet gaze of the statue of the Blessed Mother. He instantly grew in admiration for Sr. Teresa Maria, whom he already held dear. Robert knew she was special. He thought, *She was good to the witch. Maybe if people were nicer to witches, they wouldn't be quite so bad.*

As Robert knelt there pondering it all, he heard the words, "Become a priest." He had never thought of this before. He had planned to be a fireman. The following year in third grade, a Dominican nun gave him a prayer card with the inscription, "*Ora pro me.*" That night, the young boy's father told his son to ask the sister the next day why it was in Latin.

Sister Consolata looked the young lad straight in his blue eyes and said, "Because you're going to be a priest." He kept it a secret. Eventually, it became obvious to everyone that Robert was destined for the priesthood.

Father Benedict was firmly convinced that dear Sr. Teresa Maria had so much to do with his vocation. Her example of heroic love had touched him to the core. He told the story of her kindness to the "Wicked Witch" in his homily at his first Mass, at which Sr. Teresa was present. The sisters told Fr. Benedict that the old woman for whom Sr. Teresa had been so faithfully caring for seven years was hugely anti-Catholic, very irritable, and unpleasant.

Sister had had no idea about the huge impression she was making on that curious little boy until he shared it with her so many years later. She had been trying to do her works of mercy in secret. Father Benedict said that Sr. Teresa's kind deeds stayed with him all his life. She had become a spiritual mother to him and was a great and holy influence along his pilgrimage in life.[117]

"Adopting" and Praying for Others

God urges us to use the gifts He has given us so that we can spiritually mother others. I'll never forget the day I gave a talk about the Blessed Mother and the Rosary at a parish. Afterwards, I got together with a woman (I'll call her "Ella") who had attended my talk and wanted to visit with me. First, we prayed in the church together before Jesus in the Blessed Sacrament, and then decided to go out to a local diner for a bite to eat.

Afterwards, we headed outside the diner to chat a bit more on the sidewalk on that lovely, sunny autumn day. Just then, the hands displayed on the huge clock face let me know that the town clock was about to strike 3 in the afternoon. A good reminder that the day was flying by, but more importantly, it was almost the Hour of Great Mercy! When I see 3 o'clock, I know that for me, it's time to pray the Chaplet of Divine Mercy. Jesus told St. Faustina, **"At three o'clock, implore My mercy, especially for sinners; and, if only for a brief moment, immerse yourself in My Passion, particularly in My abandonment at the moment of agony. This is the hour of great mercy for the whole world"** (*Diary*, 1320).

There are many places in the *Diary* where we learn from Jesus about the Chaplet:

[E]ncourage souls to say the chaplet which I have given to you (1541).

Whoever will recite it will receive great mercy at the hour of death (687).

[W]hen they say this Chaplet in the presence of the dying, I will stand between My Father and the dying person, not as the just Judge but as the Merciful Savior (1541).

Priests will recommend it to sinners as their last hope of salvation. Even if there were a sinner most hardened, if he were to recite this Chaplet only once, he would receive grace from My infinite mercy (687).

I desire to grant unimaginable graces to those souls who trust in My mercy (687).

Through the chaplet you will obtain everything, if what you ask for is compatible with My will (1731).

On that autumn day, as the clock struck the Hour of Great Mercy, I asked Ella if she'd like to pray the Divine Mercy Chaplet together as we walked. She and I pulled out our Rosary beads and began to pray. Thinking back now, especially after what later transpired, I wish I had snapped a picture of that clock. I wish I could describe it properly. The huge round clock face seemed absolutely stunning set against the autumn trees and sky.

Around the town green we went, praying the powerful Chaplet from Jesus. We reached a place where we could cross the street. I asked Ella if she wanted to cross or continue straight. I could see that something was going on ahead. It seemed like it might have been a couple of homeless men with their gear.

Since Ella was indecisive, I suggested that we continue ahead. If they were indeed a couple of homeless men, I wanted to at least say hello to them. We continued our Chaplet: "For the sake of His sorrowful Passion, have mercy on us and on the whole world."

As we got closer, I could see a police officer standing over a man kneeling on the ground. But before we reached them, the man suddenly exited left somehow, and I could no longer see him. He'd disappeared!

I said hello to the officer and remarked about the old, abandoned house on the left that had been overgrown with foliage for some years. I assumed it was being cleaned, since some things were strewn on the sidewalk. The policeman said that the new owner would be cleaning the house up in a week or so. He did not let on about what was really transpiring.

What's Going On?

I spotted an old, collapsed pup tent on the sidewalk amid a few odds and ends. It only took another 30 seconds for me to realize what was *actually* happening: A homeless man was being evicted from his hidden shelter on the other side of the high bushes. Apparently, he had been camping out on the abandoned property.

Ella and I continued on our way. I felt there was not much I could do since the situation was being handled by the policeman. We crossed the street and headed towards our cars. I still kept wondering if I could help in any way. Then I noticed that the policeman had left the scene.

What we observed next was incredible: We watched from across the street as the man quickly disappeared behind the tall hedges. He just walked right through them! It was like he was going into a secret garden.

We saw him emerge again. I told Ella, "I wish I had something to give him."

In a flash, I remembered something. "Oh! The cake that you packaged up for me to give to my husband! I'll get a piece of that and bring it to the man."

Ella retrieved a new bottle of water from her vehicle, and we made our way back to the other side of the green.

"Jesus in the Distressing Disguise"

Suddenly, the newly "evicted" man again emerged from the bushes. He had a beard and was wearing scruffy clothes and a knitted cap. Mother Teresa would call him "Jesus, in the distressing disguise of the poorest of the poor." He seemed to be getting his belongings out from behind the bushes and onto the sidewalk.

While Ella looked on, I went over to the young man and told him that I was sorry that he had been thrown out of his "home." He nodded and quietly looked down. I asked him what he was going to do now.

"I don't know," he said, still looking at the ground.

"Where will you go?" I ventured to ask the stranger.

"I don't know."

I felt at such a loss as to what I could do or even say that would help.

"I wish there was something I could do to help," I told him. "But, here, would you like this piece of cake?"

"No," he simply replied.

"How about a bottle of water?"

"No, thank you."

I knew he must have been upset at being thrown out of the place he had called "home," and he didn't know us, so why should he trust us? Still, I felt the need to stay with him. I stood nearby and prayed silently. I asked him his name. He told us, "Chris." I eventually ventured to ask another question.

"Do you ever pray, Chris?"

"Sometimes."

"Do you want to pray now?"

He paused and then said, "Yes."

He got up from the sidewalk. Facing him, I just naturally placed my hands on his shoulders like a mother would hold her son and began to pray.

"Our Father, who art in Heaven … ."

He prayed along with me and Ella, who was standing behind me. My heart was soaring hearing Chris pray the words of the "Our Father." I moved into the "Hail Mary" next, and he quietly prayed.

"Amen!"

"Things are going to turn around, Chris. They will. You have to have hope."

"I hope so," he told me.

"It will turn around. Keep praying. Things will get better. Ask God to help you — every day. Ask God."

My Heart Went Out to Him

I started praying aloud a prayer to God as if I were Chris, asking God to help. I wanted to give Chris an idea of a simple, heartfelt prayer — something he could say anytime.

"Please help me, God. Show me the way ... help me to get better ... ."

I asked Chris if I could give him a hug. He said I could. I hugged him tight, patting his back and praying for him. Afterwards, I even made a Sign of the Cross with my thumb on his forehead, blessing him.

Chris started eating little bits of the homemade pound cake I had given to him (that Ella had baked!). It had been resting on a napkin on one of the two big black garbage bags that contained his belongings.

Our new friend went back to stuffing a few belongings into one of his bags. But he struggled. I asked if I could help.

"Do you want me to roll up your sleeping bag, Chris?"

"Okay, thanks."

Still dressed in the good clothes that I had worn for giving the presentation that morning and my dress coat, I bent down and stretched out the worn, dirty sleeping bag on the sidewalk, all the while reassuring him that I had done this countless times before for my five kids. Perhaps it could have seemed that I was making light of his terrible situation, but it was meant to be friendly, reassuring chatter. I didn't want Chris to feel bad that I had to get down and roll it up for him.

After getting Chris' "bed" into a tight roll, I asked if I should put it into the garbage bag. He approved. As I stuffed it into the tattered bag, Chris tried to help. I could then see clearly that Chris was missing all his fingers on one of his hands except for one! No wonder he was struggling with the bag.

Chris let me roll up the second sleeping bag, too. It had seen better days. The bags and all of their contents let off foul odors. I placed the second sleeping bag into the garbage bag near the other.

Then five boys walked by. Within minutes, they did an about-face and came straight towards us, huge smiles plastered across their faces.

The mama bear in me stepped out a bit in front of Chris. I became concerned as they approached, because I feared they were coming back to make fun of the unfortunate man who was kneeling on the ground putting his things in the bags and taking little bites of the pound cake.

I became a human shield. "Hi, boys! What's up?" I asked them.

The Cavalry!

"We are Boy Scouts from Troop XYZ, and we want to offer a free meal ticket to our pasta dinner at the church tonight!" one of the boys exclaimed.

Wow! How beautiful. These boys are great!

"That is so kind of you, boys!"

I believe they thought of their work of mercy all on their own. They beamed with pride, a special sort that sprang straight from their hearts. They chatted a moment with Chris to tell him where the dinner would be held. Chris acknowledged their instructions and thanked them. And off they went! But before they did, I asked if I could snap a photo of them.

Before long, they were back with a meal ticket. Chris held it in his good hand and stared down at it for a few long seconds. We all chatted, and I thanked the boys so much for being kind to Chris. I also asked them if they pray, and if they would pray for Chris to find a place to live. They agreed!

A slip of paper fell to the ground from Chris' pocket. I picked it up and saw that it was a hospital bracelet. I asked him if it was his, and what had happened. Chris told me that he had gone to the emergency room at the hospital the night before because his legs "weren't working."

I noticed from the bracelet that he was only 39 years old. He was around the same age as my oldest son. No wonder I felt like a mother to him. Initially, I wasn't sure of his age because he appeared somewhat older, most likely due to street living and a rough life.

Again, I asked him where he might go. He said for that night he would probably sleep on a park bench. I asked if he had a pillow and enough blankets, and he said that he did. I told him that if I could, I'd come back to town that night and bring something to him.

It rained that night. Unfortunately, I was unable to go out to look for Chris to bring food or clothing. I thought about Chris being out in the cold rain, as well as all the other unfortunate souls. I was up half the night praying. A lot of it was for Chris and all those in his situation.

I have a coat and an umbrella all ready in my car ready to give to him if I see Chris again. I'll bring some food. I also have a blessed Miraculous Medal and chain that I will give to him, Lord willing.

I pray that a shelter and help can be found for Chris and others like him. We must pray for and help the unfortunate. God gave us very clear instructions when He said, "Truly I tell you, just as you did it to one of the least of these who are members of my family, you did it to me" (Mt 25:40).

Jesus told St. Faustina that He *demanded* deeds of mercy (see *Diary*, 742). We not only should trust in God's great mercy, but we also need to impart that mercy to others. Ella and I could have walked the other way. Thank God that we didn't. I feel deeply grateful that our Lord unfolded this opportunity to meet a stranger in need and to offer some kind words, a little food and water, and the chance to pray together. And may God bless those boys!

Those meager actions might seem insignificant, especially due to the seriousness of the circumstances, yet we should be

sure that our little acts of love and mercy are huge in God's
eyes. He uses them to transform hearts and souls!

God provides countless opportunities for us to perform
works of mercy for others. We need to be attentive, pray, and
act when we can.

Our Relationship with Jesus is Key in Aiding Others

Saint Faustina explained in her *Diary* how she learned
that her union with Jesus was what helped souls. At one point,
one of the sisters went to see Sr. Faustina in her cell. They
had a short conversation on obedience, then the visiting sister suddenly understood something about the actions of the
saints. She told Sr. Faustina, "Thank you, Sister; a great light
has entered my soul; I have profited much" (*Diary*, 1594).

The humble mystic Faustina pondered how Jesus worked
through her to help others and wrote, "O my Jesus, this is Your
work. It is You who have spoken thus to that soul, because this
sister came in when I was completely immersed in God, and it
was just at that moment when this deep recollection left me"
(*Diary*, 1595).

She poured her heart out to Jesus: "O my Jesus, I know
that, in order to be useful to souls, one has to strive for the
closest possible union with You, who are Eternal Love. One
word from a soul united to God effects more good in souls
than eloquent discussions and sermons from an imperfect
soul" (*Diary*, 1595).

We need to earnestly seek union with our Divine Savior.

PAUSE

Take a moment to ponder the spiritual mothers in
your life. Are you a spiritual mother?

ACT

God blesses me with feminine gifts and wisdom to pass along. I will strive to be a holy and very loving spiritual mother, attentive to the needs of others!

A PRAYER OF MERCY

Dear Jesus, thank You for all the amazing blessings in my life. Please have mercy upon my soul.
I trust in You!
Mother Mary, help me to be a more loving spiritual mother to those in my midst, protect me, and guide me.
Saint Faustina, please pray for me.
Amen.

CHAPTER 30
Becoming a Grandmother

"But the steadfast love of the Lord is from everlasting to everlasting on those who fear him, and his righteousness to children's children, to those who keep his covenant and remember to do his commandments."

— Ps 103:17-18

I don't think I will ever forget holding my grandson Shepherd for the very first time. Photos of that sweet encounter grace the top of my bedroom dresser. In one photo, it looks as if I am protecting my first little grandchild with my very life — just hours old, swaddled in his blanket and nestled against my heart as he was, completely cradled in my arms, while my eyes revealed a loving determination. Words simply cannot express how a grandmother's heart soars as she showers her love upon this wonderful and miraculous extension of herself. She brims over with a special kind of pride for her child, and for his or her new child. God gifts us with such incredible miracles of life through making us grandmothers.

Grandmothers are immensely important in a grandchild's life. Jesus Himself had a grandmother: St. Anne. A grandmother's faithful life, and later on, her memory, can certainly have a considerable effect on future generations. My own grandmother (the only one I knew because the other had passed away before I was born) was an exemplary and beautiful example of living faith to me. I observed the many sacred images around her modest home. I could hear her lively faith expressed through her interactions and conversations. Even when she was speaking Polish, I could tell that her words were filled with love!

I am sure that her lessons of love and wisdom — lived out through her continuous prayers for her family, arising from her humble heart — have made a deep impression on my heart. I often recall memories of her worn Rosary beads gliding through her aged fingers even as she conversed with family members.

The light in my grandmother's sparkling hazel eyes never failed to bring warmth to my little heart as a child. Later on, as a mother, I brought my children over to see her. As she held and gazed upon her great grandchildren, Grandma's eyes gleamed with love overflowing.

I am absolutely convinced that because of God's amazing grace, grandmothers possess the tremendous ability to powerfully nurture and shape their grandchildren's consciences. Certainly my grandmother helped to shape mine. Perhaps without knowing it, she etched an exquisite image of faith upon my heart that drew me closer and closer to God.

Let's take a look at another grandmother, a very special one: Jesus' grandmother, St. Anne!

Saint Anne, a Model of Faith

God chose the devout Jews St. Anne and St. Joachim to become the grandparents of Jesus. Before meeting one another, Anne and Joachim, who were faithful to God in all things, had prayed to find a holy spouse. Their relationship came about because of God's mysterious and truly amazing providence. Each of their prayers were presented to the throne of God at the exact same time. The mystic Venerable Mary of Agreda, blessed with visions and locutions, speaks of this in *The Mystical City of God.*

Anne and Joachim, who continuously prayed for the coming of the Messiah, never dreamed that they would somehow be so closely connected to the Anointed One and actually become a part of His family (aside from the fact that they, too, were among the Chosen People).

Together in marriage, Anne and Joachim prayed that they would be blessed with a child. Even after 20 years of praying every day, still they had no child to fill their arms and their hearts, to kiss, and to teach. Anne was considered infertile. The couple never gave up praying, however. The townspeople scorned them and ridiculed them for being childless, saying it was a punishment from God. Yet all along, Anne and Joachim kept quiet, humble, and holy. They beseeched God with all their hearts and trusted in His holy will for them — no matter what it might be.

One time, as Joachim prayed in the Temple, a priest came over, rebuked him, and told him to leave, saying he was not worthy to be there and not pleasing to God, as he was childless. Joachim prayed some more and left the Temple in sorrow, returning to his farm where he spent time in solitude, begging God to be good to his wife, Anne, even if he was not worthy of a child.

Through God's Providence, love, and mercy, Anne and Joachim's prayers were miraculously answered. Their patience and perseverance were rewarded in a way that they could never have imagined — not in a million years. The Archangel Gabriel visited Anne as she was deep in contemplation of the mystery of the Incarnation. Gabriel told her that the Almighty was pleased with her prayers. Can we even imagine this? Joachim received a visit from the Archangel, as well!

Gabriel had been instructed by the Holy Trinity, "Promise them, that by the favor of our right Hand they will receive the Fruit of benediction, and that Anne shall conceive a Daughter, to whom We give the name of MARY" (emphasis in original).[118] The extraordinary impact of this news required the Holy Spirit to support Anne. Otherwise, she would have fainted from joy when she was also told by Gabriel that the baby would be the

Mother of the Messiah! Anne would keep this a secret from Joachim, who would not learn about Mary's wondrous holy role until his last days. The couple was told to continue to pray and wait.

God's appointed time arrived, and Mary was conceived in St. Anne's womb. Joachim and Anne rushed to the Temple to give thanks and praise. They were inspired to promise that very day that they would offer their daughter, Mary, to God's service in the Temple of Jerusalem. They vowed that each year on the same day, they would pilgrimage to the Temple for a day of prayer and thanksgiving, offering gifts and alms. They never ceased to return each year until their deaths.

It was at 12 in the evening, with a thousand holy angels all around, when the holy Mother of God was born of St. Anne. The angels had been assigned by God long before to protect Anne and the unborn Mary. After Mary was born, angels watched and listened as St. Anne swaddled Mary and, through tears of joy, offered her infant to God.

"Lord of infinite wisdom and power, Creator of all that exists," St. Anne lovingly cried out, "this Fruit of my womb, which I have received of thy bounty, I offer to Thee with eternal thanks, for without any merit of mine Thou hast vouchsafed it to me." She continued, "Dispose Thou of the mother and Child according to thy most holy will and look propitiously down upon our lowliness from thy exalted throne." She prayed, "Be Thou eternally blessed, because Thou hast enriched the world with a Creature so pleasing to thy bounty and because in Her Thou hast prepared a dwelling-place and a tabernacle for the eternal Word … Give me, O my Lord and King, the necessary enlightenment to know thy Will and to execute it according to thy pleasure in the service of my Daughter."[119]

Let us endeavor to call upon good St. Anne for her mighty intercession for ourselves and our families.

God Chooses Our Family

You know, God actually chooses our family. Did you ever wonder how the many different personalities of your family members ended up in one family? God chose them! He places us all within our domestic churches where we work out our salvation with one another. The *Catechism* tells us, "'The Christian family constitutes a specific revelation and realization of ecclesial communion, and for this reason it can and should be called a *domestic church.*'[120] It is a community of faith, hope, and charity; it assumes singular importance in the Church, as is evident in the New Testament" (2204, emphasis in original).

It is rather fascinating to ponder the fact that God has handpicked our family members with all their varying strengths and weaknesses to work together, complement one another, love one another, and help one another to get to Heaven. Our Christian family is very important to society. The family is the basic cell of society. As St. John Paul II pointed out, "As the family goes, so goes the nation, and so goes the whole world in which we live."[121]

We must live vibrant lives and be an example to the world. The *Catechism* states:

> The family is the *original cell of social life.* It is the natural society in which husband and wife are called to give themselves in love and in the gift of life. Authority, stability, and a life of relationships within the family constitute the foundations for freedom, security, and fraternity within society. The family is the community in which, from childhood, one can learn moral values, begin to honor God, and make good use of freedom. Family life is an initiation into life in society (2207, emphasis in original).

It is important to remember that while we are making our way to Heaven in our domestic churches, we are surely works in progress. The sparkling halos are not yet hovering over our heads! Our family might not (yet) resemble a page out of *Butler's Lives of the Saints*, but might look more like "Freaky Friday"!

We fall, we fail. We get up and try again. We need to strive for holiness, and not to become despondent when it seems like our own family is going to hell in a handbasket! We all were given free will, and so at times, some family members might stray away from or even turn their backs completely on the Catholic faith in which they were raised. We need to keep moving forward in faith and continue to pray fervently, which will set a valuable example.

I believe that grandmothers can have a tremendous effect on our families. Our earnest, loving prayers, as well as the small, ordinary sacrifices we make for the conversion or reversion of loved ones will surely pull at God's ear and tug at His Heart.

Let's also be mindful that Jesus is full of mercy! We can call upon His loving mercy often for our own souls and the souls of all of our family members, praying along with St. Faustina: "God of great mercy, who deigned to send us Your only-begotten Son as the greatest proof of Your fathomless love and mercy, You do not reject sinners; but in Your boundless mercy You have opened for them also Your treasures, treasures from which they can draw abundantly, not only justification, but also all the sanctity that a soul can attain. Father of great mercy, I desire that all hearts turn with confidence to Your infinite mercy. No one will be justified before You if he is not accompanied by Your unfathomable mercy. When You reveal the mystery of Your mercy to us, there will not be enough of eternity to properly thank You for it" (*Diary*, 1122).

Blessings Galore!

Whether you are already a grandmother or are praying for the day that you will become one, I can assure you that a great abundance of blessings is wrapped up in this wondrous vocation. Possibly you have envisioned your grandchild nestled near your grateful heart, pondered your grandchild's future, or pictured yourself teaching him or her the Catholic Faith. At every age and stage, your influence can have a powerful effect and help to shape their consciences. Your fervent prayers help establish a firm spiritual foundation in your grandchild. No matter if you live close by or far away, your loving prayers do make a huge difference.

Pause

Reflect upon your own grandmother and the blessedness of a family, which is the original cell of society. Ponder ways that you can help protect the family.

Act

There is nothing like the love of a grandmother and a grandchild! Relish it! Pray for all grandmothers.

A Prayer of Mercy

Jesus, help me to be the grandmother that
I should be (if that is Your holy will for me).
Please have mercy upon my soul.
I trust in You!
Dear St. Anne, please pray for me.
Mother Mary, help me, protect me, and guide me.
Saint Faustina, please pray for me.
Amen.

CHAPTER 31
Menopause and Retirement

"So we do not lose heart. Even though our outer nature is wasting away, our inner nature is being renewed day by day. For this slight momentary affliction is preparing us for an eternal weight of glory beyond all measure, because we look not at what can be seen but at what cannot be seen; for what can be seen is temporary, but what cannot be seen is eternal."

— 2 Cor 4:16-18

Menopause

You've surely heard of those dreaded hot flashes. Perhaps you yourself have experienced them — disturbing your sleep, waking you up, making you cranky! However, hot flashes are not the only symptom of menopause. A lot more goes on in our bodies as the production of estrogen and progesterone change: Monthly cycles transition, mood swings erupt, our bones might become more breakable, and so much more.

It's important not to think of menopause as a disease or illness. We might choose to treat some of the symptoms of menopause (hopefully in a natural way), but menopause is a natural part of our lives as women. Even so, it is a time of life that many women secretly dread because they fear it's an unmistakable sign of old age. Sometimes, a woman feels like *less* of a woman because, for instance, the severe hormonal changes cause her to no longer be able to have a baby. On the other hand, some women are immensely grateful that they'll no longer experience painful menstrual cycles and bloating.

Truth be told, we pass through menopause to embark upon a brand-new chapter in our lives. It's certainly also a time when we might experience a variety of transitions, not just physical ones. We might need to suddenly take care of elderly relatives, see our adult children out on their own, or retire from employment or be getting ready to do so. This can also be a time of added blessings — we might become a grandmother! Now, that is truly an incredible blessing, as I discussed in the last chapter!

Our lives are changing. Let's be positive, prayerful, enjoy, and keep busy!

Even with a good attitude, there are times when our lives can be lonely. It's good to ponder what we will do if we find ourselves in this situation. We might have an apathetic spouse. Adult children might not regularly stay in touch, or you might be concerned about their choices and the fact that they are away from the Church. Military women are often transplanted and might not have Catholic friends — their sisters in Christ — nearby with whom to share the faith.

There are many reasons that we might feel alone, and there will always exist trials and troubles. The important thing is how we respond. Saint Faustina wrote in her *Diary*, "O truth, O thorny life, in order to pass through you victoriously it is necessary to lean on You, O Christ, and to be always close to You" (*Diary*, 1654).

We need to lean on our Lord — always.

Retirement

Planning for our retirements could be considered a serious business. Many folks take it quite seriously because they want to be protected, to have enough put away for an oftentimes uncertain future. Others might not be as fortunate as to be able to put money aside, since they need what they have for their everyday life. That said, I believe that we can get too carried away with "socking away" for the future.

Am I irresponsible in stating such a thing? I just wish to point out that I believe it is important to be prepared and responsible, but at the same time, we need to recognize that money isn't everything. We might only have today! As you might have seen in another part of this book, I mentioned that we should live our lives in such a way that we are ready to meet our Maker today!

So, yes, plan for your future as you think prudent and necessary, but also live in the present moment, getting your soul prepared for the future. Our souls are most important. We should never neglect our soul while we provide for our body.

In Ecclesiastes (3:1-8), we learn that everything has a time. It gives us something to ponder:

> For everything there is a season, and a specific time and reason for every matter under heaven:
>
> > a time to be born, and a time to die;
> > a time to plant, and a time to pluck up
> > what is planted;
> > a time to kill, and a time to heal;
> > a time to break down, and a time to build up;
> > a time to weep, and a time to laugh;
> > a time to mourn, and a time to dance;
> > a time to throw away stones, and a time to
> > gather stones together;
> > a time to embrace, and a time to refrain
> > from embracing;
> > a time to seek, and a time to lose;
> > a time to keep, and a time to throw away;
> > a time to tear, and a time to sew;
> > a time to keep silence, and a time to speak;
> > a time to love, and a time to hate;
> > a time for war, and a time for peace.

New Adventures and Still Growing in Faith

At this time of our lives, we are still learning and growing. Hopefully, we will always be prepared for surprises as new chapters unfold.

Let's take a look at some holy advice from dear sister Faustina, as well as another favorite saint: Women learn in silence.

Turning the pages in our lives and embarking upon new chapters should give us a reason to pause and ponder ways in which to get our souls in order. Saint Faustina knew a thing or two about the necessity of silence in the spiritual life. She wrote, "Silence is so powerful a language that it reaches the throne of the living God. Silence is His language, though secret, yet living and powerful" (*Diary*, 888).

As we women search and perhaps transition to a slower pace in our later years, we can listen to some wise words from our sister Faustina. In May one year, the young mystic became very dedicated to being extra silent. She wrote, "The flower which I lay at the feet of the Mother of God for May is my practice of silence" (*Diary*, 1105).

At another time, St. Faustina wrote about what she herself had learned while silently in union with Jesus. "Silence is a sword in the spiritual struggle. A talkative soul will never attain sanctity. The sword of silence will cut off everything that would like to cling to the soul." She knew all too well that women are sensitive and might react too quickly at times. This can occur especially when we are corrected or criticized. Our mystic friend stated, "We are sensitive to words and quickly want to answer back, without taking any regard as to whether it is God's will that we should speak. A silent soul is strong; no adversities will harm it if it perseveres in silence" (*Diary*, 477).

She gives further encouragement about the workings of the Holy Spirit in silence. "The silent soul is capable of attaining the closest union with God. It lives almost always under the inspiration of the Holy Spirit. God works in a silent soul without hindrance" (*Diary*, 477).

I don't know about you, but I sure want to practice much more silence. I desire to get my soul in order.

Another Friend of Silence

Saint Teresa of Calcutta (I still like to call her Mother Teresa) was another friend of silence and spoke about it often. She taught her sisters the great need for silence in which to hear God speak to our hearts. She said, "I always begin my prayer in silence, for it is in the silence of the heart that God speaks."[122] If we are always busy and fail to pause to speak to and listen to our Lord and Creator, we will quickly become lost! Trust me: I understand a woman's hectic and sacrificial life, yet if we don't make time for prayer and Liturgy, we'll surely venture off the path.

This same petite and feisty saint reminded us, "You can pray while you work. Work doesn't stop prayer and prayer doesn't stop work." She explained, "It requires only that small raising of the mind to him: I love you God, I trust you, I believe in you, I need you now. Small things like that. They are wonderful prayers."[123]

This is really how we women can pray throughout our busy and not so busy days. In addition, we need to make sure that we carve out regular times of silent prayer wherever possible.

PAUSE

Ponder ways in which to get your soul in order. Can you plan times of quiet meditation? Will you look to Jesus, Mary, and the saints for direction?

ACT

Our Lord knows everything about your past, your present, and your future. Trust Him with all your heart.

A PRAYER OF MERCY

Dear Jesus, take me by the hand as I make
my way through this time of my life.
Please have mercy upon my soul.
I trust in You!
Mother Mary, help me, protect me, and guide me.
Saint Faustina, please pray for me.
Amen.

CHAPTER 32
Aging

"Is wisdom with the aged, and
understanding in length of days?"

— Job 12:12

When we gaze into a mirror, it's possible we see an older version of who we think we are. The years pass quickly — oh, too quickly! Perhaps more swiftly than we imagine. One time, I visited an elderly woman at a nursing home, and we took our picture together. I showed the photo to her on my cellphone, and heard a totally unexpected reaction from my 89-year-old friend.

"That's not me! How could it be? Where did you get that picture?" She just couldn't understand. Apparently, she had another version of herself in her mind — a younger self. Her disbelief about the reality of her appearance could have been caused by her progressing dementia. However, I suspect that most all of us have a younger version of ourselves in our minds, or perhaps wish that we could be younger.

Speaking of aging, you might be interested in this chapter because you desire to better prepare for the aging stage of your life. However, it's possible that you would like to learn more so that you can help other women who are in this stage of life. Whatever the case may be, allow our sister Faustina and St. Peter to impart marvelous wisdom to your heart and soul.

Let's take a look.

"Suffering is a Great Grace"

Saint Faustina explained something rather profound that could sound a bit ironic. She wrote, "Suffering is a great grace; through suffering the soul becomes like the Savior; in suffering love becomes crystallized; the greater the suffering, the purer the love" (*Diary*, 57).

Let's pray and let that sink in.

As we age, we might begin to feel sorry for ourselves. Aches and pains, sorrows, and sicknesses, as well as feelings of abandonment by friends or loved ones who do not quite understand us can be crippling. Yet our sister Faustina tells us, "Sufferings, adversities, humiliations, failures and suspicions that have come my way are splinters that keep alive the fire of my love for You, O Jesus" (*Diary*, 57).

As the young nun grew in holiness, she understood more intimately both the power of and need for redemptive suffering. This whole notion of desiring or needing suffering might seem quite odd. Why do we need suffering?

God allows us to endure sufferings in life for many reasons. One reason is to help us grow closer to Him — to depend upon Him, for He is God. Another reason is to realize that we absolutely need Him. We are not invincible! God also allows us various sufferings to help mold us into someone who is more like God!

We could pause to ponder the fact that we might not stay on the straight and narrow road to Heaven if we are distracted with too many pleasures and luxuries. It's not that He doesn't want us to be happy or enjoy pleasures. No, God is not a masochist! He wants us to get to Heaven to be happy with Him forever, but He also knows fallen human nature. He knows that we are weak and will fall many times. He wants to help us!

Another very good reason for suffering is so that we can lovingly offer it all to our Savior, our Lord Jesus Christ, and ask Him to make it redemptive so that our souls and the souls of others will benefit.

"You Shall Be Holy, for I Am Holy"

Saint Peter, when speaking of the hope of eternal life, preached, "In this you rejoice, even if now for a little while you have had to suffer various trials, so that the genuineness of your faith — being more precious than gold that, though perishable, is tested by fire — may be found to result in praise and glory and honor when Jesus Christ is revealed" (1 Pet 1:6-7).

Saint Faustina didn't always embrace suffering in her life. It frightened her. So please don't lose heart or think that it is impossible to aspire to the virtues that she eventually acquired. Take a look at what she penned in her *Diary*:

> At the beginning of my religious life, suffering and adversities frightened and disheartened me. So I prayed continuously, asking Jesus to strengthen me and to grant me the power of his Holy Spirit that I might carry out His holy will in all things, because from the beginning I have been aware of my weakness. I know very well what I am of myself, because for this purpose Jesus has opened the eyes of my soul; I am an abyss of misery, and hence I understand that whatever good there is in my soul consists solely of His holy grace. The knowledge of my own misery allows me, at the same time, to know the immensity of Your mercy. In my own interior life, I am looking with one eye at the abyss of my misery and baseness, and with the other, at the abyss of Your mercy, O God (*Diary*, 56).

Saint Faustina felt frightened and disheartened. What did she do? She "prayed continuously." She asked Jesus "to strengthen" her "and to grant" her "the power of his Holy Spirit" that she "might carry out His holy will in all things." Prayer is always the answer. Seeing ourselves for who we are (that is, a weak creature who needs God) will greatly help us on this precarious pilgrimage through life. At this point in our lives, we are heading for the finish line. We should pray for the grace we need to become more humble and open to God's graces today and every day of our lives.

During this special stage of our lives, we can heed the words of St. Peter, who preached, "Therefore prepare your minds for action; discipline yourselves; set all your hope on the grace that Jesus Christ will bring you when he is revealed" (1 Pet 1:13). He explained, "Like obedient children, do not be conformed to the desires that you formerly had in ignorance. Instead, as he who called you is holy, be holy yourselves in all your conduct; for it is written, 'You shall be holy, for I am holy'" (1 Pet 1:14-16).

During this chapter of our lives, when we are aging and getting closer to our "coronation," as Mother Teresa called it, we certainly need to pray more and to trust God. We can ask Him for the graces we need.

Mother Mary Shows Us the Cross

Saint Faustina, who often meditated upon Jesus' Passion, once saw a vision of the Mother of God holding the Infant Jesus. A moment later, the Infant vanished. Faustina wrote, "[A]nd I saw the living image of Jesus Crucified. The Mother of God told me to do what She had done." Mother Mary told her daughter that, even when she was joyful, she should always keep her eyes on the Cross. Mary told her that "the graces God was granting" her were not for her alone. They were for "other souls as well" (*Diary*, 561).

Faustina had an amazing spiritual director. Not only did our Lord supply Blessed Fr. Michael Sopoćko to be her director, a priest who finally believed her revelations, but Jesus also gave His dear mother to guide His bride. Imagine being personally led by the Blessed Virgin Mary!

Our Lady told Faustina, *"My daughter, at God's command I am to be, in a special and exclusive way your Mother; but I desire that you, too, in a special way, be my child"* (*Diary*, 1414).

Saint Faustina referred to Our Lady as her "Instructress." I will get to that in a moment, but first, a bit about the Virgin Mary. We know that from early centuries, the Blessed Mother was regarded as the perfect model of evangelical life, completely docile to the work of the Holy Spirit. She was perfectly in communion with her Son Jesus' mission and totally obedient to the will of God in all things. She was sinless and remained purely humble and holy.

On May 26, 1938, the Feast of the Ascension, the pupil Faustina wrote in her *Diary* about Mary's great love for Jesus and her complete serenity in carrying out God's plans:

> Today I accompanied the Lord Jesus as He ascended into heaven. It was about noon. I was overcome by a great longing for God. It is a strange thing, the more I felt God's presence, the more ardently I desired Him. Then I saw myself in the midst of a huge crowd of disciples and apostles, together with the Mother of God. Jesus was telling them to … **Go out into the whole world and teach in My name.** He stretched out His hands and blessed them and disappeared in a cloud. I saw the longing of Our Lady. Her soul yearned for Jesus, with the whole force of Her love. But She was so peaceful and so united to the will of God that there was not a stir in Her heart but for what God wanted (1710).

The young mystic confidently entrusted her spiritual life to the Mother of God. She had known Mary ever since she was a tiny babe. Her father, Stanislaus Kowalski, had a custom of loudly singing praise to Mary in the wee hours of the morning. The devout family also shared other customs, including praying the Rosary together. They knelt every night in front of a statue of Mary, which was next to a crucifix in their living room. In warm weather, they gathered to pray around a small shrine to Our Lady that hung from a pear tree. Our sister Faustina was accustomed to turning to Mary in every need.

I mentioned "Instructress" earlier. Saint Faustina wrote, "Mary is my Instructress, who is ever teaching me how to live for God. My spirit brightens up in Your gentleness and Your humility, O Mary" (*Diary*, 620). Mary gave her daughter guidance in her personal life and in the apostolic mission of proclaiming the great mystery of Divine Mercy to the world.

Jesus also tasked Faustina with preparing the world for His Second Coming. Can we even imagine this responsibility? The Blessed Mother told her daughter, *"I gave the Savior to the world; as for you, you have to speak to the world about His great mercy and prepare the world for the Second Coming of Him … Speak to souls about this great mercy while it is still the time for* [granting] *mercy."* And Mary gave a sobering warning. The Mother of God told her, *"If you keep silent now, you will be answering for a great number of souls on that terrible day"* (*Diary*, 635). Jesus Himself had also told the young mystic that she would be responsible for souls. As stern as this warning may seem, Heaven had a plan, and Faustina was the one chosen to carry it out. Jesus and Mary were guiding her to stay the course.

Though your life will be different in many ways from our sister Faustina's, you, too, can call upon Mother Mary's assistance and learn from the heavenly wisdom that she taught her pupil. There's much that we can all apply to our own spiritual lives.

Make Me Strong, Lord!

Since she suffered from frail health, St. Faustina asked Jesus many times to make her strong enough to receive Holy Communion. Her doctor and superiors kept a close eye on her. If her temperature was elevated by just one degree, she was to stay in her cell and not go down to the chapel. One time, St. Faustina begged Jesus, "My Master, I ask You with all my thirsting heart to give me, if this is according to Your holy will, any suffering and weakness that You like — I want to suffer all day and all night — but please, I fervently beg You, strengthen me for the one moment when I am to receive Holy Communion" (*Diary*, 876).

She went on to explain that Holy Communion was not brought to the sick at the convent. Therefore, she needed strength to get to the chapel to receive her Lord and Spouse. The young mystic beseeched Him, "O my sweet Spouse, what's the good of all these reasonings? You know how ardently I desire You, and if You so choose You can do this for me."

I think we can learn much from this young mystic who wore her heart on her sleeve for her Spouse. And her loving persistence moved Jesus' Heart! The next morning, she felt perfectly fine to receive Holy Communion. Then her suffering, fainting, and frailties returned when she was back in her cell.

Our friend Faustina wrote, "But I had no fear ... because I had been nourished by the Bread of the Strong" (*Diary*, 876).

When Suffering Exceeds Our Strength

Jesus told His bride Faustina, "**[W]hen it seems to you that your suffering exceeds your strength, contemplate My wounds, and you will rise above human scorn and judgement. Meditation on My Passion will help you rise above all things**" (*Diary*, 1184).

Jesus also told the young mystic something that should surely help us all: "**My daughter, meditate frequently on the sufferings which I have undergone for your sake, and then nothing of what you suffer for Me will seem great to you. You please Me most when you meditate on My Sorrowful Passion. Join your little sufferings to My Sorrowful Passion, so that they may have infinite value before My Majesty**" (*Diary*, 1512).

Preparing for Eternal Life

The suffering that we undergo now is a preparation for eternal life. We must remember that things did not look very good on Good Friday afternoon, when Jesus was hanging on the Cross. However, we know that the Gospels end well: Jesus rose from the dead! At times in our own lives, it seems like something we are enduring is the end of the world — everything is terrible, beyond redemption, and to all appearances, hope is lost forever. I have felt this way numerous times throughout my life. Thankfully, for the most part, they were fleeting moments of downhearted anguish, though there were times of much longer suffering. Each time, no matter the duration, I learned that it *did* pass! It was not the end of the world! God was always with me. I just couldn't see or hear Him in the darkness.

At these times, we need to endeavor to search for God with the eyes of faith and patiently wait for Him. We should never lose hope or allow the prevailing circumstances, whatever they may be, to cause us to despair. On the other hand, we need to be always ready to meet our Maker. We need to live our lives in this manner every day.

Are we ready to meet God? It's a question we must ask ourselves. If we are not ready, we need to work on it. It's essential to strive to recognize the fact that abundant grace is hidden in suffering. Grace is available to us for the asking. Jesus is all about love and mercy. He desires that we trust Him with our lives and respond to Him lovingly when facing difficult situations. Jesus, the Divine Physician, knows exactly what we need and when we need it. Let us strive to desire His holy will in our lives and not our own will.

I'm reminded of St. Claude de la Colombière, St. Margaret Mary Alacoque's spiritual director. Saint Margaret Mary had received the great Sacred Heart apparitions of Jesus. In a letter written towards the end of St. Claude's life when he was trapped in debilitating illness, he told the mystic that he was convinced that his ill health was a mercy from God, and absolutely necessary for his salvation! I am typing these words on the Solemnity of the Most Sacred Heart of Jesus. It's no wonder I'm pondering these two saints today!

Specifically, the French saint wrote:

> I cannot achieve this selflessness, which should give me access to the Heart of Jesus Christ, and I am therefore very far away from this Heart. I can see clearly that if God does not have mercy on me I will die in a state of complete imperfection. It would be

extremely sweet to me if I could at last, after so much time spent in religious life, discover by what means I could acquire complete selflessness. Ask of our good Master for me that I do nothing against his will and that in all the rest he disposed me according to his gracious will. Please thank him for the state in which he has put me. Ill health was absolutely necessary for my salvation; without it I do not know what I would have become. I am convinced that it is one of the greatest mercies that God has shown me.[124]

Set Ajar the Door of the Heart

Speaking of approaching the end of our lives, St. Faustina was absolutely convinced that God's mercy is always available to us. The humble mystic proclaimed, "All grace flows from mercy, and the last hour abounds with mercy for us" (*Diary*, 1507). Many people, after living questionable lives, give up on their salvation. They think it's too late. The truth is, though, that it's never too late, up until our dying breath.

Our Polish friend gave this encouragement: "Let no one doubt concerning the goodness of God; even if a person's sins were as dark as night, God's mercy is stronger than our misery." Saint Faustina told us what we are to do: "One thing alone is necessary: that the sinner set ajar the door of his heart, be it ever so little, to let in a ray of God's merciful grace, and then God will do the rest" (*Diary*, 1507).

However, Faustina also gave a warning: "But poor is the soul who has shut the door on God's mercy, even at the last hour." She knew how this pained our Lord. She continues, "It was just such souls who plunged Jesus into deadly sorrow in the Garden of Olives; indeed, it was from His Most Merciful heart that divine mercy flowed out" (*Diary*, 1507).

A "Drop" of Suffering at a Time

At times, the winding path of our life seems so mysterious. *How did I end up here? I did not see this coming.* We might ask ourselves. *How did I survive that crisis way back when? Why this new one?* Our loving Divine Physician, according to St. Faustina, doles out the "cup of bitterness" in drops.

I will explain.

The young mystic shared in her *Diary* her prayers to Jesus, sentiments about her life, and a message that encompasses all our lives. Faustina said, "O Christ, if my soul had known, all at once, what it was going to have to suffer during its lifetime, it would have died of terror at the very sight; it would not have touched its lips to the cup of bitterness" (*Diary*, 1655).

Saint Faustina explained further, "But as it has been given to drink a drop at a time, it has emptied the cup to the very bottom. O Christ, if You Yourself did not support the soul, how much could it do of itself?" She continued, "We are strong, but with Your strength; we are holy, but with Your holiness. And of ourselves, what are we? — less than nothing ..." (*Diary*, 1655).

Christ strengthens us! He supports us! We can be strong with Christ's strength and holy with His holiness. Saint Faustina discovered and experienced profound consolation within suffering for and with Jesus. She was a mere 33 years old when she died on October 5, 1938, succumbing to the ravages of tuberculosis. She was the same age as Jesus was when He left this world, dying for us on the Cross.

Our sister Faustina offers encouragement to us through her intimate words to her Spouse, which she recalled in her *Diary*: "Jesus, how truly dreadful it would be to suffer if it were not for You. But it is You, Jesus, stretched out on the cross, who give me strength and are always close to the suffering soul. Creatures will abandon a person who is suffering, but You, O Lord, are faithful ..." (*Diary*, 1508).

Saint Faustina's frequent meditation on her Savior's sacred wounds pleased Jesus, helped to convert souls, and gave the young mystic the strength she so desperately needed.

Our Lord is always faithful. As Faustina discovered, He is our only true Friend.

Trusting Jesus

If we haven't yet learned to trust God with our lives, it's time that we do so now. After all, the pages are turning faster in our "book of life." We must trust God with all our heart. Saint Faustina can teach us quite a bit about trusting God. As we know, she was often plagued with doubt. This wasn't simply because she didn't believe that our dear Lord was going to come through with something. The doubt that bothered Faustina came in the form of a suffocating dark cloud that spiritually descended upon her. Perhaps it was from the evil one. Nonetheless, God permitted it.

Faustina prayed and was obedient in every aspect of her religious life, but even so, doubt came to visit her. God sometimes allows us these sorts of trials in life as a reminder for us to turn to Him and to help us to grow in virtue. Most of the debilitating doubt in St. Faustina's life came during the two dark nights in the spiritual life that she experienced.

What did the young mystic do when she felt crippled under the weight of doubt? She fell to the floor (quite literally at times) in her cell or in the chapel, and she begged our Lord for help. It was usually a sincere, wholehearted prayer that burst from her heart: "Jesus, I trust in You!" Whenever she made the simplest (but sincerest) act of trust, a bit of the burden lifted. Many times, she still struggled under the weight of the burden, yet this saint in the making knew that she had to continually trust God with every detail of her life. She offers a beautiful example to aspire to.

Facing opposition from her parents to entering religious life, the sarcastic digs hurled at her from her fellow nuns, the nitpicky criticisms about her cleaning from the elderly nuns, and the dark clouds blocking her path, Faustina still wholeheartedly and courageously offered everything to God, trusting in His infinite mercy and love. I know I have mentioned this before, but I will say it again: He is the Divine Physician and always knows exactly what is needed.

Sometimes, St. Faustina would say, "Do what You will with me, O Jesus; I will adore You in everything. May Your will be done in me, O Lord and my God, and I will praise Your infinite Mercy" (*Diary*, 78). We need to consider our trust in God's mercy in our own lives.

We Wound Jesus With Our Distrust

Saint Faustina revealed the pain and suffering that Jesus experienced. In her *Diary*, she recorded Him saying, **"Distrust on the part of souls is tearing at My insides."** Jesus feels even worse when specially favored souls don't trust Him. He said, **"The distrust of a chosen soul causes Me even greater pain; despite My inexhaustible love for them they do not trust Me. Even My death is not enough for them. Woe to the soul that abuses these** [gifts]**"** (*Diary*, 50).

At another time, Jesus told Faustina, **"How painfully distrust of My goodness wounds Me! Sins of distrust wound Me most painfully"** (*Diary*, 1076).

Can we work more earnestly at trusting God with our lives? I know we can! Following our Church's teachings, frequenting the Sacraments, and staying close to Jesus and Mary will help a great deal. I'll also reiterate the importance of surrounding ourselves with faith-filled friends who will strengthen us on our journey. In addition, we need to call upon the saints for their help and intercession. Saint Faustina should be up at the top of our list! I have no doubt that she is happy to help.

We must remember that Jesus said, **"The greater the sinner, the greater the right he has to My mercy"** (*Diary*, 723). Jesus wants to bestow His unfathomable mercy upon us. Let's not hesitate to turn to Him. Let's offer to Him any doubt we might have. Let's never wound His Heart with our distrust again.

We Help Others When We Trust Jesus!

I love what happens when we really trust our Lord. Are you ready for this? I know I've mentioned it before, but I would like to emphasize something quite remarkable: Jesus told His Secretary of Mercy that when we trust Him, He fills us to overflowing with His graces (see *Diary*, 1074)! We need to approach Jesus with trust! When we trust Him, we bring graces for ourselves *and* others!

PAUSE

Ponder this beautiful stage of life. Are there areas where you should be trusting God more? What can you do? How can you help a woman in this chapter of life? Might you have regrets (small or large)? Now is the time to make a change, move your will, and ask forgiveness from God and whomever else you need to ask.

ACT

A new chapter of life is unfolding — we are older and wiser! We need to turn to God's unfathomable mercy and impart holy wisdom to others! Onward to new adventures!

A PRAYER OF MERCY

Dear Jesus, may my heart be always wide open to receive Your graces! Please open the eyes of my soul. Help me to be a vessel of grace to others who need my help. Jesus, please have mercy upon my soul. I want to grow closer to You.
I trust in You!
Mother Mary, help me, protect me, and guide me.
Saint Faustina, please pray for me.
Amen.

CHAPTER 33
Debilitating Illness

"I have given myself over to His holy will;
let Him do with me as He wishes,
and I will still love Him."

— Saint Faustina (*Diary*, 589)

Caring for ourselves or a loved one who has a debilitating illness can cause us to become depressed and fearful, and even to panic at times. It is certainly a difficult chapter in our lives. Saint Faustina encourages us: "Love casts out fear. Since I came to love God with my whole being and with all the strength of my heart, fear has left me" (*Diary*, 589).

Isn't that beautiful? Do you want the same loving fearlessness?

Our saintly friend tells us, "Even if I were to hear the most terrifying things about God's justice, I would not fear Him at all, because I have come to know Him well. God is love, and His Spirit is peace." Can we say the same?

How do we operate: in fear, or in love of God and neighbor? Saint Faustina wrote, "I see now that my deeds which have flowed from love are more perfect than those which I have done out of fear. I have placed my trust in God and fear nothing." How did she do this? She explained, "I have given myself over to His holy will; let Him do with me as He wishes, and I will still love Him" (*Diary,* 589).

During much uncertainty when we are dealing with a debilitating illness in ourselves or someone we love, we can heed St. Faustina's instruction to love God with everything we have — with our whole being and all the strength of our heart. Our fears will leave us. It most likely will not happen instantly. That is because we need to pray and to trust God that He knows exactly what we need and when we need it. He is our Divine Physician. Will we trust Him with our lives, even when it's difficult to do so? I hope and pray so.

Let us remember that God can bring much good out of suffering — even tremendous miracles! I will share an amazing true story with you.

"Everything Was God's Fault"[125]

Maureen Cahill grew up near Boston, having a basically normal childhood until the age of 15, when she learned that she had an incurable disease called lymphedema, which causes excess fluid to collect, prompting swelling due to blockages of the lymphatic system. In Maureen's case, the disease especially affected her legs.

Maureen's devastating and painful illness required more than 50 surgeries. She spent most of her teen years in hospitals. Eventually, her right leg had to be amputated — first above the knee, and later to the hip.

Even though she'd been raised Catholic by devout Irish parents, Maureen fell away from the faith. She said, "I had pushed God pretty much out of my life." She was very unhappy with her disastrous situation. Due to spending so much time in the hospital, she lost her friends along the way. They just stopped visiting.

Maureen shared, "I didn't go to confession. I would not go to Mass." She added, "I would wonder why the other kids were so happy, and I'm not. Everything was God's fault." It was the only way she could deal with such a physically devastating cross.

Maureen's parents tried to console and encourage her the best they could, telling her that God had a special plan for her. Most times, the words fell upon deaf ears. When she heard them once again, she just scoffed. God didn't love her. How could He? Like most of us, Maureen was not privy to the future. She didn't know at the time that there would come a glorious day when she would know that all of her intense suffering had been for a breathtaking and phenomenal reason.

That would have to wait.

The teenager fell into depression. She was on many medications, and stress brought on seizures. Maureen became addicted to prescription drugs. Her life became a huge, painful mess. She entertained thoughts of suicide. She confessed, "I began to want to stay in the hospital because I felt safe there, and I didn't care if I went home or not because I no longer wanted to face reality."

A certain young U.S. Marine named Bob Digan was in Maureen's life at the time. They had met many years prior, and for Bob, it had been love at first sight. Eventually, they'd started dating. Maureen's illnesses didn't scare Bob. He loved her. She loved him, too. Bob visited his girl every weekend when he was on leave. After a while, one of the nurses took it upon herself to persuade Maureen to break up with Bob, convincing her that Bob was just feeling sorry for her, and that she should cut him loose.

Maureen wondered, "How can Bob love me when God doesn't love me?" She concluded, "He's a good Catholic, and he doesn't want to hurt me." She thought he needed a girlfriend who could dance with him, not one who is in a wheelchair. She mulled it over and broke up with him. She didn't want to hold him back. Nonetheless, Maureen was miserable. Then one day, Bob walked through the door of her hospital room. It seemed he needed Maureen's advice.

"You know, there's a girl I'd like to marry, but I'm afraid to ask her because I'm afraid she might say no."

Calmly, Maureen said from her hospital bed, "Well, why don't you ask her, Bob? All she can do is say no."

Bob didn't hesitate. Instead, with a long-stemmed rose in hand, he went right to it.

"Okay," he said. "Will you marry me?"

Though Maureen was still in a dark place emotionally, feeling tortured by the ruthless progression of her illness and the deterioration of her remaining leg, she boldly accepted Bob's proposal.

Grace was moving.

A Wedding and Married Life to Plan

The newly engaged couple's hearts were filled with many hopes and dreams, though they knew that Maureen's incurable and progressive lymphedema was a serious consideration. Still, the young couple could just imagine their future children bustling around their humble home. Their hopeful vision would soon disintegrate, however, because Maureen's doctor demanded a meeting before they could marry.

He wanted to get everything on the table, especially for Bob so that he was crystal clear on what he was getting himself into. There was no cure for Maureen. On top of that, their dreams of children might be completely in vain. She might not be able to have children, the doctor firmly stated. Bob was firm as well, telling the doctor that they planned to accept whatever it was that God had planned for them.

On June 6, 1970, Maureen walked down the aisle at church to meet her groom who was standing there, steadfast, waiting. As strong and helpful as Bob had always been for his girl, he couldn't help her now. He watched and prayed as she made her way slowly towards him, her prosthetic leg hidden beneath her gown. She would be able to dance with Bob and with her father to "Daddy's Little Girl," but it would be the last time she'd wear the painful prosthetic leg.

Miraculously, shortly after their momentous wedding day, Maureen was expecting their first baby. She shared, "It was then I let God into my life. I began to trust Him a little bit more." Five months later, sadly, their baby died in utero.

Maureen was crushed to the core. She said, "The baby died, and I wanted nothing more to do with God."

Not too long after, another pregnancy commenced, and this baby, Bobby, made it to full term. Though Maureen and Bob were extremely happy, when Bobby was born, he had brain damage and would end up having multiple irregular seizures. "The doctors told us to put him in an institution," Maureen shared, "and get on with our lives, but our baby was our life — he was our miracle child."

At just shy of 2 years old, Bobby lost consciousness and experienced violent convulsions. He had had his first grand mal seizure. Seizures would become a dreaded but regular part of the Digans' lives. Bobby's health continued to deteriorate, and he lost his ability to walk and talk. On his 6th birthday, he was admitted to the hospital weighing only 35 pounds and discharged almost six months later at only 18 pounds. He had to be nourished with a feeding tube. His life expectancy at that point was pretty much nonexistent.

Bob's faith was still rock solid. However, he was weary. Maureen's left leg was getting worse. She had lost her faith completely. A surgery date was set for the amputation of her left leg. To all appearances, everything looked hopeless. Still, no matter how bad it was, Bob "felt God was calling us for something," adding, "I felt He had a plan for us."

Bob pleaded with God for an answer, hoping for guidance with their serious and complex problems, which continued to grow worse. He hoped for mercy. I'm reminded of Jesus' words to St. Faustina: **"The graces of my mercy are drawn by means of one vessel only, and that is — trust. The more a soul trusts, the more it will receive"** (*Diary*, 1578).

One evening in 1979, while Maureen and Bobby were being taken care of, Bob went to see the original film on Divine Mercy, "Divine Mercy," made in the late 1950s and released in 1978. Bob had never heard of Divine Mercy, but was intrigued upon seeing the advertising flyer. Watching the movie enlightened him about the prophetic revelations on Divine Mercy given to us by God through a Polish nun named Sr. Faustina.

"God illuminated my mind," Bob recalled, "with what the theologians would call an intellectual vision." He explained, "You don't see anything, you just know." Well, Bob couldn't stand still. There was no time to waste.

Expecting a Miracle

After seeing the movie, Bob was absolutely certain that he had to take his sickly wife and son to the tomb of St. Faustina in Poland. He was expecting a miracle! First, the Digans drove three hours to Stockbridge, Massachusetts, to meet with Fr. Seraphim Michalenko, MIC, then the North American vice-postulator for Sr. Faustina's beatification cause. Maureen was not exactly sure what Bob had in mind. As they sat in Fr. Seraphim's office, she was about to find out.

Bob spoke as Maureen and Fr. Seraphim listened. He began by stating that he had received a "collect call" from God. He added, "I understood that I was to take my family to Poland so that God's mercy then could burst forth throughout the world through Sr. Faustina," Bob explains. "And as a favor for making that trip, God would heal not one but both Maureen and Bobby."

Father Seraphim's eyes lit up, and all color drained from Maureen's face. She was flabbergasted!

"Oh my good Lord!" she thought. "My Rock of Gibraltar is crumbling! Bob's becoming a religious nut." She was immediately concerned, thinking, "He was the only solid one, and now he's falling apart!"

But no, "this wasn't wishful thinking," Bob recalled. "I knew. I was convinced."

Bob invited Fr. Seraphim to accompany them. "We want you to witness the miracle," he added. Soon after, permission was secured from Fr. Seraphim's provincial superior and from Maureen's doctors. Everything fell into place. However, Maureen did not want to go. She thought it foolish and fanatical. Still, she agreed because Bob was so certain and so fired up about it. It was perhaps the most certain he had ever been in his life.

Saint Faustina Makes Herself Known

Before setting off to Poland, Bob and Maureen would meet again with Fr. Seraphim at the Shrine of Divine Mercy in Stockbridge, Massachusetts. Personally, I feel very blessed that I met Bob one day at the Shrine when I was visiting. My friend Mariola introduced us and asked Bob if he would retell the story about what transpired before their trip to Poland.

I listened intently as Bob gave us a blow-by-blow reenactment. Before they left for Poland, Bob said, "I was invited to pray with Fr. Seraphim and some members of a prayer group the beginning day of a special novena that our pilgrimage would go well." They had gathered in a side chapel of the Shrine where, at that time, a large Image of Divine Mercy was hanging.

Standing together in that very side chapel the day I was visiting the Shrine, Bob recalled to us that while they were praying the Chaplet of Divine Mercy, "We heard a young woman's voice praying with us in the empty church." Yet they knew that no one else could be present. The doors were locked. Needless to say, they were perplexed.

"Curious, we looked out from the side chapel," Bob said, gesturing as he explained to us. I was so intrigued to hear the true story — right from the horse's mouth! Well, they looked around, peeking out from the side chapel, but no one could be found. So they got back to their prayers.

Again, the voice! The church was still empty.

"Puzzled," Bob said, "I left the side chapel and looked throughout the whole church, the choir loft, and checked everywhere. But no person could be found." After that, they felt fairly certain that there would be no more interruptions. They continued to pray.

"And once again, we heard her voice," Bob shared. He wanted to keep looking. *Who could be hiding in the church? And why? Who was "interrupting" their prayers?* Finally, Fr. Seraphim told Bob not to be concerned about searching any longer. The mystery was solved as far as he was concerned.

"He said she was Sr. Faustina praying with us!" exclaimed Bob.

Can you imagine?

Off to the Tomb of a Future Saint

The Digans and Fr. Seraphim landed in Poland on March 23, 1981, on Bobby's 8th birthday. Maureen didn't expect the trip to go well. She was right. Her brand-new wheelchair never made it on the plane, nor did the luggage, delaying their trip to Krakow by three days. All were thoroughly exhausted upon finally arriving at the convent. Maureen would prepare her heart and soul by going to Confession, even as she was still so skeptical and still angry at God.

After receiving her penance, Maureen felt a little closer to God. She had stuck her neck out through her willingness to become vulnerable before God. She received graces through that powerful Sacrament that she hadn't received since she was a young girl. Maureen had opened the door of her heart and started trusting God just a bit.

On the evening of March 28, 1981, the ninth day of a novena that the group had begun in preparation for the trip, Fr. Seraphim suggested that they all pray the Divine Mercy Chaplet together for healing. "It was about 9 o'clock at night," recalled Maureen. She thought that this kind of miraculous healing was reserved for people in the Bible, not for her. She went ahead, though, and joined the others in prayer, "just to make them happy."

"I Will Give It to You"

It was there at Faustina's tomb during that Chaplet of Divine Mercy that something incredible would happen. Inwardly, Maureen heard Sr. Faustina say: "If you ask for my help, I will give it to you."

Maureen responded, "Okay, Faustina, you dragged me to this country so far from home. If you are going to do something, do it now!"

Suddenly, every bit of pain evaporated from Maureen's sickly body, and her swollen leg shrank back to its normal size! She knew something had happened because of the way her shoe felt. However, she didn't dare look. She played it cool.

She later said, "I knew if I looked, everyone else would look, so I didn't look."

Not only did Maureen have a dramatic change, but so did Bobby! He, too, was confined to a wheelchair, and had been sitting listlessly, as was usual for him given all of his disabilities. But suddenly, he started smiling and showed increased energy. Bobby experienced a dramatic but incomplete healing. Both mother and son were radiant.

Bobby was lifted from his wheelchair. He placed flowers that Fr. Seraphim had given him on Faustina's tomb. They would all go back to their rooms for the night. Maureen secretly examined her leg and saw that it was back to its normal size. Before the trip to Poland, surgery had already been scheduled to amputate the leg. Maureen didn't say anything to Bob and went to sleep. She slept straight through until 5 p.m. the next day. Bobby did, too!

God Brings Great Good out of Suffering

When Maureen opened her eyes, Bobby was sitting up and coloring, something he had not been able to do before. Maureen checked her leg. Still no swelling. She called to Bob and showed him.

"Yeah, that's what we came here for," he said. "You've been healed."

Though Maureen could see with her own eyes the dramatic change in her leg, it would take some time to really believe and accept that she had been given this miracle. Saint Faustina had indeed given her help, as she had promised Maureen during that Divine Mercy Chaplet. Maureen had opened her heart and was healed instantly of her lymphedema. On top of that, she received a spiritual healing. Their son was able to go off of his 28 daily antiseizure pills, and his balance greatly improved. Bob shared with me, "Bobby's seizures were now under divine control as proven by medical examination, verified via electronic EEGs."

Back in the United States, Maureen was examined by five doctors independently. Each doctor concluded unequivocally that Maureen was healed. They could find no medical explanation for such a change in her incurable and progressive illness. Then came the Sacred Congregation for the Causes of Saints, who, in consultation with five doctors, examined the evidence. A team of theologians and a team of cardinals and bishops also examined all accumulated evidence. The cure was accepted by all as miraculous and to have been caused through Sr. Faustina's intercession with the Divine Mercy. Maureen's miracle led to the beatification of St. Faustina on April 18, 1993.

Maureen explained why it took time to really sink in for her. She said, "I was so scared and full of fear. I couldn't believe God could be so loving and merciful."

Though this experience was life-changing for all three, Bob and Maureen never felt they were anyone special or deserving of the honor of being the recipients of such great healings, with Maureen's actually moving Faustina's canonization cause further along. The Digans carried on with their normal lives, giving praise to God and continuing their diligent care of Bobby, while delighting in his physical changes for the better. The family also moved closer to the Shrine, where Bob and Maureen became very active in spreading the message of Divine Mercy.

They returned to Poland two years later in thanksgiving. When Faustina was beatified by St. John Paul II, Bob and Maureen also attended, and were blessed to sit with one of St. Faustina's biological sisters.

Keep Our Eyes on Jesus

The couple often pondered their experiences and the amazing wonder and mystery of Maureen's miracle being used for Faustina's beatification. They didn't feel worthy. However, they wholeheartedly accept it. Bob said, "In our day and age, when everything is so chaotic, and everything seems so discouraging and there's all this violence, the answer is still very clear: God is still with us."

Bob stated, "He allowed the healing to take place to let us know that He is still with us. But it is also a preparation for His final coming."

Maureen said, "People, even priests, think that because you received a healing that you are able to walk on water almost." But, she said, "You're not. You're no different," adding, "I mean, you're different because you have God in your life, but I'm still Maureen. I still fall. I still need confession. I still need God's help and Faustina's help."

Maureen shared, "When you have faith, your life changes," adding, "you rely on God instead of thinking you can do everything yourself."

Bob and Maureen are certain beyond doubt about the importance of the Divine Mercy message. Bob said, "We do believe this message of Divine Mercy is the prophetic message for our age, a call for people to turn back to God." He explained, "Christ told St. Faustina that before He returns as a just Judge, **'I first open wide the door of My mercy. He who refuses to pass through the door of My mercy must pass through the door of My justice'**" (*Diary*, 1146).

"We believed God had touched our lives, not for ourselves, but for a witness to the Church," Bob expressed. "We are just ordinary people living out our faith in a world needing faith."

Without a doubt, the Digans are amazing witnesses to the power of intercessory prayer. Maureen said, "Intercessory prayer is important — if it wasn't for my husband praying for me, I wouldn't be here." She added, "Suicide ran through my mind." She encourages everyone, "Pray for others. God's Divine Mercy is for everyone."

The Gift of Bobby

Bobby, the baby who was not expected to live long, lived another 10 years after his dramatic healing in Krakow at our friend Faustina's tomb. He was able to walk unassisted and learned to ride a bike. Bobby won gold and silver medals in the Special Olympics, and made his parents very proud.

In 1989, Bobby would undergo surgery to correct his scoliosis. Sadly, it did not go well. Due to a serious surgical complication, he became paralyzed. He would never walk again, nor could he eat or drink. Bobby grew progressively worse, and would be bedridden for the remainder of his short life.

One spring day in 1991, Bobby called out for his mother. Lying in bed, he explained to her, "Mommy, I have something to tell you. God is going to send His Son, Jesus, to take me to Heaven soon. Don't be sad and cry."

Bob was then called into Bobby's room while Maureen hurried to hide in the bathroom and cry her heart out. Then time sped away like a galloping horse. Soon, Fr. Seraphim and Bobby's parents were together again at Bobby's bedside, where Fr. Seraphim celebrated Holy Mass. Bobby was unresponsive. However, he responded to Fr. Seraphim when he asked the boy, "Bobby, we are ready to give you Holy Communion. Would you please open your mouth so we can put some Precious Blood in?"

Bobby complied, and Fr. Seraphim dripped a tiny bit of Precious Blood on Bobby's outstretched tongue. Father Seraphim had to ask Bobby again because it was not enough. Bobby "very slowly, and deliberately, opened his mouth. His tongue was cupped," Fr. Seraphim recalled. "He held it there long enough for me to put a spoonful into it," adding, "Slowly he withdrew his tongue, and slowly he closed his mouth." Father Seraphim remarked, "It was the most beautiful reception of the Eucharist I had ever seen."

On May 23, 1991, Bobby closed his eyes to this life on earth. He was 18 years old. As he breathed his last, color returned to his skin, and he appeared to be a healthy boy peacefully sleeping with a bit of a smile on his face.

"Bobby's vocation in life was finished," Maureen shared. "It was time for him to go home. This is a witness for others that the greatest healing comes in going to the Promised Land."

Bob shared, "Maureen said that Bobby was the one who received the ultimate healing."

Trust in God While Caring for the Ill

The Digans' story is absolutely amazing. We know that not all illnesses will end in miracles. However, we should know that everyone matters to our loving God, Who knows every hair on our heads. We might receive unseen miracles, either emotional or spiritual.

Let's take a look at some holy advice from our Lord Jesus and our sister Faustina. I mentioned it in the last chapter, but it needs to be repeated here.

One time at Adoration, Jesus told His bride St. Faustina about **"the flames of mercy"** burning Him and His desire to **"pour them out upon human souls,"** as well as the pain it caused Him **"when they don't want to accept them!"** He said, **"Tell** [all people], **My daughter, that I am Love and Mercy itself. When a soul approaches Me with trust, I fill it with such an abundance of graces that it cannot contain them within itself, but radiates them to other souls"** (*Diary*, 1074).

When we trust Jesus, He fills us up to overflowing with grace! Our trust in Him will help other souls, too! When caring for an ill loved one or when we ourselves are ill, we need to pray for the grace to wholeheartedly trust God. He will grant it!

Ask for much, my dear sister in Christ! Remember that in the Garden of Olives, Jesus asked His Father in Heaven to take the cup from Him. But He only wanted His Father's will, knowing full well that His Father knew best. Jesus trusted His Father. We must trust, too.

We must be assured that our sufferings lovingly offered to Jesus can become redemptive for our own souls and the souls of others. Jesus pours abundant graces into our hearts, graces that overflow to others!

PAUSE

Take a few moments to ponder your life. Where are you headed? Is the Divine Physician preparing you for your eternal life or urging you to help someone at that special final stage of life?

ACT

Cling to Jesus and Mary. Make acts of trust to Jesus. Be a loving intercessor and pray extra Divine Mercy Chaplets for those most in need and all who are dying.

A PRAYER OF MERCY

Dear Jesus, please help me to trust in Your great love and mercy. Please grant the graces I need to be a radiant vessel of love and Divine Mercy for others — those whom You have placed in my life. Please have mercy upon my soul.
I trust in You!
Mother Mary, help me, protect me, and guide me.
Saint Faustina, please pray for me.
Amen.

CHAPTER 34
Preparing for Death and Eternal Life

"I boldly look at everything; even
death itself I look straight in the eye."

— Saint Faustina (*Diary*, 876)

Preparing for death essentially means preparing for eternal life. Interestingly, I wrote this book during a worldwide pandemic. It was a time like nothing we have ever experienced before, stopping us in our tracks and causing many of us to ponder the state of our souls. I tried to get across through social media and my newsletters that it was time to ask ourselves an important question: Are we ready to meet our Maker? I added, "If not, we had better get ready." I was not trying to instill fear. Rather, I wanted to encourage others not to be caught off guard — to get their hearts and souls ready.

That time was indeed a life-changing experience — and still is. As I type these words, we are still in isolation, wearing masks in public, and doing social distancing. I hope that most of the world will come away from this pandemic with a new appreciation for everything — for every blessing and every comfortable thing we have ever experienced in our lifetimes.

Dr. Amedeo Capetti, an infectious diseases physician in Milan, Italy, and a consultant to the World Health Organization

(WHO), reflected on his experiences during the pandemic. He shared, "In fact, what I am living — but I believe this to be an experience shared by many others — is a phenomenon that we physicians often see in those who have survived a brush with death: the experience of opening your eyes and realizing that nothing can any longer be taken for granted." He explained he'd received "the recognition that everything is a gift: waking up in the morning, greeting your loved ones, and even all the little moments of daily life, that for some are merely time to be filled, but for others, like me, have unexpectedly become even more compelling than before."[126]

"Only One Foot Touches the Earth"

Saint Faustina, as we know, was a saint in the making all throughout her life. She strove for holiness. She dearly desired to become a saint and even consulted with another saint about it.

When she was enduring great difficulties amid spiritual darkness, St. Faustina made novenas to the saints for help, including one to St. Thérèse of Lisieux, whom she loved dearly. During the novena, St. Thérèse appeared to Faustina in a dream. Faustina's beloved saintly friend told her that her trial would end in three days. Our sister Faustina was glad to hear the reassurance, but ventured to ask St. Thérèse a question. Would she, Faustina, become a saint like St. Thérèse? The Little Flower assured her, "Yes, you will be a saint just as I am, but you must trust in the Lord Jesus" (*Diary*, 150).

Most likely, we won't be singlehandedly entrusted with so great a mission as St. Faustina, yet we are all called to sanctity. Mother Teresa always said that to become holy is not the luxury of a few, but a simple duty for each of us.

Let's pause to ask ourselves, "Do we take time to ponder how transitory life is here on earth?" When we are small children, the average life span seems like forever. Also, we often aren't very serious about the meaning of life at the start. As we get older, we begin to understand our life's purpose. One evening, while in prayer at the convent, St. Faustina was given knowledge from Jesus about "how fleeting all earthly things are, and [how] everything that appears great disappears like smoke, and does not give the soul freedom, but weariness" (*Diary*, 1141).

Saint Faustina wrote, "Happy the soul that understands these things and with only one foot touches the earth." Faustina continued, "My repose is to be united with You; everything else tires me." She felt that no one could understand her heart but God. She wrote, "Oh how much I feel I am in exile! I see that no one understands my interior life. You alone understand me, You who are hidden in my heart and yet are eternally alive" (*Diary*, 1141).

Let us strive to live with just one foot touching the earth, knowing that our eternal life lies ahead. We must get ready.

The Gift of Life and Death

No one knows the day nor the hour of their death. That is why we need to be absolutely ready to meet God each day. We need to consider whether we want Him seeing us doing whatever it is that we are doing. If not, we had better snap out of it and get crackin' on changing our lives.

Saint Faustina included a great deal about life, death, and eternity in her *Diary*. One time, she explained how Jesus told her that years of suffering for her confessor Fr. Sopoćko "would be the adornment of his priestly life." She wrote, "The days of suffering always seem longer, but they too will pass, though they pass so slowly that it seems they are moving backwards." But Faustina gives us great hope. She continued, "However, their end is near, and then will come endless and inconceivable joy. Eternity! Who can understand this one word which comes from You, O incomprehensible God, this one word: eternity!" (*Diary*, 578).

We can take comfort in these words, knowing that our Lord sees every single drop of sweat on our brow, every pain and sorrow we carry in our hearts. We can offer it all to Him with love and ask for the graces that we need. Our sufferings help us to get closer to Heaven.

In addition, as I mentioned earlier, the young mystic instructs us to leave the door of our hearts ajar. But she gave a warning, as well: "But poor is the soul who has shut the door on God's mercy, even at the last hour. It was just such souls who plunged Jesus into deadly sorrow in the Garden of Olives; indeed, it was from His Most Merciful Heart that divine mercy flowed out" (*Diary*, 1507).

Blessed Michael Sopoćko on Dying Souls

Blessed Michael Sopoćko, St. Faustina's spiritual director, shared some wise words about the dying and how we can help them to trust God.

He wrote, "Above all, trust comforts the dying, who, in their last moments, remember all the sins of their lives and are sometimes driven to despair." He gives us examples of how we can help: "Appropriate acts of trust should, then, be suggested to the dying, for it is not everyone who, at such a time, can make them for himself."[127]

I think that many times, loved ones and relatives don't wish to speak about death to the dying. They shy away from it, thinking it might cause further pain for their loved one. Sadly, the opportunity to help them get to Heaven may be lost! We should not fear. Our works of mercy in speaking to them about the reality of eternal life can help to save their soul!

Blessed Sopoćko wrote, "The dying should be reminded of their true home, now no longer distant, where the King of Mercy joyfully awaits all who trust in His Mercy." And, again, that important word — trust! He wrote, "Trust assures us of a reward after death, as we know from many examples in the lives of the Saints. We need only think of Dismas, the thief dying on the cross beside Our Lord, to whom, in his last moments, he turned with trust, to hear the blessed assurance: 'This day thou shalt be with me in Paradise' (Luke 23:43)."[128]

If we are able, we should be sure to help arrange the Sacrament of the Anointing of the Sick and the Apostolic Pardon for the dying.

Never Give Up

There are so many reasons why we might feel tempted to stop trying, but countless reasons more why we should never give up on life. I am thinking, however, that we should never give up on anyone, especially a dying soul. They really need our prayers. I am reminded right now of heroic Venerable Fulton J. Sheen and his love for a dying sinner. I've shared this story at a couple of my speaking engagements. I remember one in particular at which a man in the front row sobbed as I finished telling the story. Seeing his face soaked with tears and his shoulders heaving up and down caused me to shed a few tears too — right there at the podium.

I'll share Archbishop Sheen's story with you now.

A woman had asked the archbishop if he would visit her dying brother in the hospital. She was so concerned for his soul because he had done some very evil things in his life and was unrepentant. She threw in, "And he already kicked 17 priests out of his room!" So Sheen nicknamed himself "Last-Resort Sheen" and started praying for the man. I have no doubt that he included this man in his conversation with our Lord during his daily Holy Hour.

Sheen showed up in the man's room and visited for only 10 or 15 seconds before the man threw him out, too! That did not cause the determined archbishop to give up on him. He would continue to pray for the dying man and show up again the next night. Well, this went on for a long time — 40 nights, to be exact! Sheen committed to the time it took to reach a dying, unrepentant soul.

Finally, on the 40th night, Sheen brought Jesus in the Blessed Sacrament with him. Again, the man demanded that Sheen leave his room. However, the holy and persevering archbishop told the man that someone was with him.

"Should He leave too?" the archbishop asked.

"Who?" The man wanted to know.

"It's Jesus."

The man quieted down. But after a short while, he once again demanded that Sheen leave. Well, the archbishop was not going to give up just like that when he knew in his heart that time was running out faster than a fistful of sand falling to the beach through outstretched fingers. So he got off his knees, dashed up to the head of the bed, and put his face right next to the man's cancerous face so that he could whisper into his ear.

He told the man straight out that he was probably going to die that night, and that he should ask for God's mercy before he died. The man acknowledged that he knew he would die, but he would not ask for God's mercy.

"Get out!"

Sheen left the man's room and stopped at the nurses' station to explain that he would be waiting by his phone and would come straight back if the man needed him. His phone rang at 3 a.m. It was the nurse. The man had died! Sheen's heart must have sunk.

"What happened?"

The nurse told him that just minutes after he left the room, the man started crying out loud to God, "Lord, have mercy on me! Lord, have mercy on me! Lord, have mercy on me!"

He said this over and over again until he died! Let us never give up on anyone, and wholeheartedly strive to be more generous with our time and our prayers, for so many people absolutely need our love and intercession.

Passing From This Life to the Next

We must all bid "goodbye" to the dying, whether they be loved ones, friends, or maybe even complete strangers. Not too long ago, I happened to catch what Fr. Mitch Pacwa, SJ, said on May 27, 2020, on his television show "EWTN Live." He shared that it was always very profound for him to be at the bedside of the dying. Dr. Peter Kreeft, his guest, commented, "You are touching eternity."

When my friend Lisa's elderly mother was in hospice care, she began to decline a bit. It was during the pandemic, which meant that visits were difficult to arrange. One day, Lisa was totally surprised to hear from the caregiver that her mother would die that very day. It was so sudden. When Lisa told me, I suggested that she arrange for an immediate anointing. I prayed earnestly that it could miraculously be pulled off during the pandemic. Thanks be to God, Lisa let me know later that as soon as her dear mom was anointed, her caregiver gave her a hug, and immediately Lisa's mom breathed her last. God has perfect timing!

During the pandemic, my friend Fr. Brian felt blessed to anoint people who were dying of COVID-19. He told me that these were the most spiritual moments he had ever experienced.

"I wasn't afraid. God gave me the grace to happily be a priest, wanting to go and be an instrument of our Lord, and bring His Love and Mercy to his children most in need, and in danger of imminent death," he said, "and bring His comfort and peace, as well, to a patient's family members, reminding them of the promises Jesus offered to those who live the Way, and the Truth, and His opportunity [for them] to receive eternal life."

Yet it was very surreal, too. Father shared, "I was greeted by nurses at the entrances, vetted with questions, had my temperature taken, wore my N95 mask, gloves, and gown, and was escorted down halls that used to have a whole different feel and atmosphere." He continued, "Now it's different. It's more serious. It's all this protection." Father Brian added, "But it's not all about the body. It's about our souls. It's all about Jesus Christ, now and forever! Amen."

Father shared with me a profoundly merciful experience he had had with the dying on the very eve of Divine Mercy Sunday during the pandemic. That evening, with his handbook of devotion to Divine Mercy and St. Faustina's *Diary* nearby, Fr. Brian sat at his computer, about ready to peck away at his keyboard to write his homily. It would appear on his parish website, since churches were still closed. But before he could get anything accomplished, the phone rang. It was a call from the hospital, alerting Fr. Brian that a patient with COVID-19 was in imminent danger of death.

Father Brian quickly asked if he could visit. They agreed, and he was in his car in a flash. Along the way, my friend realized that he hadn't been out in about four weeks.

Away he went, praying the Rosary as he drove.

"You Feel It in Your Heart"

When Fr. Brian arrived at the hospital, things looked bleak. The emptiness of the parking lot matched the depressing cloudy day. Clad in protective clothing, he was greeted by several nurses at the entrance, all wearing personal protective equipment. They took his temperature and asked questions.

He followed instructions to go upstairs and was surprised to see that "there was no one along the way." It's usually quite busy. Entering, Fr. Brian couldn't help but ponder some powerful words: "Even though I walk through the darkest valley, I fear no evil; for you are with me" (Ps 23:4).

A nurse escorted him to the patient's room. Standing in the hallway, he prayed for the man as he awaited further instructions. The door opened. Father Brian recalled, "The nurse inside informed me that the patient just died — while I was praying." A lump formed in my friend's throat.

"You feel it in your heart — it's like time stopped."

"It was very powerful. And very sad," Fr. Brian recalled. "I continued my prayers for the patient, filled with emotion, as I prayed the words of God's mercy: 'May the Lord in his love and mercy help you with the grace of the Holy Spirit. May the Lord who frees you from sin save you and raise you up.'"

Father completed his prayers for the man, but his job was not finished yet. Downstairs, he removed his protective equipment and thanked all the nurses. He headed to his car to do the next tough thing: Call the man's son.

"I expressed my sorrow. I recalled my experience. I explained God's mercy, how his father had received God's blessings." Father Brian talked to the son about thinking of his father as hugged by the loving arms of our Lord; about the eternal promises of Jesus; about divine and heavenly realities, "about our hearts, and I assured him that he, the caretaking son, is not to blame. And I told him I would offer the 4 p.m. Mass for his father, and their family."

After that work of mercy, Fr. Brian went home to wash his clothes, take a shower, and write his homily. He told about his experience at the hospital and that Divine Mercy Sunday is "a day to bless and venerate the Image of Divine Mercy, and a day for priests to speak about the great and unfathomable mercy of our Lord; how Jesus wants this Feast to be a refuge and shelter for all souls, especially poor sinners; how this whole ocean of the infinite mercy of God is available by our trust in Jesus."

"Jesus, I trust in You. Jesus, I trust in You. Jesus, I trust in You," he wrote. What a powerful time it was. Father Brian recalled in his homily, "Here it is, during this pandemic, and just having gone through Lent and Holy Week, through the Paschal Mystery, the Suffering, the Death, the Resurrection, and the forthcoming Ascension, Jesus completed for each and every one of us (the grace of this feast) our redemption!" He went on with encouraging words and finished with "Jesus promised to St. Faustina that He would pour down upon us, from the very depths of His tender mercy, a whole ocean of graces!"

Father Brian said, "That's as good as it gets until that hopeful day when Jesus hopefully says, 'Well done, my good and faithful servant. Come, share your Master's joy.'"

I asked Fr. Brian to share a bit more about his hospital experience on that eve of Divine Mercy Sunday. He told me, "It's very powerful to hear someone just died and to be there." Father shared that, in seminary, he was taught that "I might have been ordained for that one confession, that one Sacrament." He said, "It's moments like those that make giving your life for God and His people so meaningful: It reinforces your vocation, and you see God's will."

Trusting God

Every day is a gift from God. We only have today in which to get ready to meet Him. Certainly, we continually meet Him in our prayers. When it is time for us to leave this earthly life, we will meet Him face-to-face. Every one of us is a work in progress — all the way up until our last breath, when we still have the opportunity to turn to God. Let's get our souls ready now. Let's not wait until tomorrow.

On April 13, 1937, Sr. Faustina wrote, "I must stay in bed all day." She had had a violent fit of coughing and was so weak from it that she couldn't walk. She wrote, "My spirit is eager to do God's work, but physical strength has left me."

She told her dear Master, "I cannot penetrate Your actions at this moment, O Lord; therefore, I keep repeating with a loving act of the will: Do with me as You please" (*Diary*, 1085). The young mystic had learned the absolute need to trust God completely. No matter what was happening to her or with her, she accepted that God knew what was going on and what was best. It's important to note that she didn't stop at this knowledge. She went further. She moved her will to make repeated loving acts of trust: "Do with me as You please."

Jesus wants us to do the same. We are to give Him our weaknesses and all that we are. Once we are able to hand everything over — completely — we will have peace. God uses everything to help our souls and convert others when we offer it all to Him with love. Pray for the grace to do so.

For further teaching about when we die and meet Jesus, you can read the *Catechism* (1021-1041).

PAUSE

Take some time to ponder your life. If possible, get to the Blessed Sacrament and pour your heart out to Jesus. Listen to Him speak to your heart.

ACT

The day is almost spent. Seek and cling to God. Don't let go. Be a radiant example of faith to others.

A PRAYER OF MERCY

Dear Jesus, help me to be more cognizant about the speed with which the years pass. Help me to truly live in the present moment of life, doing my very best to always follow Your holy will. Jesus, please have mercy upon my soul.
I trust in You!
Mother Mary, help me, protect me, and guide me.
Saint Faustina, please pray for me.
Amen.

CHAPTER 35
Onward With Divine Mercy in My Soul!

"I want to be completely transformed into
Your mercy and to be Your living reflection,
O Lord. May the greatest of all divine
attributes, that of Your unfathomable mercy,
pass through my heart and soul
to my neighbor."

— Saint Faustina (*Diary*, 163)

We women are called to evangelize in countless ways in our world today as missionaries in our own states of life. After delving deeply into the milestones of a woman's life throughout this book, our sister St. Faustina's wisdom, and dear Jesus' profound teachings about His unfathomable mercy, I hope and pray that your soul is bursting with Divine Mercy! Remember, we women are to be the aroma of Christ! With God's grace, that holy aroma should waft throughout the world like billowing incense! It's our job as women with Divine Mercy in our hearts and souls to impart it to others!

I love what dear St. John Paul II said about how we women nurture society and the Church. He said, "Without the contribution of women, society is less alive, culture impoverished, and peace less stable. ... In fact, woman has a genius all her own, which is vitally essential to both society and the

Church."[129] We should never underestimate the immense value of our feminine contributions.

What Should We Do and How Shall We Do It?

Jesus told St. Faustina, **"My daughter, do whatever is within your power to spread devotion to My mercy. I will make up for what you lack."** Jesus loves us more than we will ever understand this side of Heaven. He told His Secretary of Mercy, **"Tell aching mankind to snuggle close to My merciful Heart, and I will fill it with peace"** (*Diary*, 1074).

What are we waiting for? We absolutely need to share Jesus' love and great mercy! We need to snuggle up to His merciful Heart ourselves and receive His abiding peace!

Throughout this final chapter, I will offer many ways in which we can help "aching mankind."

Divine Mercy Now

We should start our holy work first within our families and then reach out to our neighbors. Let's look at a powerful passage from the *Diary*:

> **How very much I desire the salvation of souls! My dearest secretary, write that I want to pour out My divine life into human souls and sanctify them, if only they were willing to accept My grace. The greatest sinners would achieve great sanctity, if only they would trust in My mercy. The very inner depths of My being are filled to overflowing with mercy, and it is being poured out upon all I have created. My delight is to act in a human soul and to fill it with My mercy and to justify it. My kingdom on earth is My life in the human soul. Write, My secretary, that I Myself am the spiritual guide of souls — and I guide them indirectly through the priest, and lead each one to sanctity by a road known to Me alone** (*Diary*, 1784).

It's no coincidence that God's Secretary of Mercy came to us during the 20th century, and it's no fluke that you are reading this book right now. God has always been merciful. But because our world is in such need of Divine Mercy, Heaven arranged to raise up a humble farm girl to accept the mission to teach the world about that mercy.

When Jesus appeared to Faustina on February 22, 1931, in the Image of the Divine Mercy, everything changed. Certainly, Faustina's life was completely transformed. Through her obedience to her confessor in writing her *Diary* and the prayerful support of Blessed Michael Sopoćko, among others, the essential message of God's mercy has made its way to you and me. Now that we have learned about it and received it into our hearts and souls, we must help others to understand and receive Divine Mercy, too.

We need to be instruments of God's mercy. We can learn so much from St. Faustina, who deeply desired to be completely transformed into God's mercy so that she could impart it to others. She earnestly prayed:

> I want to be completely transformed into Your mercy and to be Your living reflection, O Lord. May the greatest of all divine attributes, that of Your unfathomable mercy, pass through my heart and soul to my neighbor.
>
> Help me, O Lord, that my eyes may be merciful, so that I may never suspect or judge from appearances, but look for what is beautiful in my neighbors' souls and come to their rescue.
>
> Help me, O Lord, that my ears may be merciful, so that I may give heed to my neighbors' needs and not be indifferent to their pains and moanings.
>
> Help me, O Lord, that my tongue may be merciful, so that I should never speak negatively of my neighbor, but have a word of comfort and forgiveness for all.

> Help me, O Lord, that my hands may be mer-
> ciful and filled with good deeds, so that I may do
> only good to my neighbors and take upon myself
> the more difficult and toilsome tasks.
>
> Help me, O Lord, that my feet may be merciful,
> so that I may hurry to assist my neighbor, over-
> coming my own fatigue and weariness. ...
>
> Help me, O Lord, that my heart may be mer-
> ciful so that I myself may feel all the sufferings of my
> neighbor. ... May Your mercy, O Lord, rest upon
> me (*Diary*, 163).

Let us strive to pray her prayer with an earnest heart so
that, like Faustina, our eyes, ears, tongue, hands, feet, and
heart may come to the rescue of those in need of God's mercy.

Let's take a look at the Great Mercy Pope, St. John Paul
II, and ponder his insights on Divine Mercy. After that, we will
discuss the practical ways in which we can live a life of mercy
and impart mercy to others.

The Church Cries Out for God's Mercy

Divine Mercy was a very important theme in St. John
Paul II's life and pontificate. In 1980, in his second encyclical
letter *Dives in Misericordia* (*Rich in Mercy, DM*), he discussed
the great need for God's mercy, as well as the need to cry out
for God's mercy, especially in our day and age. The Great
Mercy Pope described the mercy of God as the presence of
love that is greater than evil, greater than sin, and greater
than death.

He stated, "The Church proclaims the truth of God's
mercy revealed in the crucified and risen Christ, and she professes it in various ways. Furthermore, she seeks to practice
mercy towards people through people, and she sees in this an
indispensable condition for solicitude for a better and 'more
human' world, today and tomorrow" (*DM*, 15).[130]

Saint John Paul II urges us on, underscoring the great
need for mercy in our time, as well as the role of the Church in

obtaining it. The pontiff proclaimed, "However, at no time and in no historical period — especially at a moment as critical as our own — can the Church forget the prayer that is a cry for the mercy of God amid the many forms of evil which weigh upon humanity and threaten it. Precisely this is the fundamental right and duty of the Church in Christ Jesus."

He continued, "The more the human conscience succumbs to secularization, loses its sense of the very meaning of the word 'mercy,' moves away from God and distances itself from the mystery of mercy, the more the Church has the right and the duty to appeal to the God of mercy 'with loud cries.'"

Saint John Paul II explained, "These 'loud cries' should be the mark of the Church of our times, cries uttered to God to implore His mercy, the certain manifestation of which she professes and proclaims as having already come in Jesus crucified and risen, that is, in the Paschal Mystery." He added, "It is this mystery which bears within itself the most complete revelation of mercy, that is, of that love which is more powerful than death, more powerful than sin and every evil, the love which lifts man up when he falls into the abyss and frees him from the greatest threats" (*DM*, 15).

We must never hesitate to cry out for God's most powerful mercy.

Divine Mercy as Refuge and the Light of Hope

At St. Faustina's beatification (on Divine Mercy Sunday, April 18, 1993), St. John Paul II spoke about St. Faustina's mission after her death yielding "astonishing fruit." He mentioned living in a time of "deep restlessness and a fear of the future," and highlighted the need for the Divine Mercy message and devotion as a place for us to "find refuge and the light of hope."[131]

At St. Faustina's canonization, April 30, 2000, St. John Paul II declared the Second Sunday of Easter "Divine Mercy Sunday" for the universal Church. The Great Mercy Pope said in his homily: "It is important then that we accept the whole message that comes to us from the word of God on this Second Sunday of Easter, which from now on throughout the Church *will be called "Divine Mercy Sunday"*. ... [B]y this act, I intend today to pass this message on to the new millennium."[132]

Later, on August 17, 2002, St. John Paul II solemnly entrusted the world to Divine Mercy. He spoke of the "spark" mentioned in St. Faustina's *Diary* that would ready the world for the final coming of Jesus, declaring:

> Today, therefore, in this Shrine, I wish *solemnly to entrust the world to Divine Mercy*. I do so with the burning desire that the message of God's merciful love, proclaimed here through Saint Faustina, *may be made known to all the peoples of the earth* and fill their hearts with hope. May this message radiate from this place to our beloved homeland and throughout the world. May the binding promise of the Lord Jesus be fulfilled: from here there must go forth "the spark which will prepare the world for his final coming" (cf. *Diary*, 1732).
>
> This spark needs to be lighted by the grace of God. This fire of mercy needs to be passed on to the world. *In the mercy of God the world will find peace and mankind will find happiness!* I entrust this task to you, dear Brothers and Sisters, to the Church in Kraków and Poland, and to all the votaries [devotees] of Divine Mercy who will come here from Poland and from throughout the world. *May you be witnesses to mercy!*[133]

Providentially, the Great Mercy Pope went home to his eternal reward on Saturday, April 2, 2005, the Vigil of Divine Mercy Sunday. He had prepared a message for Divine Mercy Sunday that was shared posthumously on April 3, 2005, and read by Archbishop Leonardo Sandri, substitute of the Vatican Secretariat of State, following the Mass for his eternal repose.

On the Sunday after Easter, through the words he drafted before he passed away, St. John Paul II proclaimed to the faithful, "As a gift to humanity, which at times seems bewildered and overwhelmed by the power of evil, selfishness and fear, the Risen Lord offers his love that pardons, reconciles and reopens hearts to love." The deceased pontiff's stirring words go on to explain the power of Christ's love: "It is a love that converts hearts and gives peace. How much the world needs to understand and accept Divine Mercy!"[134]

And his heartfelt prayer cried out to Jesus: "Lord, who reveal the Father's love by your death and Resurrection, we believe in you and confidently repeat to you today: Jesus, I trust in you, have mercy upon us and upon the whole world."[135]

Now, let's take a look at the practical and holy ways in which we can spread Divine Mercy.

Saving Souls Every Day!

Women pray for mercy, receive mercy with wholehearted surrender, and offer God's mercy. There is no doubt about it. Women are meant to show God's mercy to others. We women were entrusted with the human being, after all! Therefore, we must take very good care of the people whom God has given us. We must show God's great mercy to them.

We are given many opportunities in our daily lives to impart God's mercy to others during our encounters and conversations with our family, neighbors, and those we happen to meet. Our everyday situations and experiences can be viewed through the light of faith. We should come to recognize that God has His hand in every detail of our lives and wants us to help other souls however we can.

How can I help this person? How might my response to this person impart God's love and mercy, which will, with God's grace, ultimately bear fruit and may even save their life? These are questions we should ponder.

Can we discern that God is present even in the painful struggles, trials, and sufferings we experience? It's essential for us to do so, for we are never alone. God loves us and allows us to come closer to Him, especially through suffering. No matter how painful the struggle might be, it can be used for a great deal of good, so let us not waste our trials and pain.

Certainly we can answer Jesus' call to St. Faustina and endeavor to help save souls. It is His holy will for all souls to be saved. God created every human being to enjoy everlasting happiness with Him in Heaven one day, and Jesus laid down His life for each one of us!

Through her messages at Fatima, Mother Mary encourages us to pray for the salvation of souls. Remember, Our Lady of Fatima asked us to offer much for the conversion of souls. She told the Fatima visionaries Lúcia, Francisco, and Jacinta that many souls are going to hell because they don't have anyone to sacrifice for them. Most times, we will not need to search for penances to perform because they come to visit us each day.

The heart of Our Lady's message at Fatima is to offer up daily prayers (the Rosary) and sacrifices for the conversion of sinners, and to tell others about her requests. Our Lady of Fatima said, "Sacrifice yourselves for sinners, and say many times, especially whenever you make some sacrifice: 'O Jesus, it is for love of Thee, for the conversion of sinners and in reparation for the sins committed against the Immaculate Heart of Mary.'"[136]

Our Lady said, "If what I say to you is done, many souls will be saved and there will be peace." She also told the children, "Pray, pray very much, and make sacrifices for sinners; for many souls go to hell, because there are none to sacrifice themselves and pray for them."

The Angel of Peace who appeared to the children in 1916, the year before the apparitions of Our Lady of Fatima, instructed the children to "accept and bear with submission" their daily troubles and offer them for the conversion of sinners. The angel taught the young shepherds a simple prayer: "O my God, I believe, I adore, I hope and I love Thee; and I beg pardon for those who do not believe, do not adore, do not hope and do not love Thee." He instructed them to pray this prayer often.

Saint John Paul II said that the message of Fatima is more important today than ever. Pope Emeritus Benedict XVI said that Fatima is not just a private devotion. He said that the message of Fatima is a call from Our Lady to all of her children, beseeching them to participate in the salvation of souls.[137] She promised the blessing of peace for the world if her request was fulfilled. So we see the great need for praying for the salvation of souls.

"Every Conversion of a Sinful Soul Demands Sacrifice"

Sacrifice is necessary for the conversion of sinners. God has given us a sure way to help save souls. It might seem surprising or maybe even a bit shocking, but Jesus told His bride, **"[E]very conversion of a sinful soul demands sacrifice"** (*Diary*, 961). Chances are good that if we are associated with the person who needs converting, God will ask us to lovingly (not reluctantly or begrudgingly) offer sacrifice to help save that soul.

Remembering the directives from the Angel of Peace to "accept and bear with submission" our daily troubles, we can lovingly offer our present sufferings to God, uniting them all to His Passion and death on the Cross, and ask that He use them in a redemptive way to save souls (our own and others). In addition, we can offer sacrifices and penances, as well as special fervent prayers, for their conversion. We also do this in our Morning Offering prayer.

Saint Faustina prayed:

O Jesus, stretched out upon the cross, I implore You, give me the grace of doing faithfully the most holy will of Your Father, in all things always and everywhere. And when this will of God will seem to me very harsh and difficult to fulfill, it is then I beg You, Jesus, may power and strength flow upon me from Your wounds, and may my lips keep repeating, "Your will be done, O Lord." ... O most compassionate Jesus, grant me the grace to forget myself that I may live totally for souls, helping You in the work of salvation, according to the most holy will of Your Father ... (*Diary*, 1265).

Let us endeavor to possess this same attitude with regard to the conversion of sinners.

Jesus again and again told St. Faustina that suffering plays an essential role in calling down Divine Mercy upon others. He succinctly said, **"There is but one price at which souls are bought, and that is suffering united to My suffering on the cross"** (*Diary*, 324).

Jesus also told her, **"The loss of each soul plunges Me into mortal sadness. You always console Me when you pray for sinners."** He also told the young mystic that praying for the conversion of sinners is the prayer that most pleases Him (see *Diary*, 1397). Jesus reveals an amazing truth to us, telling us that such a prayer never fails to capture His attention.

"Know, My daughter," Jesus told St. Faustina, **"that this prayer is always heard and answered"** (*Diary*, 1397). Our Lord's powerful and revealing words to St. Faustina give us much hope in praying for sinners. Let us go to Him continuously with our loving and sacrificial prayers, begging His Mercy on all sinners.

Are we up to the task? I sure hope so, because Heaven depends upon us!

Let's listen up about how we can truly help to save souls, benefiting from Jesus' instructions to St. Faustina.

Imparting God's Mercy Through Sacrifice and Prayer

In June of 1938, Jesus arranged a three-day retreat for His Apostle of Mercy, Sr. Faustina. Throughout the duration of the retreat, He taught her many things that she needed to know and practice in the spiritual life. Jesus instructed His student about His great love and reminded her that it never changes. He also taught her about spiritual warfare; the use of treasures of grace for the sanctification of souls; love of neighbor; Jesus' love through the Blessed Sacrament; God's

Mercy; and how sacrifice and prayer can rescue souls. What an amazing retreat it was! We will focus on the last topic for now.

Jesus told Faustina, **"My daughter, I want to instruct you on how you are to rescue souls through sacrifice and prayer"** (*Diary*, 1767). The young mystic was about to be enlightened by God Himself with regard to the efficacy of prayer and suffering. Jesus then called on Faustina to *become* a sacrifice.

Her Master said, **"You will save more souls through prayer and suffering than will a missionary through his teachings and sermons alone."** During this retreat, Jesus got down to the nitty-gritty details and taught His bride every single aspect of what it means to "deny" herself as His disciple. Denying ourselves is something we are all called to do. You might recall that I have mentioned Jesus' instructions to would-be disciples several times throughout this book: "Let them deny themselves and take up their cross and follow me" (Mt 16:24).

Jesus had been leading Faustina every step of the way throughout her life. Even when she felt as if she was in complete darkness, groping blindly towards the light, He was there with her, granting graces to her and burnishing her soul. Now He was giving very clear instructions on how to make perfect sacrifices — the pure kind that will give the most pleasure to Him. Is this because God loves to see Faustina or any one of us suffer? No, not at all. We are talking about valuable sufferings that, when offered to God, are made holy to save souls.

We should let that sink in. Our cooperation with grace can truly save souls!

Let's take a look at what Jesus specifically asked His bride to do. He said, **"I want to see you as a sacrifice of living love, which only then carries weight before Me. You must be annihilated, destroyed, living as if you were dead in the most secret depths of your being."** He continued, **"You must be destroyed in that secret depth where the human eye has never penetrated; then will I find in you a pleasing sacrifice, a holocaust full of sweetness and fragrance"** (*Diary*, 1767).

Jesus' words seem so strong. They might even sound crazy, scary, or unattainable. After all, who would like to be "destroyed"? But let's look at the rewards Jesus has promised. Most importantly, Jesus said that this kind of sacrifice will be pleasing to Him. But He also said, **"And great will be your power for whomever you intercede."**

He continued, **"Outwardly, your sacrifice must look like this: silent, hidden, permeated with love, imbued with prayer."** Jesus said to His bride, **"I demand, My daughter, that your sacrifice be pure and full of humility, that I may find pleasure in it. I will not spare My grace, that you may be able to fulfill what I demand of you."**

Jesus is crystal clear. He supplies every single grace that we need. He went on to enlighten St. Faustina as to what her everyday sacrifices would consist of. He instructed her to **"accept all sufferings with love"** and told her not to be afflicted if her **"heart often experiences repugnance and dislike for sacrifice."**

I'll pause here to say that I believe that all of us at one time or another (most likely, many times!) have recoiled (whether in our hearts or physically) from sacrifice. Jesus tells us not to worry. **"All its power rests in the will,"** He told Faustina. What power? Our Lord is talking about the power of sacrifices. **"[A]nd so these contrary feelings,"** Jesus continued, **"far from lowering the value of the sacrifice in My eyes, will enhance it."** Jesus gives us amazing gems to pray over and ponder. Let us not be concerned about the feelings of repugnance or dislike for a sacrifice, but rather rejoice in those feelings if possible. Push through it all with God's grace. We must move our wills!

Jesus cautioned St. Faustina, **"Know that your body and soul will often be in the midst of fire. Although you will not feel My presence on some occasions, I will always be with you. Do not fear; My grace will be with you …"** (*Diary*, 1767).

Wow. I believe that we can take Jesus' words straight to our hearts. We can pray in a pure and loving way for a greater desire to save souls and the graces we need to obtain for them through sacrifices. Jesus promises us the graces we need. Remember: We never do this alone! He will always be with us when we choose Him. We should never fear. Let's try our best to accept the sufferings that come our way, asking Jesus to help us and to transform our sufferings into graces for our own souls and the souls of others.

Remember, Jesus told Faustina, **"And great will be your power for whomever you intercede."** Let us keep this in mind!

Divine Mercy Through Daily Details

At times, we might lament that we are so busy each day with the care of others or our work that we aren't praying enough or making sufficient extra sacrifices for the sake of saving souls. Saint Faustina lamented about this, too.

One evening, St. Faustina saw Jesus on the Cross. She wrote, "From His hands, feet, and side the Most Sacred Blood was flowing." Jesus spoke to His bride: **"All this is for the salvation of souls. Consider well, My daughter, what you are doing for their salvation"** (*Diary*, 1184).

What a wakeup call to Faustina, and to you and me! Faustina sincerely answered her dear Lord, "Jesus, when I look at Your suffering, I see that I am doing next to nothing for the salvation of souls." Jesus answered immediately. He reassured her, **"Know, My daughter, that your silent day-to-day martyrdom in complete submission to My will ushers many souls into heaven"** (*Diary*, 1184).

We busy women can take Jesus' words right into our hearts. When we follow God's will according to our duties as a Catholic woman in whatever state of life we are immersed in, He sees us. He sees every bead of sweat on our brows. He knows of every difficulty we endure. He sees that we are taking care of the people He has entrusted to us. This pleases our Lord. All of this loving work and the living martyrdom we are experiencing means an awful lot to Jesus. He tells us that by His grace, we save souls even in the everyday details of our lives, as long as we are in complete submission to His will.

Deeds of Mercy

Jesus told His bride St. Faustina that **"even the strongest faith is of no avail without works"** (*Diary*, 742). We know that this same teaching is found in Scripture: "What good is it, my brothers and sisters, if you say you have faith but do not have works? Can faith save you? If a brother or sister is naked and lacks daily food, and one of you says to them, 'Go in peace; keep warm and eat your fill,' and yet you do not supply their bodily needs, what is the good of that? So faith by itself, if it has no works, is dead" (Jas 2:14-17).

With Divine Mercy in our hearts and souls, we need to go forth to impart God's mercy to the world! God's mercy is preached powerfully in our works of mercy towards others, which we impart to them through deed, word, and prayer. First, our merciful works should be carried out for our family members. Then, if we are able, our outreach spreads further.

Jesus succinctly articulated His demands for mercy to Faustina:

> **My daughter, if I demand through you that people revere My mercy, you should be the first to distinguish yourself by this confidence in My mercy. I demand from you deeds of mercy, which are to arise out of love for Me. You are to show mercy to your neighbors always and everywhere. You must not shrink from this or try to excuse or absolve yourself from it.**
>
> **I am giving you three ways of exercising mercy toward your neighbor: the first — by deed, the second — by word, the third — by prayer. In these three degrees is contained the fullness of mercy, and it is an unquestionable proof of love for Me. By this means a soul glorifies and pays reverence to My mercy** (*Diary*, 742).

Jesus gives us very clear instructions. We should not make excuses for not doing what He has asked (actually, has demanded). Everyone can at least pray for their neighbors and souls in need. However, we should also try very hard to move beyond what is comfortable in order to impart Divine Mercy through deed and word. Jesus is counting on us and tells us that these deeds contain the fullness of mercy. By imparting His mercy through these works, we glorify and revere God's mercy. We show God our love for Him!

Remember, Jesus emphasized to His dear Faustina the essential importance of trust for receiving His Divine Mercy. Through our trust in God's holy will, we are strengthened and given a deeper understanding of His mercy. We become more confident and gain the graces we need to perform works of mercy.

Praying for Priests and Religious

Priests and religious are on the front lines in the spiritual battle for souls. They need our prayers and support. Jesus told St. Faustina, **"I place in your care two pearls very precious to My Heart: these are the souls of priests and religious. You will pray particularly for them; their power will come from your diminishment"** (*Diary*, 531).

The Catholic Church has been persecuted down through the ages and will continue to be until the end of time. Why? Because we are immersed in a battle of good versus evil. The devil wants to drag as many people as possible to the never-ending torments of hell. The evil one will always cause trouble and tempt the just to doubt the Church and to persecute priests and religious. He will also deploy intense temptations to bombard good and holy priests and religious.

The evil sown through priests and religious who have caused harm will not go unnoticed, and will cause good priests and religious to be persecuted for the deeds of the others. Let us call to mind Jesus' words to St. Faustina, entrusting her with prayers for them. We need to know that Jesus requests these prayers of us, as well, because the temptations of the world are rampant, evil, and insidious.

Priests and religious need our prayers. It's the least that we can do for them for professing vows to serve God and us.

Praying for the Dying and Souls in Purgatory

Saint Faustina recorded in her *Diary* that every single soul absolutely needs God's mercy all throughout life, but especially at the hour of death. That is why we need to pray the Divine Mercy Chaplet for the dying. We can all pray it. We should not make excuses. Not only should we pray it at the Hour of Great Mercy, but when we wake up in the middle of the night or at any other time we feel inspired to do so. Souls are dying all of the time, and they need our prayers.

The young mystic revealed, "I realize more and more how much every soul needs God's mercy throughout life and particularly at the hour of death. This chaplet mitigates God's anger, as He Himself told me" (*Diary*, 1036).

Our sister Faustina learned that most of the souls who are suffering eternal damnation are those who had not believed in the existence of hell! She was shown this when an angel led her to the chasms of hell! Faustina wrote in detail about the various tortures destined for particular souls (see *Diary*, 741).

She revealed, "Each soul undergoes terrible and indescribable sufferings, related to the manner in which it has sinned" (*Diary*, 741). She would have died at the sight of the horrendous tortures if God had not supported her. Faustina wrote all of her descriptions at the command of God, Who wanted mankind to know of the existence of hell and the consequences for sin, after which she wrote a solemn testimony to hell's existence. Her testimony of hell and the devils there is quite compelling.

Further, she said, "What I have written is but a pale shadow of the things I saw." And here is the clincher! She added, "But I noticed one thing: that most of the souls there are those who disbelieved that there is a hell. ... How terribly souls suffer there!" Because of this experience, St. Faustina prayed all the more earnestly, pleading with God to have mercy upon sinners.

She cried out to her Lord and Savior, "O my Jesus, I would rather be in agony until the end of the world, amidst the greatest sufferings, than offend You by the least sin" (*Diary*, 741).

I'd like to remind us of Jesus' important words to Faustina and about how we are to pray for the dying. Jesus told His bride, "Pray as much as you can for the dying." He explained to her that her prayers would obtain for them trust in His mercy — what they needed most at the hour of death. Jesus said, "Be assured that the grace of eternal salvation for certain souls in their final moments depends on your prayer," adding, "You know the whole abyss of My mercy, so draw upon it for yourself and especially for poor sinners. Sooner would heaven and earth turn into nothingness than would My mercy not embrace a trusting soul" (*Diary*, 1777).

You might recall that I quoted Blessed Michael Sopoćko in the previous chapter. He explained that souls in their last hours need prayers from others so that they will trust God. Get into the habit of praying for the souls of the dying every day and every evening.

Saint Faustina's pure heart wanted to save every soul. She has set a powerful example for us all. She prayed, "O my God, how I pity those people who do not believe in eternal life; how I pray for them that a ray of mercy would envelop them too, and that God would clasp them to His fatherly bosom" (*Diary*, 780).

Praying for the Holy Souls

Our sister Faustina is a mighty example of Divine Mercy in action. She toiled away at saving souls. Numerous places in her *Diary* speak of sacrifice, prayer, trials, tribulations, and God's mercy to redeem sinners. She also prayed for those who had died in the state of grace, but hadn't yet atoned for their former sins. Therefore, they were in Purgatory — a place of purification. They were in need of the prayers of willing intercessors. Some of these souls visited Faustina and begged for her prayers. Faustina recalls numerous such visits throughout her *Diary*.

Early on in the religious life, St. Faustina asked our Lord for whom she should pray. Jesus told His bride that He would tell her the following night. Faustina recounted what happened in her *Diary*:

> I saw my Guardian Angel, who ordered me to follow him. In a moment I was in a misty place full of fire in which there was a great crowd of suffering souls. They were praying fervently, but to no avail, for themselves; only we can come to their aid. The flames which were burning them did not touch me at all. My Guardian Angel did not leave me for an instant. I asked these souls what their greatest suffering was. They answered me in one voice that their greatest torment was longing for God. I saw Our Lady visiting the souls in Purgatory. The souls call her "The Star of the Sea." She brings them refreshment. I wanted to talk with them some more, but my Guardian Angel beckoned me to leave. We went out of that prison of suffering. [I heard an interior voice] which said, **My mercy does not want this, but justice demands it.** Since that time, I am in closer communion with the suffering souls (20).

At another time, St. Faustina recorded, "The Lord said to me, **Enter into purgatory often, because they need you there.**" The young mystic cried out to her Lord, "O my Jesus, I understand the meaning of these words which You are speaking to me, but first let me enter the treasury of Your mercy" (*Diary*, 1738).

Our sister Faustina urges us on to be like her — to desire to assist our Lord in saving souls and in praying for the Holy Souls in Purgatory.

The Chaplet of Divine Mercy

The Chaplet of Divine Mercy is a powerful prayer! Jesus asked St. Faustina and asks us, as well, to help Him save souls. The Chaplet of Divine Mercy is an intercessory and atonement prayer through which our Lord pours amazing graces. Endeavor to pray it every day at 3 p.m., the Hour of Great Mercy (when Jesus died on the Cross). However, it is very good to try to find other times to pray the Chaplet as well. It will help those in need.

Another powerful way to help others, especially hardened sinners, is by praying the "O Blood and Water" prayer with a contrite heart. Here is what Jesus told His bride:

> Today Jesus said to me, **I desire that you know more profoundly the love that burns in My Heart for souls, and you will understand this when you meditate upon My Passion. Call upon My mercy on behalf of sinners; I desire their salvation. When you say this prayer, with a contrite heart and with faith on behalf of some sinner, I will give him the grace of conversion. This is the prayer:**
>
> **"O Blood and Water, which gushed forth from the Heart of Jesus as a fount of Mercy for us, I trust in You"** (*Diary*, 186-187).

Arm yourself, dear sister in Christ, with these powerful prayers. You can pray them for your family, loved ones, and complete strangers. Don't hesitate to pray them often with a contrite heart. All things are possible with God!

Praying for Children

As someone who is all about the family (as you might be able to tell when reading this book!), I couldn't help but be deeply touched when I read what Faustina recorded in her *Diary* about praying for children:

As I walked about, inspecting everything, I suddenly saw a crowd of children who seemed to be no older than five to eleven years of age. When they saw me they surrounded me and began to cry out: Defend us from evil, and they led me into the chapel which was in this convent. When I entered the chapel, I saw the distressful Lord Jesus. Jesus looked at me graciously and told me that he is **gravely offended over children: You defend them from evil.** From that moment, I pray for children, but I feel that prayer alone is not enough (*Diary*, 765).

We should take St. Faustina's words to our hearts, and in addition to our earnest prayers, endeavor to do whatever we can to protect our innocent children.

Onward, Dear Sister!

Remember, Jesus instructed Faustina, **"Tell aching mankind to snuggle close to My merciful Heart, and I will fill it with peace"** (*Diary*, 1074). Let's be sure to do that ourselves and to lead others to our dear Lord's loving, merciful Sacred Heart. Our Lord told His bride Faustina, **"Souls who spread the honor of My mercy I shield through their entire lives as a tender mother her infant, and at the hour of death I will not be a Judge for them, but the Merciful Savior"** (*Diary*, 1075).

Dear sister in Christ, we Catholic women are called to be the aroma of Christ. We are entrusted with the human being! We are called to aid mankind! Let us, with Divine Mercy in our hearts and souls, be led by the Holy Spirit to be that spark to touch the hearts of those in need. Let us imitate dear Mother Mary, our Mother of Mercy, to go "in haste" to bring the Divine Mercy message to the world — one-on-one and one-by-one to our families and to all we meet.

Saint Faustina tells us, "Happy the soul that understands these things and with only one foot touches the earth." We are leaping towards Heaven, dear sister, one foot in flight! God is counting on us to impart His Divine Mercy to save souls! Be a "spark," a holy witness of His mercy and love!

PAUSE

Take some time to ponder God's amazing love for you and the exquisite gifts He has given you as a Catholic woman.

ACT

Ask Jesus to use you to help others. Ask Him to make you a blazing spark of His love and mercy so you can impart it to others.

A PRAYER OF MERCY

O Jesus, may I be a witness to Your mercy! Along with St. Faustina, I raise my heart to You and pray: "I want to be completely transformed into Your mercy and to be Your living reflection, O Lord. May the greatest of all divine attributes, that of Your unfathomable mercy, pass through my heart and soul to my neighbor" (*Diary*, 163).
Jesus, please have mercy upon my soul.
I trust in You!
Mother Mary, help me, protect me, and guide me.
Saint Faustina, you said your mission will begin after your death (see *Diary*, 281).
Please help me to live and share the Divine Mercy message. Please pray for me.
Amen.

AFTERWORD

So, here we are now as I finish this labor of love for you, my sister. In God's Providence, today is the eighth anniversary of my sister Barbara's entrance into her eternal reward. She was like a second mother to me. How fitting it is to finish today.

I have thought of you and prayed for you while I wrote this book. Every book is a journey for me. I have called upon the Holy Spirit for His great and unfailing aid as I have written. I have called upon mighty, saintly intercessors to help me. My relic of our dear sister Faustina was always with me as I wrote.

During the months that I put pen to paper and fingers to the keyboard to write this book, sheltered from the world for the most part due to the worldwide pandemic, a lot has happened. As much as I tried to avoid it, I ended up getting COVID-19 and offered the suffering for the love of God, the conversion of sinners, and in reparation for the sins committed against the Immaculate Heart of Mary. Thankfully, churches are slowly reopening with safety measures in place. I was able to go on pilgrimage to the National Shrine of The Divine Mercy in Stockbridge, Massachusetts, with my husband on our wedding anniversary. There, on hallowed ground and during Holy Mass, I drank in many graces, continuing to ask our Lord, Our Lady, and St. Faustina for help in writing this book.

God is full of surprises. Remember Susan, who gave me the daisies (Chapter 25: Single Motherhood)? I must say, God is certainly present in every single detail of our lives! After I'd not heard from her in years, Susan got in touch one day. It was during the writing of the story about her! She said that as hard as it was for her to go through so much suffering during her separation, divorce, and resulting court battle, she could see now that it had brought her to her knees to pray. She is getting closer to God.

Finally, my dear sister, let us be mindful of Pope St. Paul VI's encouraging words to women. He said, "That is why, at this moment when the human race is undergoing so deep a transformation, women impregnated with the spirit of the Gospel can do so much to aid mankind in not falling."[138] Let us strive to do our very best. Let us pray to be the holy "spark" that St. John Paul II spoke of.

Jesus, I trust in You!

With a grateful heart,
God bless you,
Your sister, **Donna-Marie**
July 27, 2020

APPENDIX OF PRAYERS

"O my Jesus, teach me to open the bosom
of mercy and love to everyone who asks
for it. Jesus, my Commander, teach me
so that all my prayers and deeds
may bear the seal of Your mercy."

— Saint Faustina (*Diary*, 755)

The Divine Mercy Chaplet[139]

The Chaplet of Mercy is recited using ordinary Rosary beads
of five decades. The Chaplet is preceded by two opening
prayers from the *Diary of Saint Maria Faustina Kowalska* and
followed by a closing prayer.

How to Pray the Chaplet of Divine Mercy

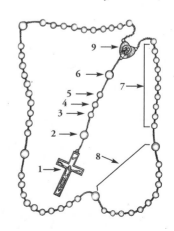

1. Make the Sign of the Cross.
2. Say the optional Opening Prayer.
3. Say the "Our Father."
4. Say the "Hail Mary."
5. Say the Apostles' Creed.
6. Say the "Eternal Father."
7. Say 10 "For the sake of His sorrowful Passion" on the "Hail Mary" beads.

8. Repeat for four more decades, saying "Eternal Father" on the "Our Father" bead and then 10 "For the Sake of His sorrowful Passion" on the following "Hail Mary" beads.

9. At the conclusion of the five decades, on the medallion say the "Holy God," the concluding doxology, three times.

10. Say the optional Closing Prayer.

Prayers of the Chaplet of Divine Mercy

1. The Sign of the Cross: In the name of the Father, and of the Son, and of the Holy Spirit. Amen.

2. Opening Prayers *(optional)*: You expired, Jesus, but the source of life gushed forth for souls, and the ocean of mercy opened up for the whole world. O Fount of Life, unfathomable Divine Mercy, envelop the whole world and empty Yourself out upon us (*Diary*, 1319).

O Blood and Water, which gushed forth from the Heart of Jesus as a fount of mercy for us, I trust in You! *(three times)* (84).

3. The Our Father: Our Father, who art in heaven, hallowed be Thy name; Thy kingdom come; Thy will be done on earth as it is in heaven. Give us this day our daily bread; and forgive us our trespasses as we forgive those who trespass against us; and lead us not into temptation, but deliver us from evil. Amen.

4. The Hail Mary: Hail Mary, full of grace. The Lord is with thee. Blessed art thou among women, and blessed is the fruit of thy womb, Jesus. Holy Mary, Mother of God, pray for us sinners, now and at the hour of our death. Amen.

5. The Apostles' Creed: I believe in God, the Father almighty, Creator of heaven and earth, and in Jesus Christ, his only Son, our Lord, who was conceived by the Holy Spirit, born of the Virgin Mary, suffered under Pontius Pilate, was crucified, died, and was buried; he descended into hell; on the third day he rose again from the dead; he ascended into heaven, and is seated at the right hand of God the Father almighty; from there he will come to judge the living and the dead. I believe in the Holy Spirit, the holy catholic Church, the communion of saints, the forgiveness of sins, the resurrection of the body, and life everlasting. Amen.

6. On the "Our Father" *bead before each decade:* Eternal Father, I offer You the Body and Blood, Soul and Divinity of Your dearly beloved Son, Our Lord Jesus Christ, in atonement for our sins and those of the whole world (476).

7. On the "Hail Mary" *beads of each decade:* For the sake of His sorrowful Passion, have mercy on us and on the whole world.

8. Repeat "Eternal Father" and **"For the Sake of His sorrowful Passion"** *(Numbers 6 & 7)* prayers for four more decades.

9. After 5 decades, the concluding doxology *(three times)*: Holy God, Holy Mighty One, Holy Immortal One, have mercy on us and on the whole world.

10. Closing Prayer *(optional)*: Eternal God, in whom mercy is endless, and the treasury of compassion inexhaustible, look kindly upon us, and increase Your mercy in us, that in difficult moments, we might not despair, nor become despondent, but with great confidence, submit ourselves to Your holy will, which is Love and Mercy Itself. Amen (950).

The wording of the Apostles' Creed conforms with the *Roman Missal.*

How to Pray the Rosary

1. Make the Sign of the Cross and say the "Apostles' Creed."

2. Say the "Our Father."

3. Say three "Hail Marys."

4. Say the "Glory be to the Father."

5. Announce the First Mystery; then say the "Our Father."

6. Say 10 "Hail Marys" while meditating on the Mystery.

7. Say the "Glory be to the Father." After each decade, say the following prayer requested by the Blessed Virgin Mary at Fatima: "O my Jesus, forgive us our sins, save us from the fires of hell. Lead all souls to Heaven, especially those in most need of Thy mercy."

8. Announce the Second Mystery: then say the "Our Father." Repeat 6 and 7 and continue with the Third, Fourth, and Fifth Mysteries in the same manner.

9. Say the "Hail, Holy Queen" on the medal after the five decades are completed.

As a general rule, depending on the season, the Joyful Mysteries are said on Monday and Saturday; the Sorrowful Mysteries on Tuesday and Friday; the Glorious Mysteries on Wednesday and Sunday; and the Luminous Mysteries on Thursday.

Prayers of the Rosary

The Sign of the Cross: In the name of the Father, and of the Son, and of the Holy Spirit. Amen.

The Apostles' Creed: I believe in God, the Father almighty, Creator of heaven and earth, and in Jesus Christ, his only Son, our Lord, who was conceived by the Holy Spirit, born of the Virgin Mary, suffered under Pontius Pilate, was crucified, died, and was buried; he descended into hell; on the third day he rose again from the dead; he ascended into heaven, and is seated at the right hand of God the Father almighty; from there he will come to judge the living and the dead. I believe in the Holy Spirit, the holy catholic Church, the communion of saints, the forgiveness of sins, the resurrection of the body, and life everlasting. Amen.

The Our Father: Our Father, who art in heaven; hallowed be Thy name; Thy kingdom come; Thy will be done on earth as it is in heaven. Give us this day our daily bread; and forgive us our trespasses as we forgive those who trespass against us, and lead us not into temptation; but deliver us from evil. Amen.

The Hail Mary: Hail Mary, full of grace. The Lord is with thee. Blessed art thou among women, and blessed is the fruit of thy womb, Jesus. Holy Mary, Mother of God, pray for us sinners, now and at the hour of our death. Amen.

Glory be to the Father: Glory be to the Father, and to the Son, and to the Holy Spirit. As it was in the beginning, is now, and ever shall be, world without end. Amen.

Hail, Holy Queen: Hail, Holy Queen, Mother of Mercy, our life, our sweetness and our hope, to thee do we cry, poor banished children of Eve; to thee do we send up our sighs, mourning and weeping in this valley of tears; turn, then, most gracious Advocate, thine eyes of mercy towards us, and after this, our exile, show unto us the blessed fruit of thy womb, Jesus. O clement, O loving, O sweet Virgin Mary!

Pray for us, O holy Mother of God, that we may be made worthy of the promises of Christ.

The wording of the Apostles' Creed conforms with the *Roman Missal.*

Mysteries of the Rosary
JOYFUL MYSTERIES

FIRST JOYFUL MYSTERY
THE ANNUNCIATION

And when the angel had come to her, he said, "Hail, full of grace, the Lord is with you" (Lk 1:28).

One Our Father, Ten Hail Marys, One Glory Be, etc.

FRUIT OF THE MYSTERY: *HUMILITY*

SECOND JOYFUL MYSTERY
THE VISITATION

Elizabeth, filled with the holy Spirit, cried out in a loud voice and said, "Most blessed are you among women, and blessed is the fruit of your womb" (Lk 1:41-42).

One Our Father, Ten Hail Marys, One Glory Be, etc.

FRUIT OF THE MYSTERY: *LOVE OF NEIGHBOR*

THIRD JOYFUL MYSTERY
THE BIRTH OF JESUS

She gave birth to her firstborn Son. She wrapped Him in swaddling clothes and laid Him in a manger, because there was no room for them in the inn (Lk 2:7).

One Our Father, Ten Hail Marys, One Glory Be, etc.

FRUIT OF THE MYSTERY: *POVERTY IN SPIRIT*

FOURTH JOYFUL MYSTERY
THE PRESENTATION

When the days were completed for their purification according to the law of Moses, they took Him up to Jerusalem to present Him to the Lord, just as it is written in the law of the Lord, "Every male that opens the womb shall be consecrated to the Lord" (Lk 2:22-23).

One Our Father, Ten Hail Marys, One Glory Be, etc.

FRUIT OF THE MYSTERY: *OBEDIENCE*

FIFTH JOYFUL MYSTERY
FINDING THE CHILD JESUS IN THE TEMPLE

After three days they found Him in the temple, sitting in the midst of the teachers, listening to them and asking them questions (Lk 2:46).

One Our Father, Ten Hail Marys, One Glory Be, etc.

FRUIT OF THE MYSTERY: *JOY IN FINDING JESUS*

LUMINOUS MYSTERIES

FIRST LUMINOUS MYSTERY
BAPTISM OF JESUS

After Jesus was baptized, ... the heavens were opened [for Him], and he saw the Spirit of God descending like a dove [and] coming upon Him. And a voice came from the heavens, saying, "This is My beloved Son, with whom I am well pleased" (Mt 3:16-17).

One Our Father, Ten Hail Marys, One Glory Be, etc.

FRUIT OF THE MYSTERY: *OPENNESS TO THE HOLY SPIRIT*

SECOND LUMINOUS MYSTERY
WEDDING AT CANA

His mother said to the servers, "Do whatever He tells you." ... Jesus told them, "Fill the jars with water." So they filled them to the brim (Jn 2:5-7).

One Our Father, Ten Hail Marys, One Glory Be, etc.

FRUIT OF THE MYSTERY: *TO JESUS THROUGH MARY*

THIRD LUMINOUS MYSTERY
PROCLAIMING THE KINGDOM

"As you go, make this proclamation: 'The kingdom of heaven is at hand.' Cure the sick, raise the dead, cleanse lepers, drive out demons. Without cost you have received; without cost you are to give" (Mt 10:7-8).

One Our Father, Ten Hail Marys, One Glory Be, etc.

FRUIT OF THE MYSTERY: *REPENTANCE AND TRUST IN GOD*

FOURTH LUMINOUS MYSTERY
TRANSFIGURATION

While He was praying His face changed in appearance and His clothing became dazzling white. Then from the cloud came a voice that said, "This is My chosen Son; listen to Him" (Lk 9:29, 35).

One Our Father, Ten Hail Marys, One Glory Be, etc.

FRUIT OF THE MYSTERY: *DESIRE FOR HOLINESS*

FIFTH LUMINOUS MYSTERY
INSTITUTION OF THE EUCHARIST

Then He took the bread, said the blessing, broke it, and gave it to them, saying, "This is My body, which will be given for you ..." And likewise the cup after they had eaten, saying, "This cup is the new covenant in My blood" (Lk 22:19-20).

One Our Father, Ten Hail Marys, One Glory Be, etc.

FRUIT OF THE MYSTERY: *ADORATION*

SORROWFUL MYSTERIES

FIRST SORROWFUL MYSTERY
THE AGONY IN THE GARDEN

He was in such agony and He prayed so fervently that His sweat became like drops of blood falling on the ground. When He rose from prayer and returned to His disciples, He found them sleeping from grief (Lk 22:44-45).

One Our Father, Ten Hail Marys, One Glory Be, etc.

FRUIT OF THE MYSTERY: *SORROW FOR SIN*

SECOND SORROWFUL MYSTERY
THE SCOURGING AT THE PILLAR

Then Pilate took Jesus and had Him scourged (Jn 19:1).

One Our Father, Ten Hail Marys, One Glory Be, etc.

FRUIT OF THE MYSTERY: *PURITY*

THIRD SORROWFUL MYSTERY
CROWNING WITH THORNS

They stripped off His clothes and threw a scarlet military cloak about Him. Weaving a crown out of thorns, they placed it on His head, and a reed in His right hand (Mt 27:28-29).

One Our Father, Ten Hail Marys, One Glory Be, etc.

FRUIT OF THE MYSTERY: *COURAGE*

FOURTH SORROWFUL MYSTERY
CARRYING OF THE CROSS

And carrying the cross Himself, He went out to what is called the Place of the Skull, in Hebrew, Golgotha (Jn 19:17).

One Our Father, Ten Hail Marys, One Glory Be, etc.

FRUIT OF THE MYSTERY: *PATIENCE*

FIFTH SORROWFUL MYSTERY
THE CRUCIFIXION

Jesus cried out in a loud voice, "Father, into Your hands I commend My spirit"; and when He had said this He breathed His last (Lk 23:46).

One Our Father, Ten Hail Marys, One Glory Be, etc.

FRUIT OF THE MYSTERY: *PERSEVERANCE*

GLORIOUS MYSTERIES

FIRST GLORIOUS MYSTERY
THE RESURRECTION

"Do not be amazed! You seek Jesus of Nazareth, the crucified. He has been raised; He is not here. Behold the place where they laid Him" (Mk 16:6).

One Our Father, Ten Hail Marys, One Glory Be, etc.

FRUIT OF THE MYSTERY: *FAITH*

SECOND GLORIOUS MYSTERY

THE ASCENSION

So then the Lord Jesus, after He spoke to them, was taken up into heaven and took His seat at the right hand of God (Mk 16:19).

One Our Father, Ten Hail Marys, One Glory Be, etc.

FRUIT OF THE MYSTERY: *HOPE*

THIRD GLORIOUS MYSTERY

DESCENT OF THE HOLY SPIRIT

And they were all filled with the Holy Spirit and began to speak in different tongues, as the Spirit enabled them to proclaim (Acts 2:4).

One Our Father, Ten Hail Marys, One Glory Be, etc.

FRUIT OF THE MYSTERY: *LOVE OF GOD*

FOURTH GLORIOUS MYSTERY

THE ASSUMPTION

"You are the glory of Jerusalem! ... You are the great boast of our nation! ... You have done good things for Israel, and God is pleased with them. May the Almighty Lord bless you forever!" (Jud 15:9-10).

One Our Father, Ten Hail Marys, One Glory Be, etc.

FRUIT OF THE MYSTERY: *GRACE OF A HAPPY DEATH*

FIFTH GLORIOUS MYSTERY

THE CORONATION

A great sign appeared in the sky, a woman clothed with the sun, with the moon under her feet, and on her head a crown of twelve stars (Rev 12:1).

One Our Father, Ten Hail Marys, One Glory Be, etc.

FRUIT OF THE MYSTERY: *TRUST IN MARY'S INTERCESSION*

Saint Faustina's Prayers

Praises of Divine Mercy

(*Diary*, 949-950)

Let the doubting soul read these considerations on
    Divine Mercy and become trusting.
Divine Mercy, gushing forth from the bosom of the
    Father, I trust in You.
Divine Mercy, greatest attribute of God, I trust in You.
Divine Mercy, incomprehensible mystery, I trust in You.
Divine Mercy, fount gushing forth from the mystery of
    the Blessed Trinity, I trust in You.
Divine Mercy, unfathomed by any intellect, human and
    angelic, I trust in You.
Divine Mercy, from which wells forth all life and
    happiness, I trust in You.
Divine Mercy, better than the heavens,
    I trust in You.
Divine Mercy, source of miracles and wonders,
    I trust in You.
Divine Mercy, encompassing the whole universe,
    I trust in You.
Divine Mercy, descending to earth in the Person of the
    Incarnate Word, I trust in You.
Divine Mercy, which flowed out from the open Wound
    of the Heart of Jesus, I trust in You.
Divine Mercy, enclosed in the Heart of Jesus for us,
    and especially for sinners, I trust in You.
Divine Mercy, unfathomed in the institution of the
    Sacred Host, I trust in You.
Divine Mercy, in the founding of Holy Church,
    I trust in You.
Divine Mercy, in the Sacrament of Holy Baptism,
    I trust in You.
Divine Mercy, in our justification through Jesus Christ,
    I trust in You.

Divine Mercy, accompanying us through our whole life,
I trust in You.

Divine Mercy, embracing us especially at the hour of
death, I trust in You.

Divine Mercy, endowing us with immortal life,
I trust in You.

Divine Mercy, accompanying us every moment of our
life, I trust in You.

Divine Mercy, shielding us from the fire of hell,
I trust in You.

Divine Mercy, in the conversion of hardened sinners,
I trust in You.

Divine Mercy, astonishment for Angels,
Incomprehensible to Saints, I trust in You.

Divine Mercy, unfathomed in all mysteries of God,
I trust in You.

Divine Mercy, lifting us out of every misery,
I trust in You.

Divine Mercy, source of our happiness and joy,
I trust in You.

Divine Mercy, in calling us forth from nothingness to
existence, I trust in You.

Divine Mercy, embracing all the works of His Hands,
I trust in You.

Divine Mercy, crown of all of God's handiwork,
I trust in You.

Divine Mercy, in which we are all immersed,
I trust in You.

Divine Mercy, sweet relief for anguished hearts,
I trust in You.

Divine Mercy, only hope of despairing souls,
I trust in You.

Divine Mercy, repose of hearts, peace amidst fear,
I trust in You.

Divine Mercy, delight and ecstasy of holy souls,
I trust in You.

Divine Mercy, inspiring hope against hope,
   I trust in You.

Eternal God, in whom mercy is endless and the treasury of compassion inexhaustible, look kindly upon us and increase Your mercy in us, that in difficult moments we might not despair nor become despondent, but with great confidence, submit ourselves to Your holy will, which is Love and Mercy itself. Amen (*Diary*, 950).

O Jesus, eternal Truth, our Life, I call upon You and I beg Your mercy for poor sinners. O sweetest Heart of my Lord, full of pity and unfathomable mercy, I plead with You for poor sinners. O Most Sacred Heart, Fount of Mercy from which gush forth rays of inconceivable graces upon the entire human race, I beg of You light for poor sinners. O Jesus, be mindful of Your own bitter Passion and do not permit the loss of souls redeemed at so dear a price of Your most precious Blood. O Jesus, when I consider the great price of Your Blood, I rejoice at its immensity, for one drop alone would have been enough for the salvation of all sinners. Although sin is an abyss of wickedness and ingratitude, the price paid for us can never be equalled. Therefore, let every soul trust in the Passion of the Lord, and place its hope in His mercy. God will not deny His mercy to anyone. Heaven and earth may change, but God's mercy will never be exhausted. Oh, what immense joy burns in my heart when I contemplate Your incomprehensible goodness, O Jesus! I desire to bring all sinners to Your feet that they may glorify Your mercy throughout endless ages (*Diary of Saint Maria Faustina Kowalska*, 72).

O Greatly Merciful God, Infinite Goodness, today all mankind calls out from the abyss of its misery to Your mercy — to Your compassion, O God; and it is with its mighty voice of misery that it cries out. Gracious God, do not reject the prayer of this earth's exiles! O Lord, Goodness beyond our understanding, Who are acquainted with our misery through and through, and know that by our own power we cannot ascend to You, we implore You: anticipate us with Your grace and keep on increasing Your mercy in us, that we may faithfully do Your holy will all through our life and at death's hour. Let the omnipotence of Your mercy shield us from the darts of our salvation's enemies, that we may with confidence, as Your children, await Your [Son's] final coming — that day known to You alone. And we expect to obtain everything promised us by Jesus in spite of all our wretchedness. For Jesus is our Hope: through His merciful Heart, as through an open gate, we pass through to heaven (*Diary*, 1570).

A Prayer of Trust by
Blessed Fr. Michael Sopoćko

Holy Spirit, give me the grace of unwavering trust when I think of Our Lord's merits, and of fearful trust when I think of my own weakness. When poverty comes knocking at my door: Jesus, I Trust in You, when sickness lays me low, or injury cripples me. Jesus, I Trust in You, when the world pushes me aside, and pursues me with its hatred. Jesus, I Trust in You, when I am besmirched by calumny, and pierced through by bitterness. Jesus, I Trust in You, when my friends abandon me, and wound me by word and deed. Jesus, I Trust in You, Spirit of love and Mercy, be to me a refuge, a sweet consolation, a blessed hope, that in all the most trying circumstances of my life I may never cease to trust in You.[140]

ACKNOWLEDGMENTS

I wish to thank the Sisters of Life for allowing me to share their beautiful "Litany of Trust" prayer, composed by Sr. Faustina Maria Pia, SV, in this book. May God reward them!

I am deeply grateful to my parents, Eugene Joseph and Alexandra Mary Cooper, for bringing me into the world and raising me in a large Catholic family. To my brothers and sisters — Alice Jean, Gene, Gary, Barbara, Tim, Michael, and David — thank you for being a wonderful part of my life.

My heartfelt gratitude goes to my dear husband, Dave, and my beloved children — Justin, Chaldea, Jessica, Joseph, and Mary-Catherine — for their continued love and support, and to my precious grandsons, Shepherd and Leo. I love you all dearly!

Special thanks to my sisters in Christ for their continual prayers, to my friend Fr. John Hardon, SJ, who spiritually directed and encouraged me, and I believe continues from Heaven! An exuberant thank you to dear Mother Teresa for playing a huge role in shaping me spiritually, which I know she continues even now. Thank you to my sister and friend St. Faustina who, no doubt, has helped me to write this book for you!

I owe special thanks to Marian Press for asking that I write this book, and to Fr. Chris Alar, MIC; Chris Sparks; Mary Clark; and all of the wonderful team at Marian Press that helped get this book out to you!

Finally, I am extremely thankful for my readership, viewership, and listenership, and to all those I meet in my travels. I pray for you every day. Thank you for being part of my fascinating journey through life! Please pray for me, too. I pray that God will continue to bless you in great abundance!

About the Author

Donna-Marie Cooper O'Boyle enjoys nature, gardening, telling stories, and teaching the faith. She is a Catholic wife, mother, grandmother; an award-winning and best-selling author and journalist; and an international speaker. She is the host of three EWTN television series she created to teach and encourage Catholic families. Donna-Marie enjoyed a decade-long friendship with Mother Teresa and was invited by the Holy See to participate in an international Vatican women's congress. She is the author of more than 30 books, lives with her family in New England, and lectures throughout the world.

She can be reached at her websites DonnaCooperOBoyle.com and FeedingYourFamilysSoul.com, where you can learn more about Donna-Marie's books, apostolate, retreats, pilgrimages, and blogs.

REFERENCES

[1] St. John Paul II, Homily, April 18, 1993, published in *L'Osservatore Romano*, April 21, 1993, accessed March 4, 2021, https://www.thedivinemercy.org/message/john-paul-ii/homilies/1993-04-18.

[2] St. John Paul II, Homily, April 18, 1993.

[3] St. John Paul II, Address to the Bishops of the Church in the States of Minnesota, North Dakota and South Dakota (U.S.A.) on Their "Ad Limina" Visit, June 6, 1998, n. 1, http://www.vatican.va/content/john-paul-ii/en/speeches/1998/june/documents/hf_jp-ii_spe_19980606_ad-limina-usa-vii.html.

[4] St. John Paul II, General Audience, July 26, 2000, n. 4, http://www.vatican.va/content/john-paul-ii/en/audiences/2000/documents/hf_jp-ii_aud_20000726.html.

[5] Beth Skwarecki, "Babies Learn to Recognize Words in the Womb," *Science*, August 26, 2013, https://www.sciencemag.org/news/2013/08/babies-learn-recognize-words-womb.

[6] Janet L. Hopson, "Fetal Psychology," *Psychology Today* 31, no. 5 (September-October 1998), 44-48, 76, https://www.psychologytoday.com/us/articles/199809/fetal-psychology.

[7] St. Alphonsus Liguori, "Discourses for the Novena of Christmas," in Discourse II, *The Incarnation, Birth and Infancy of Jesus Christ, or the Mysteries of the Faith*, 2nd ed., ed. Eugene Grimm (1886, repr., St. Athanasius Press, 2014), 26.

[8] Belinda Luscombe, "Making Eye Contact With a Baby Changes Both Your Brain Waves, Study Says," *Time*, November 30, 2017, https://time.com/5043217/baby-eye-contact-brain-waves/.

[9] Luscombe, "Making Eye Contact."

[10] Cf. Council of Florence: DS 1314: *vitae spiritualis ianua*.

[11] *Roman Catechism* II,2,5; Cf. Council of Florence: DS 1314; CIC, cann. 204 § 1; 849; CCEO, can. 675 § 1.

[12] Pope Benedict XVI, Homily, Feast of the Baptism of the Lord, January 7, 2007, http://www.vatican.va/content/benedict-xvi/en/homilies/2007/documents/hf_ben-xvi_hom_20070107_battesimo.html.

[13] Pope Benedict XVI, *Angelus*, January 8, 2012, http://www.vatican.va/content/benedict-xvi/en/angelus/2012/documents/hf_ben-xvi_ang_20120108_battesimo.html.

[14] Mt 19:14.

[15] St. Augustine, quoted in Rev. John Henry Hanson, "Growing Young: St. Therese of Lisieux and Spiritual Childhood," October 1, 2019, https://stjosemaria.org/growing-young/. See St. Augustine's *Commentaries on the Psalms*: Psalm 149, i. Augustine's original sentence: "*Inveteravit homo per peccatum, innovatur per gratiam.*"

[16] *St. Thérèse of Lisieux: Her Last Conversations*, trans. John Clarke, OCD (Washington, DC: Institute of Carmelite Studies, 1977), 139.

[17] St. John Paul II, Encyclical Letter *Mulieris Dignitatem* (*On the Dignity and Vocation of Women*), August 15, 1988, n. 30, http://www.vatican.va/content/john-paul-ii/en/apost_letters/1988/documents/hf_jp-ii_apl_19880815_mulieris-dignitatem.html, emphasis in original.

[18] *Code of Canon Law*, Canon 913, §1 (Vatican City: Libreria Editrice Vaticana, 1983), http://www.vatican.va/archive/cod-iuris-canonici/eng/documents/cic_lib4-cann879-958_en.html#Art._1.

[19] *LG* 11.

[20] *PO* 5.

[21] St. Louis de Montfort, *True Devotion to Mary: With Preparation for Total Consecration* (Charlotte, NC: St. Benedict Press, TAN Books, 2010), n. 53.

[22] Venerable Fulton J. Sheen, quoted in Donna-Marie Cooper O'Boyle, *Rooted in Love: Our Calling as Catholic Women* (Notre Dame, IN: Ave Maria Press, 2012), 11.

[23] Helen Keller, *Let Us Have Faith* (New York: Doubleday, Doran & Co., 1940), 51.

[24] Helen Keller, *The Story of My Life* (1903, repr., Mineola, NY: Dover Thrift, 1996), 11.

[25] St. John Paul II, Homily, Dar-es-Salaam, Jangwani Grounds, September 2, 1990, n. 2, http://www.vatican.va/content/john-paul-ii/en/homilies/1990/documents/hf_jp-ii _hom_19900902_dar-es-salaam.html, emphasis in original.

[26] St. John Paul II, Homily, Eucharistic Concelebration in the Grounds of the Papal Seminary in Pune, February 10, 1986, n. 3, https://w2.vatican.va/content/john-paul-ii/en/homilies/1986/documents/hf_jp-ii_hom_19860210_pont-ateneo-pune.html.

[27] I wrote a memoir about it titled *The Kiss of Jesus: How Mother Teresa and the Saints Helped Me to Discover the Beauty of the Cross* (San Francisco, CA: Ignatius Press, 2015). I'm not trying to leave you on a cliff wondering. You can be sure that I will weave in anecdotes throughout this book.

[28] St. John Paul II, Homily, Holy Mass for the Representatives of the International Youth Forum, Chapel of the University of Santo Tomás, Manila, January 13, 1995, n. 6, https://www.vatican.va/content/john-paul-ii/en/homilies/1995/documents/hf_jp-ii_hom_19950113_forum-giovani-gmg.html, emphasis in original.

[29] Venerable Fulton J. Sheen, quoted in Donna-Marie Cooper O'Boyle, *By Dawn's Early Light: Prayers and Meditations for Catholic Military Wives* (Manchester, NH: Sophia Institute Press, 2017), 187-188.

[30] Venerable Fulton J. Sheen, quoted in Cooper O'Boyle, *By Dawn's Early Light*, 187-188.

[31] Donna-Marie Cooper O'Boyle, *52 Weeks With Saint Faustina* (Stockbridge, MA: Marian Press, 2018), 57.

[32] *Compendium: Catechism of the Catholic Church* (Vatican City: Libreria Editrice Vaticana, 2005), https://www.usccb.org/prayer-and-worship/prayers-and-devotions/ prayers/acts-of-faith-hope-and-love.

[33] Blessed Fr. Michael Sopoćko, "Trust in God," n.d., https://www.divinemercy.org/elements-of-divine-mercy/trust-in-divine-mercy/114-trust-in-god-by-fr-sopocko.html.

[34] St. John Bosco, quoted in Joan Carroll Cruz, *Angels and Devils* (Charlotte, NC: TAN Books, 1999), 126.

[35] Thomas á Kempis, *The Imitation of Christ*, trans. Aloysius Croft and Harold Bolton, bk. 1, chap. 13 (Milwaukee, WI: Bruce Publishing Co., 1940), http://catholicarchive. org/thomas_a_kempis/the_imitation_of_christ/1/13.html.

[36] Francis Xaviêr Nguyễn Văn Thuận, *Prayers of Hope, Words of Courage* (Boston: Pauline Books and Media, 2002), 114.

[37] Cooper O'Boyle, *By Dawn's Early Light*, 87.

[38] Military Council of Catholic Women, "Faith Formation," n.d., http://mccw.org/ faith-formation/.

[39] Cf. St. Augustine, *De diversis quaestionibus octoginta tribus* 64,4:PL 40,56.

[40] Mother Teresa, quoted in *One Heart Full of Love: Mother Teresa*, ed. José Luis González-Balado (Ann Arbor, MI: Servant, 1998), 8.

[41] St. Teresa of Avila, *The Way of Perfection*, trans. and ed. E. Allison Peers (New York: Sheed and Ward, 1946), chap. 19, https://www.ecatholic2000.com/stteresa/way26.shtml.

[42] St. John Paul II, Apostolic Exhortation *Familiaris Consortio* (*On the Role of the Christian Family in the Modern World*), November 22, 1981, n. 11, http://www.vatican.va/content/john-paul-ii/en/apost_exhortations/documents/hf_jp-ii_exh_19811122_familiaris-consortio.html.

[43] *FC* 85; cf. *Mt* 11:28.

[44] St. John Paul II, "May Christ Be Your Total and Exclusive Love," International Conference of Consecrated Virgins, Rome, June 2, 1995, https://consecratedvirgins.org/usacv/sites/default/files/documents/VocRes/pjp2-a.pdf, emphasis in original.

[45] Cf. *Mk* 16:16.

[46] Cf. *SC* 67.

[47] *Code of Canon Law*, Canon 892.

[48] International Committee on English in the Liturgy, Inc., *Rite of Confirmation*, English translation, Introduction, n. 5 (Washington, DC: ICEL, 1975), accessed March 8, 2021, http://www.liturgyoffice.org.uk/Resources/Rites/Confirmation.pdf.

[49] St. John Paul II, *Angelus*, Apostolic Journey to the Far East and Oceania, Adelaide, Australia, November 30, 1986, http://www.vatican.va/content/john-paul-ii/en/angelus/1986/documents/hf_jp-ii_ang_19861130.html.

[50] Thomas á Kempis, *Imitation of Christ*, bk. 1, chap. 13.

[51] Á Kempis, *Imitation of Christ*, bk. 1, chap. 13.

[52] Mother Teresa, said to the author.

[53] St. Louis de Montfort, *Treatise on True Devotion*, n. 225, quoted in St. John Paul II, Letter of John Paul II to the Montfort Religious Family, http://www.vatican.va/content/john-paul-ii/en/letters/2004/documents/hf_jp-ii_let_20040113_famiglie-monfortane.html.

[54] Cooper O'Boyle, *52 Weeks With Saint Faustina*, 132-133.

[55] St. Thérèse of Lisieux, *Manuscrits autobiographiques* [*Autobiography of St. Thérèse of the Child Jesus*] (Lisieux: Carmel de Lisieux, 1957), 227-229. This excerpt appears in the Roman Office of Readings for the memorial of St. Thérèse on October 1.

[56] St. Thérèse of Lisieux, *Manuscrits autobiographiques,* 227-229, emphasis in original.

[57] Letter of Pope John Paul II to Women, June 29, 1995, n. 2, http://www.vatican.va/content/john-paul-ii/en/letters/1995/documents/hf_jp-ii_let_29061995_women.html.

[58] Mother Teresa, quoted in *Love: A Fruit Always in Season: Daily Meditations From the Words of Mother Teresa* (San Francisco: Ignatius Press, 1987), 112.

[59] St. Thérèse of Lisieux, quoted in "Selected Prayers and Quotes of the Little Flower," EWTN.com, https://www.ewtn.com/catholicism/devotions/selected-prayers-and-quotes-of-the-little-flower-13776.

[60] Pope Paul VI, Address of Pope Paul VI to Women, Closing of the Second Vatican Ecumenical Council, December 8, 1965, http://www.vatican.va/content/paul-vi/en/speeches/1965/documents/hf_p-vi_spe_19651208_epilogo-concilio-donne.html.

[61] St. Ambrose, quoted in Abbot Guéranger, trans. Dom Laurence Shepard, *The Liturgical Year, Paschal Time*, vol. I (New York: Benziger Brothers, 1908), 280.

[62] Edith Stein, quoted in Lucy Gelber and Romaeus Leuven, OCD, ed., trans. Freda Mary Oben, *The Collected Works of Edith Stein*, vol. 2, *Essays on Woman* (Washington, DC: ICS Publications, 1987).

[63] Sr. Bernadette Mary Reis, FSP, "Spiritual Exercises: Jesus' Thirst and Woman's Tears," February 21, 2018, https://www.vaticannews.va/en/pope/news/2018-02/spiritual-exercises-pope-thirst-jesus-women-tolentino.html.

[64] Reis, "Spiritual Exercises: Jesus' Thirst and Woman's Tears."

[65] John Montgomery, Ph.D., *Psychology Today*, "Emotions, Survival, and Disconnection: Our Emotions Can Both Help Us and Disconnect Us," September 30, 2012, https://www.psychologytoday.com/us/blog/the-embodied-mind/201209/emotions-survival-and-disconnection.

[66] Montgomery, "Emotions, Survival, and Disconnection."

[67] St. Teresa of Calcutta in a letter to the author of this book, February 18, 1988.

[68] St. John Paul II, Apostolic Letter *Salvifici Doloris* (*On the Christian Meaning of Human Suffering*), n. 2, http://www.vatican.va/content/john-paul-ii/en/apost_letters/1984/documents/hf_jp-ii_apl_11021984_salvifici-doloris.html.

[69] Venerable Fulton J. Sheen, *Fulton J. Sheen's Guide to Contentment* (New York: Simon & Schuster, 1967), 74.

[70] St. Francis De Sales, quoted in Paul Thigpen, ed., *A Dictionary of Quotes from the Saints* (Charlotte, NC: TAN Books, 2001), 211, accessed February 18, 2021, https://qdoc.tips/a-dictionary-of-quotes-from-the-saints-paul-thigpen-pdf-free.htm.

[71] Sheen, *Guide to Contentment*, 74.

[72] Sheen, *Guide to Contentment,* 75.

[73] Venerable Fulton J. Sheen, *Three to Get Married* (New York: Appleton-Century-Crofts, Inc. 1951), https://www.ewtn.com/catholicism/library/three-to-get-married-11222.

[74] Sheen, *Three to Get Married.*

[75] Donna-Marie Cooper O'Boyle, "Unexpected Discovery," *Magnificat*, June 2015.

[76] St. John Paul II, "Reverence for Christ the Basis of Relationship Between Spouses," General Audience, August 11, 1982 (*Theology of the Body* lecture n. 89), https://www.catholicnewsagency.com/document/89-reverence-for-christ-the-basis-of-relationship-between-spouses-908.

[77] St. John Paul II, "Reverence for Christ."

[78] Sheen, *Three to Get Married.*

[79] Sheen, *Three to Get Married.*

[80] St. John Paul II, Apostolic Exhortation *Familiaris Consortio* (*On the Role of the Christian Family in the Modern World*), November 22, 1981, n. 14, http://www.vatican.va/content/john-paul-ii/en/apost_exhortations/documents/hf_jp-ii_exh_19811122_familiaris-consortio.

[81] Vatican Council II, *Lumen Gentium*, Dogmatic Constitution on the Church, November 21, 1964, n. 11, https://www.vatican.va/archive/hist_councils/ii_vatican_council/documents/vat-ii_const_19641121_lumen-gentium_en.html.

[82] St. John Paul II, Encyclical Letter *Evangelium Vitae* (*The Gospel of Life*), n. 92, http://www.vatican.va/content/john-paul-ii/en/encyclicals/documents/hf_jp-ii_enc_25031995_evangelium-vitae.html.

[83] Cf. *Acts* 16:31; *Acts* 11:14

[84] Pope Benedict XVI, General Audience, Feb. 7, 2007, http://www.vatican.va/content/benedict-xvi/en/audiences/2007/documents/hf_ben-xvi_aud_20070207.html.

[85] Stanford Children's Health, "Family Meals: More Than Good Nutrition," accessed February 19, 2021, https://www.stanfordchildrens.org/en/topic/default?id=family-meals-more-than-good-nutrition-1-2152.

[86] Sr. Lúcia of Fatima, quoted in "The Children," World Apostolate of Fatima, USA, accessed February 19, 2021, http://www.bluearmy.com/newsite/about-fatima/the-children/.

[87] St. John Paul II, *Angelus*, July 23, 1995, 1.

[88] 56 CDF, instruction, *Donum vitae*, intro. 5.

[89] Thomas à Kempis, *The Imitation of Christ,* bk. 1, chap. 13.

[90] United States Conference of Catholic Bishops, *Book of Blessings* (Washington, DC:

USCCB, 1988), http://www.usccb.org/prayer-and-worship/bereavement-and-funerals/blessing-of-parents-after-a-miscarriage-or-stillbirth.cfm.

[91] Cf. CDF, *Dúnum vitae* I,1.

[92] St. John Paul II, Homily, Apostolic Journey to the United States of America: Eucharistic Celebration for the Young People, October 7, 1995, Central Park, New York, n. 6, http://www.vatican.va/content/john-paul-ii/en/homilies/1995/documents/hf_jp-ii_hom_19951007_central-park.html, emphasis in original.

[93] William Grimes, "B. N. Nathanson, 84, Dies; Changed Sides on Abortion," *The New York Times*, February 21, 2011, https://www.nytimes.com/2011/02/22/us/22nathanson.html.

[94] Grimes, "B. N. Nathanson, 84, Dies."

[95] International Theological Commission, *The Hope of Salvation for Infants Who Die Without Being Baptised,* January 19, 2007, no. 82 b, http://www.vatican.va/roman_curia/congregations/cfaith/cti_documents/rc_con_cfaith_doc_20070419_un-baptised-infants_en.html.

[96] International Theological Commission, *The Hope of Salvation for Infants.*

[97] St. John Paul II, Address to the Bishops and Apostolic Administrators of Albania on Their "Ad Limina" Visit, February 3, 2001, n. 5, http://www.vatican.va/content/john-paul-ii/en/speeches/2001/february/documents/hf_jp-ii_spe_20010203_albania-ad-limina.html.

[98] John M. Haas, United States Conference of Catholic Bishops, "Begotten Not Made: A Catholic View of Reproductive Technology," 1998, http://www.usccb.org/issues-and-action/human-life-and-dignity/reproductive-technology/begotten-not-made-a-catholic-view-of-reproductive-technology.cfm.

[99] Haas, "Begotten Not Made."

[100] St. Thérèse of Lisieux, *Story of a Soul: The Autobiography of St. Thérèse of Lisieux*, trans. Michael Day (Charlotte, NC: Saint Benedict Press, TAN Books, 2010), 4-5.

[101] *Magnificat*, August 17, 2015, https://aleteia.org/daily-prayer/monday-august-17/prayer-for-this-morning-0.

[102] Mother Teresa, quoted in Alan Drake, *Doing the Works of Jesus: Book 1: Becoming a Disciple Who Loves* (Dallas, TX: Spirit of Wisdom Publications, 2013), chap. 10, Kindle.

[103] Pius XII, Address to Italian Women, October 21, 1945, *Acta Apostolicae Sedis* 37 (1945), 287.

[104] Sr. Maria Faustina Pia, SV, "Litany of Trust," Sisters of Life, www.sistersoflife.org.

[105] Mother Teresa, quoted in *Love: A Fruit Always in Season*, 77.

[106] Chris Alar, MIC, and Jason Lewis, MIC, *After Suicide: There's Hope for Them and for You* (Stockbridge, MA: Marian Press, 2019), 59.

[107] Donna-Marie Cooper O'Boyle, *A Catholic Woman's Book of Prayers* (Brewster, MA: Paraclete Press, 2017), 74.

[108] Pope Francis, Extraordinary Moment of Prayer Presided Over by Pope Francis, March 27, 2020, http://www.vatican.va/content/francesco/en/homilies/2020/documents/papa-francesco_20200327_omelia-epidemia.html.

[109] Pope Francis, Extraordinary Moment of Prayer.

[110] Pope Francis, Extraordinary Moment of Prayer.

[111] Saint Teresa of Calcutta, from a letter to the author dated October 26, 1991.

[112] Venerable Fulton J. Sheen, "Women Who Do Not Fail," 1953, The Catholic World, YouTube video, 4:08, June 24, 2014, https://www.youtube.com/watch?v=_tfGHvap0fQ.

[113] Edith Stein, *Collected Works of Edith Stein,* vol. 2, 258.

[114] Stein, *Collected Works*, vol. 2, 258-259.

[115] Venerable Mary of Agreda, *The Mystical City of God: The Divine History and Life of the Virgin Mother of God*, vol. II, *The Incarnation*, trans. Rev. George J. Blatter (Fiscar Marison) (So. Chicago, IL: The Theopolitan; Hammond, IN: W.B. Conkey Co., 1914), chap. XIX, n. 249.

[116] Mary of Agreda, *The Mystical City of God*, chap. XIX, n. 249.

[117] Fr. Benedict Groeschel, *The Virtue Driven Life* (Huntington, IN: Our Sunday Visitor, 2006).

[118] Mary of Agreda, *The Mystical City of God: A Popular Abridgment of the Divine History and Life of the Virgin Mother of God* (Charlotte, NC: TAN Books, 1978), 39. The private revelations given even to a holy soul, such as Ven. Mary of Agreda, are not completely trustworthy in the same way that Holy Scripture is completely trustworthy; nevertheless, they contain many insights that are fruitful subjects for contemplation. Thus, as Catholics, we do not have to accept these private revelations and all their details as matters of faith, but we can read and meditate upon them with prudence, and find much profit for our souls in doing so.

[119] Mary of Agreda, *The Mystical City of God: A Popular Abridgment*, 57.

[120] *FC* 21; cf. *LG* 11.

[121] St. John Paul II, Homily, Perth, Australia, November 30, 1986, n. 4, https://w2.vatican.va/content/john-paul-ii/en/homilies/1986/documents/hf_jp-ii_hom_19861130_perth-australia.html.

[122] Mother Teresa, quoted in Elaine Murray Stone, *Mother Teresa: A Life of Love* (Mahwah, NJ: Paulist Press, 1999), 10.

[123] Mother Teresa, quoted in Jaya Chaliha and Edward Le Joly, comps., *The Joy in Loving: A Guide to Daily Living with Mother Teresa* (New York: Penguin Compass, 1996), 73.

[124] Father Gerard DuFour, *Perfect Selflessness According to Saint Claude La Colombière*, ed. Maison la Colombière (Paray-le-Monial: Editions Emmanuel, n.d.), 11.

[125] Quotations from Maureen and Bob Digan on the following pages are taken from conversations with the author and from the following sources: Felix Carroll, "Life After the Miracle," Marian.org, March 28, 2011, https://www.marian.org/news/Life-After-the-Miracle-3204; Felix Carroll, "Life After the Miracle: Part II," Marian.org, June 9, 2008, https://www.thedivinemercy.org/articles/life-after-miracle-part-2; Iris Alderson, "Maureen Digan's Miracle of Mercy with Sister Faustina," April 28, 2012 (updated March 24, 2019), MassLive.com, https://www.masslive.com/living/2012/04/iris_alderson_maureen_digans_miracle_of_mercy_with_sister_faustina.html.

[126] Amedeo Capetti, MD, "Letter From the Trenches," trans. Renzo Canetta and Letizia Mariani, *CL Newsletter*, March 24, 2020, originally published in *Il Foglio*, March 18, 2020, https://www.clnewsletter.org/post/letter-from-the-trenches.

[127] Sopoćko, "Trust in God."

[128] Sopoćko, "Trust in God." '

[129] St. John Paul II, *Angelus*, July 23, 1995.

[130] St. John Paul II, Encyclical Letter *Dives in Misericordia* (*Rich in Mercy*), November 30, 1980, n. 15, http://www.vatican.va/content/john-paul-ii/en/encyclicals/documents/hf_jp-ii_enc_30111980_dives-in-misericordia.html.

[131] St. John Paul II, Homily, April 18, 1993.

[132] St. John Paul II, Homily, Mass in St Peter's Square for the Canonization of Sr Mary Faustina Kowalska, April 30, 2000, n. 4, http://www.vatican.va/content/john-paul-ii/en/homilies/2000/documents/hf_jp-ii_hom_20000430_faustina.html, emphasis in original.

[133] St. John Paul II, Homily, Dedication of the Shrine of Divine Mercy, Apostolic Voyage to Poland, Kraków-Łagiewniki, August 17, 2002, n. 5, http://www.vatican.va/content/john-paul-ii/en/homilies/2002/documents/hf_jp-ii_hom_20020817_shrine-divine-mercy.html, emphasis in original, emphasis in original.

[134] St. John Paul II, *Regina Caeli,* Eucharistic Celebration for the Repose of the Soul of Pope John Paul II, posthumously on April 3, 2005, n. 2, http://www.vatican.va/content/john-paul-ii/en/angelus/2005/documents/hf_jp-ii_reg_20050403_divina-misericordia.html.

[135] St. John Paul II, *Regina Caeli,* n. 2, posthumously on April 3, 2005.

[136] William Sockey, "Offer It Up! The Most Important Message of Fatima," World Apostolate of Fatima, USA, January 3, 2019, https://www.bluearmy.com/offer-it-up-the-most-important-message-of-fatima/.

[137] Sockey, "Offer It Up!".

[138] Pope Paul VI, Address to Women, December 8, 1965.

[139] "How to Pray the Chaplet," DivineMercy.org, accessed March 6, 2021, https://www.thedivinemercy.org/message/devotions/pray-the-chaplet.

[140] Sopoćko, "Trust in God."

ESSENTIAL DIVINE MERCY RESOURCES

Diary of Saint Maria Faustina Kowalska:
Divine Mercy in My Soul

Also available
as an ebook —
Visit shopmercy.org

The *Diary* chronicles the message that Jesus, the Divine Mercy, gave to the world through this humble nun. In it, we are reminded to trust in His forgiveness — and as Christ is merciful, so, too, are we instructed to be merciful to others. Written in the 1930s, the *Diary* exemplifies God's love toward mankind and, to this day, remains a source of hope and renewal. Keep the *Diary* next to your Bible for constant insight and inspiration for your spiritual growth! Also available in Spanish.

Large Paperback: Y96-NBFD   Compact Paperback: Y96-DNBF
Deluxe Leather-Bound Edition: Y96-DDBURG
Audio Diary MP3 Edition: Y96-ADMP3

The Divine Mercy Message and Devotion
Our most popular pocket-size handbook on Divine Mercy covers every aspect of the message and devotion. By Fr. Seraphim Michalenko, MIC, with Vinny Flynn and Robert A. Stackpole, STD. 88 pages. Y96-M17

The Divine Mercy

Message and Devotion

Divine Mercy 101 DVD
The popular presentation by Fr. Chris Alar, MIC, is better than ever: all the basics of Divine Mercy in a clear, one-hour presentation. Also available as a CD. Y96-DM102 AUDIO CD: Y96-NE101

For our complete line of books, prayercards, pamphlets, Rosaries, and chaplets, visit ShopMercy.org or call 1-800-462-7426 to have our latest catalog sent to you.

FREE!

THE OFFICIAL DIVINE MERCY APP

Perfect for bringing the Divine Mercy message with you anywhere you go. This free app from the authorities on Divine Mercy puts a world of Divine Mercy info and resources at your fingertips.

Also available from the Marian Fathers: the complete MARY APP

Download now!

Download on the **App Store**

ANDROID APP ON **Google** play

DivineMercyArt.com

Top Quality Religious Art ...
at *Merciful Prices*!

Handmade at the National Shrine of The Divine Mercy with top-quality wood, canvas, and inks.

- Lowest prices
- Many sizes available
- Framing options

Canvas images starting at $19.95!

Y96-PV10GW

DivineMercyArt.com or call 1-800-462-7426
Prices subject to change.

Y96-PH10GW

Y96-PB10GW

Friends of Mercy

Marians of the Immaculate Conception ‖ Association of Marian Helpers

Friends of Mercy is a group of Marian Helpers who are committed to living the message of Divine Mercy and sharing it with others by deed, by word, and by prayer. Friends of Mercy will inspire you to grow deeper in faith and allow God's mercy to transform your life and the lives of those around you.

**To join or for more information, visit
TheDivineMercy.org/friends
or call 1-800-462-7426**

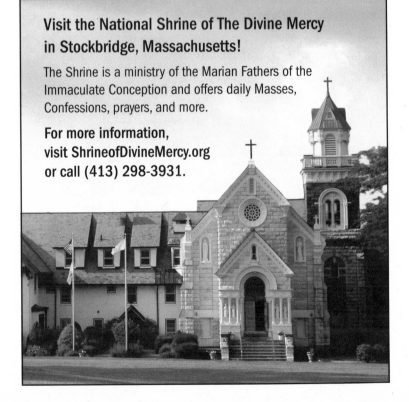

**Visit the National Shrine of The Divine Mercy
in Stockbridge, Massachusetts!**

The Shrine is a ministry of the Marian Fathers of the Immaculate Conception and offers daily Masses, Confessions, prayers, and more.

**For more information,
visit ShrineofDivineMercy.org
or call (413) 298-3931.**

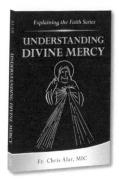

Explaining the Faith Series

Understanding Divine Mercy
by Fr. Chris Alar, MIC

Pope St. John Paul II said there is nothing the world needs more than Divine Mercy, yet few people understand exactly what Divine Mercy is and why it is so critical for our times. Now there's one book that summarizes it all in an easy-to-understand way! Have you ever wondered "What exactly is Divine Mercy and who is St. Faustina?" Would you like to know how to receive the extraordinary promise Jesus offers only one day a year, on Divine Mercy Sunday? Have you ever asked, "How could a merciful God allow so much suffering in the world?" If you answered yes to any of these questions, *Understanding Divine Mercy* by Fr. Chris Alar, MIC, is for you. In this first volume of his *Explaining the Faith* series, Fr. Chris shares, in his engaging style, the elements of the Divine Mercy message and devotion and explains why Jesus told St. Faustina that Divine Mercy is "mankind's last hope of salvation." Paperback. 184 pages. Y96-EFBK

Explaining the Faith – DVD
by Fr. Chris Alar, MIC

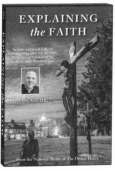

Jesus' promise of Divine Mercy Sunday. Catholic devotion to Mary. Church teaching about suffering and suicide. Are you able to defend our faith when questioned about these topics and others? In this new DVD series, Fr. Chris Alar, MIC, offers his favorite 13 talks to address all of these topics and explains the Mass in a way you have never heard before. Running time: 10 hours. Y96-EXDVD

After Suicide
There's Hope For Them And For You

In this Catholic best-seller, Fr. Chris Alar, MIC, and Jason Lewis, MIC, address the hard issue of suicide simply and pastorally. Drawing from the teaching of the Church, the message of Divine Mercy, and their own experience of losing a loved one, they offer readers two key forms of hope: hope for the salvation of those who've died by their own hand, and hope for the healing of those left behind. This book is a must-read for all those trying to make sense out of such a difficult subject. Remarkably, the spiritual principles of healing and redemption apply not only to a loss from suicide, but by any means of death. Paperback. 195 pages. Y96-ASTH

For our complete line of books, prayercards, pamphlets, Rosaries, and chaplets, visit ShopMercy.org or call 1-800-462-7426 to have our latest catalog sent to you.

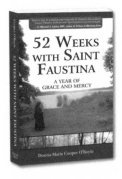

52 Weeks with Saint Faustina:
A Year of Grace and Mercy
By Donna-Marie Cooper O'Boyle

Spend a year with St. Faustina! Perfect to begin any time of the year, this collection of weekly meditations and activities by EWTN TV host Donna-Marie Cooper O'Boyle, author of *The Domestic Church: Room by Room*, guides readers on a 52-week spiritual pilgrimage through the life and teachings of the Secretary and Apostle of Divine Mercy, St. Faustina Kowalska (1905-1938). Paperback. 390 pages. Y96-WEEKS

Our Friend Faustina:
Life Lessons in Divine Mercy
Edited by Michele Faehnle and Emily Jaminet

Michele Faehnle and Emily Jaminet, the writing team behind *Divine Mercy for Moms*, have assembled an extraordinary collection of essays by modern women, all joined by their common friendship with one extraordinary person: St. Faustina Kowalska (1905-1938), the Secretary and Apostle of the Divine Mercy. This collection will help introduce you to a friend for life (and afterlife!) in extraordinary, ordinary St. Faustina. Paperback. 176 pages. Y96-FFRD

Faustina: The Mystic and Her Message
In this major biography, award-winning author and historian Dr. Ewa Czaczkowska pursues Faustina Kowalska and her roots, tracking the saint's riveting life and her extraordinary call to bring the message of Divine Mercy to the world. Get to know the "real" Faustina as the author uncovers new information and rare photos. Paperback. 456 pages. Y96-BIOSF

Divine Mercy Essentials
From the John Paul II Institute comes an in-depth course on the theology and spirituality of devotion to Divine Mercy. This 30-session course explores every major aspect of the message and devotion to the Divine Mercy.

10-DVD SET: Y96-DMEDVD
30-SESSION ONLINE PROGRAM: Y96-MODME
Visit onlinecourse.marian.org for more
information on the online program.

For our complete line of books, prayercards, pamphlets, Rosaries, and chaplets, visit ShopMercy.org or call 1-800-462-7426 to have our latest catalog sent to you.

Divine Mercy 101 Kit

Includes *Divine Mercy Explained* booklet, *Divine Mercy 101* DVD, *Now Is The Time For Mercy* Book, "Father, Forgive Them" Prayercard, Tri-Fold Card, 5" x 7" Vilnius Divine Mercy Image Canvas print.

Also includes
bonus materials.
Y96-DMKIT

PAMPHLETS: "Works of Mercy," "How to Make a Good Confession," "The Devotion to the Divine Mercy," "The Message of Divine Mercy," "Father, Forgive Them," "Novena to Saint Faustina," "Novena to St. John Paul II."

33 Days to Merciful Love

A Do-It-Yourself Retreat in Preparation for Consecration to Divine Mercy
by Fr. Michael Gaitley, MIC

Live Divine Mercy to the full! Get your copy of *33 Days to Merciful Love* by Fr. Michael Gaitley, MIC, the stirring sequel to the international sensation, *33 Days to Morning Glory*. Using the same 33-day preparation format, *33 Days to Merciful Love* journeys with one of the most beloved saints of modern times, St. Thérèse of Lisieux, and concludes with a consecration to Divine Mercy. So whether you want to deepen your love of Divine Mercy or have a devotion to St. Thérèse, *33 Days to Merciful Love* is the book for you. Paperback. 216 pages. Y96-33DML

No Turning Back: A Witness to Mercy
10th Anniversary Edition

For the past 10 years, the story of Donald Calloway's journey from runaway teen to Marian priest has touched the hearts and changed the lives of thousands of people. Now, in this 10th anniversary edition of *No Turning Back*, the Very Rev. Fr. Donald Calloway, MIC, looks back on the past decade in a new introduction to this Christian classic, a perennially powerful witness to the transforming grace of God and the Blessed Mother's love for her children. His witness proves a key truth of our faith: Between Jesus, the Divine Mercy, and Mary, the Mother of Mercy, there's no reason to give up hope on anyone, no matter how far they are from God. Paperback. 288 pages. Includes color photo section. Y96-ANTBK

For our complete line of books, prayercards, pamphlets, Rosaries, and chaplets, visit ShopMercy.org or call 1-800-462-7426 to have our latest catalog sent to you.

Join the

Association of Marian Helpers,

headquartered at the
National Shrine of The Divine Mercy,
and share in special blessings!

**An invitation from
Fr. Joseph, MIC, director**

**Marian Helpers is an Association of
Christian faithful of the Congregation
of Marian Fathers of the Immaculate
Conception.** By becoming a member,
you share in the spiritual benefits
of the daily Masses, prayers, and
good works of the Marian priests
and brothers.

This is a special offer of grace given to you by the Church
through the Marian Fathers. Please consider this opportunity
to share in these blessings, along with others whom you
would wish to join into this spiritual communion.

**The Marian Fathers of the Immaculate Conception of the Blessed
Virgin Mary is a religious congregation of nearly 500 priests and
brothers around the world.**

Call 1-800-462-7426 or visit marian.org

Give a Consoling Gift: *Prayer*

Enroll your loved ones in the Association of Marian Helpers, and they will participate in the graces from the daily Masses, prayers, good works, and merits of the Marian priests and brothers around the world.

1-800-462-7426 • marian.org/enrollments

Enrollments can be offered for the living or deceased. We offer a variety of enrollment cards: wedding, anniversary, First Holy Communion, birthday, get well, and more.

Request a Mass
to be offered by the Marian Fathers for your loved one

Individual Masses
(for the living or deceased)

Gregorian Masses
(30 days of consecutive Masses for the deceased)

**1-800-462-7426
marian.org/mass**